IF YOU CAN'T TAKE A JOKE…

To Jen,

Hope you enjoy it

Jordan Gray

IF YOU CAN'T TAKE A JOKE…

The travels of a naval salesman

Gordon Gray

Copyright © 2014 Gordon Gray

The moral right of the author has been asserted.

Apart from any fair dealing for the purposes of research or private study, or criticism or review, as permitted under the Copyright, Designs and Patents Act 1988, this publication may only be reproduced, stored or transmitted, in any form or by any means, with the prior permission in writing of the publishers, or in the case of reprographic reproduction in accordance with the terms of licences issued by the Copyright Licensing Agency. Enquiries concerning reproduction outside those terms should be sent to the publishers.

Matador
9 Priory Business Park,
Wistow Road, Kibworth Beauchamp,
Leicestershire. LE8 0RX
Tel: (+44) 116 279 2299
Fax: (+44) 116 279 2277
Email: books@troubador.co.uk
Web: www.troubador.co.uk/matador

ISBN 978 1783064 687

British Library Cataloguing in Publication Data.
A catalogue record for this book is available from the British Library.

Typeset in 11pt Times New Roman by Troubador Publishing Ltd, Leicester, UK
Printed and bound in the UK by TJ International, Padstow, Cornwall

Matador is an imprint of Troubador Publishing Ltd

This book is dedicated to all the 'good guys' in Sales and Marketing at the former Decca Radar Co; especially Frank Headington, Ernie Cast and Louis Foy who all taught me so much in my early days in sales.

Contents

1	Learning the Ropes in the UK	1
2	Hong Kong	20
3	China. (People's Republic of China)	42
4	Korea	70
5	Thailand	117
6	Malaysia	124
7	Singapore	137
8	Saudi Arabia	144
9	Egypt	172
10	Oman and the UAE	181
11	India	201
12	USA	247
13	Some Final Thoughts	257

Brief CV of Gordon Gray	269

– ORIGIN –

In the Royal Navy when everything is going wrong and can only get worse, a sympathetic shipmate will say "If you can't take a joke you shouldn't have joined.

CHAPTER 1

Learning the Ropes in the UK

"Gordon, will you come through to my office? I think I may have a trip for you." My heart leapt. A trip at last? But to where? I had been working in the Harbour Radar Sales and Marketing Department of Decca Radar in their Head Office in London for about 6 months and was eager for my first overseas sales trip. Our department, with our technical colleagues at the research department adapted Decca's commercial marine radars for specialised use in ports, harbours and coastal areas all over the world. It seemed to me that Simon had visited most of them. At my interview he had assured me that if I joined then we would share the international projects and travel equally, no matter where the projects were. Now, at last, I was to go on a trip.

Simon was in his early thirties, a boisterous, noisy, larger than life chap who was full of bonhomie. He had a "full set" black beard, smoked like a chimney and had a loud laugh that could be heard streets away. I went through and sat down in Simon's office, which overlooked the River Thames. The sun shone brightly and sparkled as it reflected off the brown muddy waters. I tried to remember if I had any sun cream at home or would need to buy it at the airport. No more old, muddy Thames for me – I am going travelling. But where was he about to send me? Simon got into his flow.

"We have been approached by a firm of international port and harbour consultant engineers who would like to know about how our radars can help their port and harbour plans and what we can offer for their various projects. I would like you to go and talk to them.

IF YOU CAN'T TAKE A JOKE...

Their office is in Bradford, so you can get there and back in a day," Simon proudly told me.

"Bradford! A day trip to Bradford! My long-awaited trip is to Bradford?" Nothing wrong with Bradford, of course; but not quite what I had hoped to hear him say and not exactly a leading port of the world! Even though we had lived in Yorkshire for four years, I had never even been to Bradford. All I knew about Bradford was that a 1970s pop group called "Smokie" came from there. Oh well, I guess you have to start somewhere and deep in my head, a voice was saying: "Today Bradford, tomorrow the world." But it was not a very loud, or convincing, voice. A Royal Naval saying came to mind: "If you can't take a joke – you shouldn't have joined." It was a saying that events allowed to be repeated throughout my career and helped to keep me sane.

Simon continued to do all the international travelling and I was kept back in the office. "Well, Gordon, I need you here to run things when I am away," Simon used to say, often. Eventually he did send me overseas but it was only after we had been asked to discuss a project in Saudi Arabia, which just happened to be Simon's least favourite place in all the world. I got the message. If this is what it is all about, then I may as well still be an office boy across the Thames in the Marylebone Lane office of the architects where I had started out my working life ten years before as a nineteen-year-old. How did I end up here?

My first job in Marylebone Lane had led me to seek excitement and go to sea, so I joined the Royal Navy for a Short Service Commission. That was followed by marriage to Doreen – a lovely, blue-eyed Scots girl who I met when I was on a ship based in Scotland and Doreen was a Wren who worked in the Base Pay Office. We set up home in Yorkshire where I had taken a management job in the deep sea trawling industry in Hull. Unfortunately, a few years later, the trawling industry collapsed and a new career had to be found. My work in the trawling industry had led to an interest in international sales and marketing and that led me to try and find a job with a marine or naval company.

So, I wrote to Decca Radar and was asked to come to London for interviews. I was interviewed by four people, including Simon, and one with John, the general manager. John was a serious faced, correct and academic sort of guy who actually seemed a bit shy. Knowing that I was then working in the fishing industry, he produced from his pocket a couple of small rolls of paper which he unrolled on the desk. They were clearly from a fish-finding echo sounder.

"Now then, can you tell me what those are?" he said, pointing at marks on the paper.

"Fish" I told him.

"You can tell that can you from these marks?"

"Yes. On this sheet these are bottom feeding fish, probably cod or haddock feeding close to the seabed here and those on that paper trace are midwater fish, maybe herring or mackerel. They are much lighter in tone and in the midwater area." "Oh, I see" he said. He didn't ask me anything else and just got up and left. I was introduced to the sales director, Charles Taylor, whose message was: "You will have to start at the bottom you know and learn how to sell." A few days later, I was offered a job in their harbour radar department.

I was brought back from my musings by Simon droning on about train times to Bradford. I realised that if the extent of my travel in Simon's department was going to be Bradford, then I could not see the job providing me with any real selling experience and certainly no overseas work. I had heard a whisper on the office grapevine that there might be a salesman's position on offer in the London area office of the UK Marine Radar Sales Department and although it would not involve any overseas work, it was one that would certainly get me out and about. I would be learning real selling and I would be dealing directly with shipowners and ships again. So, I applied for the job to the UK Sales Manager, Frank Headington. Frank was a smart, dapper gentleman; kind and friendly and we had met a few times when I worked in Hull. He had run the UK sales operation for many years and was well known and respected in the marine industry.

After a few weeks of worry, rumour and counter rumour about

who was going to get the job, I was delighted when Frank called me in to say that I had got the job.

Ernie

I would be now the Deputy London Area Sales Manager and moved into the London Area Sales Department which dealt with all the shipowners, yacht chandlers and agents in London and the South East. I was now working for a very fine gentleman called Ernie Cast, who was the London Area Sales Manager and reported to Frank. Ernie had been doing the job since he left the RAF after the war, where he had been a navigator in Lancaster bombers. In spite of the horrific losses the RAF bomber crews incurred, Ernie always said that looking back it was the best time of his life. He was a big, genial man with real presence. If Ernie said no, then it was NO. He always wore a three-piece suit and he was always pleasant, friendly and his advice was always helpful and wise. Although I was very much the baby salesman, I never felt it with him as he always encouraged me and backed me up when needed. In private he may offer a word or two of advice, but never in public. We seemed to get on well together from day one.

Ernie had learnt his trade well and taught me a lot about the dark arts of selling and the integrity of a handshake on a deal. We operated in the London shipping market which is centred on the Baltic Exchange and where deals are done on a handshake, and the phrase "My word is my bond" is as good as any written contract. "That is the way we operate too," said Ernie. "Most of the people we meet day to day are either the shipowners themselves or senior masters who have been promoted to superintendent jobs ashore and are bright and wily people." He would repeat to me: "Sell yourself first, then the company, and then the radar and never the other way round and always be totally honest. If you don't know the answer, say so. Never knock the competition and never bull the customer. He will always find you out." How right he was.

He had a number of useful tips which he always followed and which stood me in good stead, too. No one ever heard Ernie say: "I sold three radars today." The word "I" did not exist in Ernie's salesman's dictionary. It was always "We". He took the correct view that the customer ordered the radars because they were well designed by good design engineers, worked well thanks to the production teams, maintained well at sea by the service department and competitively priced thanks to the commercial department. Ernie was merely the man who made the customer aware of all these things, explained the benefits and shared his enthusiasm for the radar with the customer. The sale was the result of the customer appreciating all these factors and responding to Ernie's enthusiasm. I still cringe whenever I hear anyone saying "I sold X, Y or Z".

He also never carried a briefcase. "Never go into their offices with a briefcase," he would say as I polished my new burgundy, red leather briefcase with brass corners.

"Why on earth not?" I asked.

"Because the customer will assume that it is full of brochures and you are going to bore him to death with technical jargon. Without a briefcase, you look as though you have just popped in and he will relax and offer you a coffee. Over the coffee is when you get the information you want or make the deals; when the customer is relaxed and not being bored rigid by some brochure fanatic."

"But what if he does want a brochure though?" I naively asked.

"Firstly, you should know what the brochure says and tell him what he wants to know and, secondly, that is then the opportunity to say 'I will bring one in for you tomorrow, I have a meeting across the road so it is no problem, is 10 o'clock convenient?'; which, of course, is the opportunity for you to chat more and get to know him even better, hopefully over another coffee and a custard cream."

"Always remember that in the customer's office you represent the company, but in the company's office you represent the customer, and do both as well as you can" was another of his pearls of wisdom.

In fact, when I joined him, he said to me that all he expected me to do for the first year was to get to know my customers personally and not to think about "trying to sell" them anything. "If they want to buy one they will let you know, but if you try too hard, too early, it will put them off. That will all come naturally later." I like to think it did.

In addition to the "Big Boys" of the London shipowners, companies like BP Tankers and P&O as well as Sealink Ferries – the biggest shipowners in the UK at that time – Ernie had on his client list the major London-based Greek shipowners of whom there were still many in the 1970s. He had been working with them for years. The London Greek shipping community was big and they either owned or managed a huge amount of tonnage. In addition to the big names such as Onassis and Niarchos, there were many relatively large fleets run from London by the Greek families. It was a close-knit community and they all knew each other well – often they had family ties with other Greek owners. If one of them died, then they all knew about it. Ernie had picked up on this and would always try to attend their funerals and come in with his black tie. "I am off to so and so's funeral later on." Nothing elaborate; he did not tell the Greeks that he was going nor did he attend the social side afterwards. He would just attend the service at the back of the church and quietly leave after paying his respects to the family. Word always spread that Ernie had been at the funeral and he was respected as an honourable man by the Greek community and many doors opened for him because of it.

When I told Ernie that one of the masters of a Sealink ferry Horsa, who we both knew well, had died suddenly, Ernie and I both went down to Folkestone for the funeral. We sat at the back and afterwards paid our respects to his widow after all the family and friends, then we left. I was amazed when some weeks later I was chatting to one of the chief officers on one of the ships, when he said, "Oh, I hear you were at Peter's funeral last month. That was really good of you." It would never have occurred to me to do such a thing, but it did to Ernie and he was well thought of because of it.

My grand title then was "Deputy London Area Sales Manager." Ernie insisted that our names were the first thing you read on the card, in large letters in the middle. "If your name is printed so small that they cannot read it, they will think you are not important and will probably forget it." He would say, "It is you they are talking to and your name is what they want to know."

After the person's name, the title on the business card is important. Any customer being handed a card forms an impression of the person from what he sees before him in person and from what he then reads on the card. The title on a card paints a picture for the customer and if he does not understand it, he will feel negative. He likes to feel that he knows who to expect coming through his door from the job title of the visitor. Later on, when I worked for Plessey, I noticed that the company had a subtle way of keeping salesmen's egos in check. No matter what your business card said your title was, your payslip each month always just said: "Sales Rep".

After I had been with Ernie a few months, I arranged a first meeting with the Marine Superintendent of a small Greek shipping company in the City that Ernie had asked me to get to know. I duly arrived at his office five minutes early and handed my card to the young, slim, dark-haired secretary sitting behind the reception desk.

I smiled and said, "Hello, my name is Gray. I have an appointment with Captain Theodakis."

She barely looked up at me. She glanced briefly at the card in a bored way, then said, "Wot company do I say?"

"Decca Radar," I replied.

She dialled a number on the phone and while still studying the letter she was typing, said in her best London estuary accent, "Captain Feo? The decorators 'ere."

Demonstration Van

Decca had a demonstration van that was fitted out with a range of radars, fish finders, radios etc and was used to mount demonstrations at the fishing ports around the coast. This normally tied in with the fishing season so that the van would follow the fleets that followed the shoals of herring, so to speak. A visit was planned for Eyemouth on the East coast of Scotland. The Scotland Sales Manager, Eric Anderson, was tasked with ensuring all the skippers knew about the visit. Eric was a fine Aberdonian Scot who was well loved and respected around the coast. He had been doing the job for many years and had a lovely, gentle way with him. Frank had sent me up to Glasgow for a week to see how Eric operated and dealt with his customers, who were predominantly fishermen and ferry companies. His sales technique was brilliant in its simplicity. He would listen carefully to the skipper, then say in his slow, soft Scottish accent, "Ah, yes, I see, now what you will be wanting, skipper, is one of these excellent new fish sounders and two of these super new radars. Now, shall I deliver them to the boat next Monday or Tuesday?" Sale done!

On the day of the Eyemouth demonstrations, the Sales Director Charles Taylor and Frank Headington arrived in Eyemouth from London and met up with Eric.

"Now, is it all arranged?" growled Charles. "Do all the skippers know about this?"

"Yes, of course, Mr Taylor, I have spoken to them all myself," assured Eric.

A short while later, Charles and Frank were chatting with Eric outside the van, when two skippers spotted the van and wandered along the quayside towards them. Eric, keen to welcome the guests, moved towards the skippers. "Good Morning, Good Morning. Glad you could make it," welcomed Eric.

The skippers both stopped in their stride and stared. The bigger one put his hands on his hips and said in a west highland drawl, reminiscent of Private Fraser in *Dad's Army*, "Wheel, wheel, wheel, Airick Undersun!... We thought you were deeead!"

Charles and Frank saw the funny side but poor Eric was mortified.

We have all heard the stories of business men meeting gorgeous blondes on flights and having mad, passionate flings at their destination. Just once, in over thirty years of business travelling around the world, have I ended up sitting next to a gorgeous blonde and it was on that famous, romantic long-haul route: London to Douglas in the Isle of Man. I was asked to go across and help the demonstration van team during the Isle of Man herring season. The aircraft was an old Vickers Viscount, if anyone can remember them. It had four propeller engines and lovely big round windows. As I boarded the aircraft on a warm summer's day at Heathrow, I counted the seat rows and realised that this gorgeous creature was actually sitting in my window seat. However, being the old smoothie that I am, I ignored her protests and let her sit in my window seat in the sunshine while I sat in the aisle seat next to her. She was about my age, with a ready and pleasant smile, very shapely and dressed in a colourful summer frock. I took the plunge and introduced myself. I discovered she was called Sheila. I splashed out and ordered a British Airways complimentary gin and tonic for her and as the warm sun shone through the window and the planes engines droned happily away, we chatted on and even had two more each before we got to the island.

"Your first time here?" "Are you here on business, too?" I learnt that she worked in PR for a major electronic timing company. "What lovely weather!" You know the really heavy seductive talk. James Bond could have learnt a few things that day.

At Douglas airport when we arrived, we even shared a baggage trolley. *Here we go*, I thought as I helped her through the exit door and we headed for the taxis. We had gone no more than four paces when three big bruisers in black leathers and white T-shirts appeared in front of me and grabbed the trolley. "Hi Sheila! How are you?" They warmly greeted her with hugs and familiar, friendly banter. Then, the penny dropped. It was Isle of Man Motorbike TT the following week and she was there on a company business and was to be looked after by her leather-clad gentlemen biker friends.

"Goodbye Gordon, have a nice stay," she called sweetly as I grabbed my case off the trolley and the three heavies carried her off to their van like a TT Trophy.

James Bond? Not a hope in hell, Gray.

IF YOU CAN'T TAKE A JOKE...

Boat Shows

Decca always exhibited on a large stand at the annual London Boat Show, which then was held at Earl's Court, just after Christmas. For anyone with a sales position, this was a "three-line whip" occasion as the company needed everyone they could get to man the stand. Two things I remember about my time at the Boat Show. One was sore feet, the other was some of the amusing characters that we met. The old hands were able to spot various sailing and yachty types at 20 paces. You knew when one of the more unusual visitors was about when all your senior colleagues suddenly vanished from the stand.

As a new boy, I was left to hold the fort. *Huh*, I thought, *I can do this! What is there to it?* Then, I saw this person approaching. His eyes were fixed on me as he shambled towards me with a slight stoop. He was wearing a grubby-looking raincoat, had a brown beret perched on top of his head and had a dark green canvas rucksack across his shoulder. He wandered slowly up without taking his eyes off me. He was of medium height and he spoke softly, but seriously.

"What are these?" he asked, looking at our range of small radar scanners for boats and yachts mounted along the stand top. He peered intently into my face eager to hear my answer.

"Radar scanners," I replied.

"Hmmm," he said in a very unimpressed way. Then, he said, "I built a radar, you know, in my garage."

Had I heard him correctly? My senses were now working overtime. What on earth was he talking about?

"Did you?" I asked. "What sort of range did you get on it?"

"Oh, about 5 miles," he replied, seriously.

I looked round for some support but only caught sight of two of my older colleagues peering round the edge of the stand giggling like schoolboys.

"Very good," said I. "Did you sell many?"

"No, but it's still there though." He looked at the scanners on the stand again. "Rubbish," he said. "Just modern rubbish."

Then, without another word, he just wandered off, disappearing into the crowd.

Luckily, the vast majority of visitors were genuinely nice people, interested and eager to learn or to seek advice about radars and what sort of equipment was best for their particular boat. Most were genuinely struggling to balance the demands for safety with the different navigation systems available and the horrors of the price of modern electronics to do the job. There was, however, one small group we found tiresome. They tended to be males in their fifties or sixties, pompous and often on the portly side with ruddy cheeks. They would invariably be wearing a blazer or other obviously yachting type clothes and always wore deck shoes – the flat blue ones with leather laces and white soles. All that was missing was the glass of gin and tonic and binoculars round their necks. Why they dressed this way when they were in central London on a cold January day with snow and slush outside was a mystery we never resolved.

They would walk up to you and command your attention, often interrupting conversations. They would say loudly and proudly: "I have a Burgerflip 32 (or some such type of boat), which of your radars do I need for it? Quite a big one, I imagine." The tone and look made it clear that they saw us as no different from boatyard cleaners.

Now, most of us working at the show spent the rest of the year selling big ship radars to the fleet owners and often sold radars in fleet size quantities. These radars cost anything from ten or twenty times the price of a small yacht radar, and merchant ships normally had two radars; so one small yacht radar was not really that important in our normal daily life. But, if the owner of a "Burgerflip 32" thought it was, then we had better give him our undivided attention.

"Firstly, sir (they loved the sir and it softened them up), how many masts has your yacht?"

"It's a Burgerflip 32, I told you."

"Yes, I know, but I am sorry, you must forgive me, I am not familiar with that particular yacht myself."

"Oh goodness," he would sigh. "Well, it has one mast."

"Ah, I see, just a single mast then. Is it a Bermudan rig or gaff rig?"

"Bermudan, of course, with a self furling jib," he said proudly.

"Oh dear, what a shame. Had it been gaff rigged, then there is often enough clear room on the mast above the foresails, but a Bermudan rig, oh dear, no, that is difficult. You see sir, it is always very difficult to fit any radar to a single mast Bermudan sloop as the foresails prevent any clear mast space for the radar to be fitted and then if you did, there is a real danger of the jib or genoa taking the radar with it when you tack."

"Why can't you fit it on the cabin top?" he barks.

"Well, that is a possibility, but we then run into radiation issues as well as boom movements or a loose spinnaker boom could knock it flying, and of course there may be halyard or sheet runs across the top of the cabin."

As he drew breath to interrupt, we would continue, "I imagine though that you stow your dingy on the cabin roof don't you? Crucially though, the radar must obviously be fitted high enough above the water to get a sufficient radar range to be of any real use and we find that the cabin top is just too low, only about 4 or 5 feet above the water. Of course, had it been a larger yacht, such as a ketch or even a yawl, then we could certainly have offered you a radar that could have been easily installed on forward side of the mizzen mast."

By now, the poor guy would be fuming. He would grunt something unintelligible and sulk off towards the Guinness stand.

"When you buy a proper ship, do call back," we would mutter pleasantly as he left. However, as I say, the vast majority were good, decent folk who we thoroughly enjoyed chatting to and helping out if we could, but as in all walks of life there were always those who asked for it.

The Boat Show was a great time for catching up with other guys and listening to stories. The North West area manager was an old and bold merchant master mariner called Gordon Roberts. He was a big, bluff man who took no nonsense and he told us a couple of amusing stories.

At his interview for his master's exam, the examiner asked, "At what speed should a ship go in thick fog?"

Gordon, a young and eager officer said, correctly, "A reasonable speed for the conditions and visibility."

"And what do you consider to be a reasonable speed, Mr Roberts?"

"Oh, about 8 knots," replied Gordon.

"8 Knots!" screeched the examiner.

"We were in a ship in fog doing just 4 knots and we had a collision!"

Gordon was unphased by this and replied, "Well, if you had been doing 8 knots, you would not have been there, would you!"

Later on in life, he took a job as a harbour pilot in Freetown in West Africa. The new French liner 'France' had berthed there and the next day Gordon was sent out to bring in a small merchant ship that was a regular visitor to Freetown. Gordon and the captain of this ship, who was a pompous fellow, did not get on and had had a few 'words' in the past.

As they rounded the last bend before the harbour, the captain said, "What ship is that, pilot?"

"It's the 'France', captain."

"Well," said the Captain, "I bet they had the best senior pilot out to bring her in?"

"Oh, they did, sir. Me. But actually, captain, I could have done with you here yesterday."

The captain puffed up his chest expecting a compliment on his skill and knowledge, "Oh really, pilot, and why is that?"

"We could have used you as a bloody tug." Gordon had to write several letters of apology for that one!

Cross Channel

Having spent a couple of years with Ernie, I was offered my first chance of a proper overseas role. It was to run a series of presentations and demonstrations of a new radar system that incorporated a computer to track other ships. It was called an Automatic Radar Plotting Aid (or ARPA for short). In time, this type of equipment would become a compulsory fit on all large merchant ships under International Maritime law. The new computer-based radar automatically tracked the radar echoes of ships, and gave the operator key information on their courses and speeds to assist collision avoidance as well as providing useful navigation information.

A few of us were sent on a two-week technical course on the new radar so we could understand how it worked and then move on to be able to present it in a way that demonstrated its main features and benefits. The course was well designed and given by Tony Brookes and enabled non technical salesmen to understand the technical benefits of the radar. Initially, the demonstrations were to be done on a cross-channel ferry before we could start demonstrating the system worldwide. We had to demonstrate and sell it to the UK and European markets first. We installed the radar on the bridge of the Horsa, a Sealink ferry that ran from Folkestone to Boulogne. My role was to base myself in Folkestone. I stayed in the Burlington Hotel. It was a pleasant, relaxed and comfortable hotel with a good restaurant and a cosy downstairs cocktail bar with easy chairs, and which always had a blazing fire burning during the cold, damp winter months. They also had a friendly Danish barmaid called Anna, whose pleasant smile made it even nicer. Many of the visiting customers used to spend the night there, either before or after the crossing. I would meet customers coming down from London by train or drive them down myself, then take them onto the ferry for the return crossing to Boulogne. After an introductory talk to explain the system, we would move onto the bridge and demonstrate the functions and features of the radar as we sailed across the channel. Then, after the trip, they would either stay in Folkestone or I would take them to the station for a train to London. Customers were invited from all the London shipping companies as well as from all over Europe and Scandinavia, so we had a busy time of it and the trips went on during summer and winter.

This was my first exposure to giving structured presentations and demonstrations to customers. I discovered very early on that while it all seems very straightforward running through the slides sitting in the office, onboard the ship in front of the customers it was very different. I should know what the next slide was going to show and which words I would utter to enhance the slide. In the real world, however, my memory would go blank, the correct technical word would vanish from my head and those I found would not form properly. I found myself stopping and pausing while I tried to work out what to say next. Even on a ferry with people I knew, stage fright could strike. I learnt quickly that it was imperative to carefully write the script and have an intimate knowledge of both the script and the slides I was about to present – to the point that I knew what the next three or four slides were going to show and which words I would use to describe them. I also tried to ensure that I knew the answers to the next two technical levels of questions that were likely to be asked. Then, with repeated rehearsals for timing and content at home and in the office, I slowly gained the confidence to be able to give, what I hope were, passable presentations and demos. This experience was to prove invaluable throughout my career and I never forgot the horrors of forgetting my lines and the cold sweat that accompanied it during some of those early attempts.

The trip across to Boulogne took about an hour and a half. On the way over, I would present and demonstrate the radar system to them on the bridge, then answer their questions and let them use the radar themselves. Hopefully, all the while trying not to distract or get in the way of the ship's officers as they sailed the ship across one of the busiest shipping lanes in the world. The Straits of Dover provided plenty of ships to track and test the system, so it was an ideal situation. When we were not onboard, the ship's officers used the radar, so we got vital firsthand feedback from them when we next went onboard. By the time we reached Boulogne, most customers had seen all that they needed to and so we would go down for a leisurely lunch in the ship's restaurant during the turnaround when it was empty and quiet. Then they were able enjoy a stroll on deck or to carry on with any questions and discussions on the return leg to Folkestone.

One day, I had driven down to Folkestone with the senior technical superintendent of a large London-based shipping company. I shall call him Bob. I knew Bob well and we got on fine together. He was a pleasant north country fellow who had spent many years at sea before getting a senior management position ashore some years before. We often met in London and we were starting to achieve some sales successes with his company – so I felt that this should be a relatively easy day, but still knew it was an important one.

We arrived in Folkestone on a sunny summer's morning but there was a stiff southwesterly breeze blowing and a few white horses out in the Channel. By the time we got down to the ferry berth, the wind was rising and I could see more white horses foaming out at sea. Bob saw them too and said, "It's not going to be rough, is it, Gordon?"

"Oh, I'm sure it will be fine, Bob, just a summer squall blowing through."

We went onboard and I took him up to the bridge and introduced him to the captain. Then, we set sail. I could see that the waves were beginning to sweep round the end of the breakwater as we let go the ropes. We had not gone more than 50 yards when there was a crash and a bang from forward as the ship met the first of the rollers from this summer gale. As we headed out into the Channel, we turned south to clear the Varne sandbanks. In doing so, we turned more into the wind and sea. The seas were picking up and the ship pitched and heaved as she fought her way across, and waves crashed against the bow.

We struggled through the presentation, but I could see that Bob had lost all interest in the radar and me and was intently watching for the next wave and crash of spray across the bridge windows. I was not sure what to do. Did I carry on and pretend that I thought he was fine; even though it was clear he was not? Or did I call off the demo and take him for a coffee indicating that it was obvious to me that he was seasick? I suggested the coffee but he said, "No, I would rather stay up here. Can we go out on deck for a minute?" We went out onto the bridge wing and while, to his credit, he was not actually seasick, he was decidedly queasy and a little green about the gills. However, the fresh air helped him and he had perked up by the time we were approaching the Boulogne breakwater.

As we moved onto our berth in Boulogne harbour, I thought that he was getting back to normal. However, he surprised me as he had made a decision.

"Gordon, I cannot go back today on this ship. I must get off. I will spend the night here and sail back tomorrow when it is fine. Why don't you come too, as I do not know Boulogne? I shall buy you dinner. There must be a good hotel here?"

"Bob, I really would love to do that but I honestly can't. I have to go back on this sailing as I have to meet some Swedish customers off the train at Folkestone later on tonight. They are staying in the Burlington Hotel and we are coming across tomorrow morning. But don't worry, Bob, you will be fine; come and have some lunch and the gale will have blown through by the time we sail."

"No, there is no way I am going back. I appreciate that you can't stay here tonight, but never mind, I will find a hotel and be fine."

By this time, we had moved back inside and I followed him down to the car deck where he said a brisk "Thank you". And with that and without any chance to talk him round, he walked briskly – if unsteadily – along the car deck and out into the sunshine through the big bow doors. I have had customers fall asleep on me; I have had customers walk out of my presentations; but I had never had one jump ship.

When I went back up to the bridge, the captain said, "Where's Bob gone?"

"Ashore, sir," I said. "He does not like too much sea time in one day so he is saving some for tomorrow!"

By the time we sailed, the gale had blown through and we had a beautiful, sunny, calm afternoon's return sail.

Having now cut my sales teeth on UK activities, I was still itching to spread my wings a bit. The ARPA radar sales were now going well and the product manager, Louis, decided it was time to take it overseas. Louis was one of life's gentlemen. He was smart, efficient and always calm. I never saw him lose his temper. He had served in the Royal Navy during the Korean War and worked as a product manager on marine radars since the late 1950s. What he did not know about radar was not worth worrying about. He offered me a job doing all the overseas presentations and demonstrations with the radar. It would mean another two-week course on the new radar and how it all worked, as well as learning how to give good presentations and demonstrations. Then I would be off and travelling non-stop with the radar. I jumped at it. Over the coming years, I was to learn that international selling is not as easy as leaping on a plane and coming home with the order and a suntan.

The first port of call for the "ARPA Radar World Tour" was Hong Kong. We shipped the radar to our agents there – a division of the Swire's organisation in Hong Kong. I followed the radar out a week later. Swires were one of the old and respected Hong Kong companies and were also our customers in that they owned the China Navigation Shipping Co, which was a major shipping line in Asia.

Louis and I had been dealing with a Hong Kong Chinese gentleman in Swires called Ted Toyit, who Louis knew well. Ted had been with Swire's marine agency business for years and knew all the Hong Kong shipowners. He had told us that he now had a new boss, an expat Brit, who had just come out to Hong Kong to join the company. He had decided to place the responsibility for all the local arrangements for the radar demonstrations in the hands of a young Chinese manager called Mr Raymond Leung, who had also only recently joined Swires. Ted explained that Mr Leung had been told to meet me off the flight on Saturday morning and arrange for the radar equipments to be delivered to the hotel on the Sunday morning.

Hong Kong and foreign travel. Here I come!

M V Horsa – Mr. G At The ARPA

Eyemouth harbour

CHAPTER 2

Hong Kong

The Arrival of Mr Gary

"Please ensure that your seat belt is securely fastened and your tray table locked away in the upright position. We are about to land at Hong Kong's Kai Tak International Airport."

It had been a long flight from Gatwick via Bahrain – sixteen hours' flying time and heaven knows how many since I got up yesterday morning. The petite Cathay Pacific air stewardesses, in their red uniforms, dashed around the Business Class cabin making their final checks and collecting up the last few glasses before strapping themselves into their seats. The engines roared again as the big jumbo banked to the right to start its approach across the harbour. I hoped that Mr Leung would be there to meet me as I flexed my legs and looked forward to a shower and a few hours to sleep and relax before the work started tomorrow.

The engine roar decreased as the plane straightened and levelled out. We emerged from the low clouds; below us lay Hong Kong Harbour and then the rooftops and the bustling early morning streets of Kowloon. As we got lower, I caught flashes of the green and cream taxis and red buses and the early morning crowds down in the busy streets. We arrived at traffic lights on the corner of a busy crossroads near the airport; luckily, the lights were green and the plane's engines roared again as it banked sharply to the right at the green grocers. Then, we suddenly dropped the last 100 feet onto Kai Tak runway.

The plane bounced, the tyres screeched and reverse thrust screamed. Our seat belts bit into our laps as the plane slowed dramatically and stopped just before the end of the runway and the harbour beyond. We had arrived in Hong Kong.

As I walked out of the customs hall, I looked around for any signs of this Mr Leung. I eventually spotted a young Chinese guy in a grey suit standing towards the back of the hall holding a piece of paper down by his side that just had "Decca" written on it. I went over and asked him if he was meant to be meeting me. He was. We introduced ourselves. Mr Leung's first comment surprised me a little.

"I am glad you have come now, I have been up long time as I come to meet you and not had any breakfast; so, we will now go to airport restaurant for breakfast."

"Sorry, Mr Leung, but I do not want any breakfast. I want to get to the hotel," I retorted. I may as well have said nothing as he had already turned round and was heading back into the terminal and up the stairs towards the main Chinese restaurant. All I could do was follow, carrying my suitcase.

Mr Leung proceeded to enjoy a "full Chinese" breakfast in the clattering cacophony of a canteen with its shiny, chrome-framed, formica-topped tables and hard chairs. It was full of Chinese airport workers and passengers with their families and bags, all yelling at each other as tea was slurped noisily, bowls of noodles and congee were devoured and rattled down onto the tables. I only saw one other European in there and he looked as hacked off as I felt.

As soon as Mr Leung had finished his fish congee – a type of rice soup with lumps of fish in it – I got up and said, "Right. Can we go to the hotel now, please."

"OK," said Mr Leung, "but no hurry, radar will not be at hotel until after 12 o' clock."

I turned round and glared down at him. "What? You were asked to arrange that for tomorrow. Why are you doing it today?"

I got an insolent Chinese look that said 'because I, Raymond

Leung, do not want to mess about on Sunday and there is nothing that you can do about it "round eyes".' I was angry as he was right and I would now have to stay up all day and sort it all out. This trip was not starting well.

The drive from the airport though Kowloon's teeming, hot and humid streets was frosty. We emerged from the Cross Harbour Tunnel on the Hong Kong Island side and were approaching the hotel. Mr Leung spoke, " I will leave you at hotel and go to warehouse to make sure radar is ready to come here, then I return here, very soon." I got out of the car into the hot morning air and he roared off into the traffic.

I entered the lobby through the big glass doors and was immediately hit by a wall of refreshing, cool, air-conditioned air. I looked around. The lobby was busy with people checking out and others hanging around waiting for colleagues or friends. Everyone looked clean, fresh and efficient. Everyone seemed to be fully charged up for another day's holiday explorations, shopping or work – as Saturday was a normal work day in Hong Kong then. I felt tired, dirty, jet-lagged, and not a little angry at Mr Leung's attitude. I should have been looking forward to a shower and a sleep, but now had to wait for Mr Leung and the radar. I sighed, resigned myself to my fate and walked over to the reception desk.

"Good morning, I think you have a reservation for me. My name is Gray."

The trim, young Hong Kong girlie, dressed in a full-length, deep red cheongsam tapped away at the keyboard. I noticed she had a cute little smile that made her look quite vulnerable.

"Ah, so sorry, sir, no reservation."

"Oh? Are you sure? Our agent's office made it some time ago. There is meant to be a room for me and a conference room booked as well?"

"Yes, sir, very sure. No reservation in that name, no conference room booked also."

"OK, but I know the reservation was made; can you please check again? The name is Gray, G.R.A.Y., Gordon Gray?"

"No, sir, nothing, so sorry."

"Do you think that you could check with your supervisor or duty manager?"

She scurried away into the back office. I knew the reservation must be there as Ted had telexed me to confirm it. A few moments later, an older, black suited Chinese lady appeared from the back office. "Is there a problem, sir?"

I explained what had happened and gave her the company name, agent's name and details. She tapped away, then smiled.

"Ah, yes, we have the reservation made by Swire, but it is for a Mr Gary Gordon."

"Could that not be for Mr Gordon Gray?" I asked, hopefully.

"Oh I see! Your name is Gray! So sorry, on the computer screen Gray is Gary."

Gray is an unusual name for the Chinese but Gary is a much more familiar name to them. Also when two apparent Christian names appear together, the receptionists do not know which name is the surname, so they can get transposed!

"OK, that's me; Mr Gordon Gray."

"I am so pleased sir, now my colleague will check you in. Have a nice stay, Mr Gary." I was too tired to worry about it so I just said thank you, took my key and headed for the lifts. I did not realise it at the time but I was now Mr Gary, forever. I smiled, *Oh well, if you can't take a joke!* Over the following years, the number of times that I appeared on hotel computers around the world as Mr Gary was countless. It got to the point that my wife could ring a hotel and ask for Mr Gary and get put straight through.

The hotel, the Furama, was a fine modern one in the business centre and was handy for our customers to get to. The room that Swires had booked was called a junior suite, but it was just a large room. Half of it had a bed in the middle and the other half was just open space with the bathroom to one side. I stood and stared at it. Was this meant to be just my room or was there another room booked for the demonstrations – and, if so, where? If not, then there was no way I was sleeping beside the radar. I would need another room. There was nothing I could do until Mr Leung chose to return. At least the room had a fantastic harbour view. I stood and watched the activity out on the harbour while I waited.

I recalled my very first visit there in 1973 when I was in the Royal Navy. From the sea, Hong Kong is fascinating and full of contrast. The ships pass silent, hilly, tree-clad islands with little sign of habitation; then, as they round the end of Hong Kong Island, the mass of buildings and glistening glass-clad skyscrapers appears through the heat haze. Ships are everywhere, coming, going, anchored, while tugs and barges are constantly moving freight through the harbour. 'Where did all that come from?' is the normal reaction. Here, around one smallish island, it seems that half of Asia is working non-stop and the atmosphere, noises and smells of the harbour and the city convey that.

Our frigate had arrived in the main harbour area in the early morning and we rolled gently in the wakes and washes of the many tugs, freighters and ferries that churned across the "Fragrant Harbour", turning it into a churning turmoil of water. We waited while a small tug, towing a huge barge with a big red derrick crane and a two-storey deck house on one end, slowly chugged along the quay side where we were meant to berth. We slowly approached our berth at HMS *Tamar*, the RN base on Hong Kong Island. It was situated right in the middle of the busy business district and set amid the growing forest of skyscrapers. As I concentrated on my bridge duties, I tried to absorb the atmosphere, the noises, the scents and smells that drifted across the harbour. It was like nowhere else that I had ever seen. It was just as I remembered it. The green and white double-ended Star ferry boats still plied across from Kowloon to Central, the tugs and lighters still churned up and down the harbour and the freighters still moored between Hong Kong Island and Kowloon.

Local ferries plied all over the harbour and surrounding waterways, linking all the other islands to Central and Kowloon.

Hong Kong is one of only two major cities in the world that were exactly as I imagined they would be before I visited them. The other one was New York. Hong Kong is manic; there is a smell to Hong Kong – a scent of money and hard work as six million Chinese try to earn a bowl of rice or a new Rolls Royce. Everyone is working, working all hours; everywhere, there is bustle and activity. Everywhere, there are people carrying, pulling, pushing, driving, rushing, selling, buying, moving things. Produce from the PRC, electronics from Japan, machinery from Europe, ducks and vegetables from the New Territories.

While physically it was constantly changing, the atmosphere and excitement of Hong Kong never changed. I always loved Hong Kong. There is a "Must Win" atmosphere about the place. To lose in Hong Kong is a sin. The Hong Kong Chinese strive to better themselves and losing is not on their agenda. They all seem to respect the other person's right to strive in his own way – be it as a grocer or a banker, a bar girl or a bus driver. They all have the same goal: to make money to improve their lot. The streets are a mass of shops and stalls. From the high fashion houses in the posh Central shopping malls to the souvenir stalls in the side alleys of Kowloon. All that Mainland China can produce finds its way to Hong Kong. From cheap plastic toys to beautiful arts and crafts; huge silk carpets, lacquer vases, painted porcelain, ginger jars, silks of all sorts, cheap silk underwear, paintings of misty green hills with the Great Wall stretching away into the distance – they all jostle for space in the shops and stalls. Hong Kong used to be a great place to buy cameras, stereo or HiFi sets and watches. 'Johnny, you come back. I give you better price!'

I have spent many hours bargaining with stall holders to get an extra $10 discount; always great fun, if done in a happy friendly way. I was with a pal in one of the underground markets looking at watches one day when he saw one he liked. After an hour of negotiating, he got one poor lady shopkeeper so frustrated that she went off and came back with her stock ledger and waved the page in front of him shouting, "Look! You see I pay more than what you offer for watchy!" In the end, he did a deal at cost price plus $10 – but it took three days and it was a long time ago.

There was a knock on the door. Mr Leung walked in and stood in the empty part of the room. "Crate is coming. Is now on lorry. It will stand there," he said, pointing at a blank piece of wall.

"Hang about, the radar presentations are meant to be in a proper business meeting room or conference room, not my bedroom!"

"None available, bed there for you is OK," was all he said in a haughty way. He lifted his nose in the air and hurried out knowing that by now I was blazing.

Mr Leung had shown himself to be arrogant, confrontational and determined that his way was the only way. He clearly had absolutely no idea how to stage a series of demonstrations and I was sure he had not met any of the people that had been invited and knew nothing about marine radar.

"Mr Leung, I am not sleeping with the radar and its equipment in my room, nor am I having all the shipowners of Hong Kong tramping through my bedroom. This is meant to be my home for the next two weeks. Is there not another room booked for the presentations? 'No' was his reply. "Right, you wait here, I am going to see reception."

The supervisor who had found my booking earlier was still there. She quickly checked her computer. "Unfortunately there are no free conference rooms for Monday or the next two weeks, so sorry."

"Can you tell me when the room was booked?"

"Room booked last week. If you had booked even two week ago, then we had conference room available." She then managed to find me a standard bedroom two floors below the suite.

I went back up. Raymond was looking out at the view. "If your company had done what we asked you, when we asked you over a month ago, we could have had a proper function room. Now we are stuck with this room for the demonstrations, but I will be staying in another room. This is my new room number."

Raymond ignored me. There was a noise outside in the corridor and a babble of Chinese. The radar crate had now arrived. I stood aside as three sweaty, T-shirt clad Chinese labourers manhandled the large wooden case into the room.

Raymond took this as his cue that his job was done and left calling over his shoulder, "See you at the cocktail party."

"Hold on! What cocktail party, Raymond?"

"The one that I have arranged on Monday morning at 0930, before your demonstration."

I was speechless. "You have done what? No one has a cocktail party at that time anywhere! You must change it to a proper time."

"It is arranged. Invitations sent out. It is too late" – and with that, he was gone.

I decided that I needed to talk to Ted before I got to work setting up the radar. I rang Ted at home. Before I had a chance to say anything, he said, "Oh Gordon, I am sorry about things."

"What's going on Ted? This guy Leung is a lunatic and an arrogant one, too."

"Yes, I know, but he is being groomed for higher management and the new managing director wanted something to test him, so he was given the Decca radar demonstrations to organise."

"Well, what is done is done," I said, "but, Ted, I need you here on Monday as you know all the shipowners. Also, we will expect your company to pay for this farce of a cocktail party he has arranged and I am afraid that Louis will not be happy either. We are not your new managing director's guinea pigs for Raymond Leung to play with!"

Ted agreed and promised that he would be there on Monday. The demonstrations were scheduled to run for two full weeks with morning and afternoon sessions each day.

I then set to unpacking the radar, the video player and the slide projector; connecting it all up and hoping it was all OK. This was the first time I had set the whole thing up from scratch so I was a bit anxious. I should not have worried as when I switched it all on, it worked like a dream. I heaved a huge sigh of relief. I did a few function checks to make sure all was well, then rang Louis back in the UK where he was enjoying a lazy Saturday morning at home. I related events to him and he was as disgusted as I was, but agreed we would not say anything until the end of the demos as Louis was due to come out for the last few days and had a meeting planned with the new managing director anyway. As it was now after 6 o'clock, I shut the radar display down, went down and found my new room and, gratefully, finally had the shower I had promised myself on the plane nearly twelve hours ago.

This trip was my first real experience of jet lag and I struggled to get myself alert and 'switched on' in the mornings. I found, however, that I was fine in the afternoons but started to fall asleep at about 6 o'clock at night. I had once asked John Gunner, the USA manager in Decca how long it took to get over jetlag.

"Gordon, it takes one day for every hour of time difference."

"No, surely not? You are winding me up, John."

"No, I'm not. Seriously you should plan not to be 100% for at least a few days. If you ever have to go to the Far East then it will be a full week before you feel normal." John was right.

The cocktail party was a fiasco with coffee, tea, alcohol and peanuts all on offer. Not surprisingly, the only people who came were those coming to the first morning session. People were naturally a bit bemused by a cocktail party at 0930, but thankfully after half an hour, Ted and I gently moved everyone up to the room where we had the radar. After that, the demonstrations actually went quite well. Thankfully, someone must have said something to Raymond as he failed to appear. After Louis had arrived at the end of the following week, we had an interesting meeting with Raymond Leung's boss – a guy called Tony and a former director of a security business in London. He seemed to be a really nice guy but admitted knowing nothing about handling the Chinese or about the shipping industry. However, Louis, in his gentle but forceful manner, explained the importance of the demonstrations to our company and our frustrations with Mr Leung. The managing director had the grace to accept what we said and apologised for not letting Ted run with it.

Chek Lap Kok

On our last Saturday in Hong Kong, Ted took Louis and I over to Lantau Island for a seafood lunch at a restaurant on the west side of the island. Tai O was a small fishing village built by a muddy river mouth and an inlet of the sea where the fishing community had settled, building their houses on stilts above the tides reach but close enough to their boats. The small family-run restaurant was tucked a couple of rows back from the water but was full of fish tanks with all sorts of fish in them. We sat down and were served a selection of foods that Ted negotiated with the small but fierce lady owner. After a lunch of prawns, crab and other unidentified fish that Ted recommended, all washed down with chilled San Miguel beers, he suggested that we go up into the hills for a walk.

As we climbed higher and looked down at the deserted hills and bays that stretched all the way up the island, he pointed out the area that was due to be flattened and pushed into the sea to make the "new" Hong Kong airport to be called Chek Lap Kok. In 1981, it was a beautiful, remote piece of coastline with steep-sided lush green hills cascading down to an empty sea from their mist-shrouded summits. The area was virtually uninhabited and hidden from the main Hong Kong harbour which lay off the East side of the island. On the face of it, the area was an unlikely site for a major airport. Little did we know then what a difference twenty years would make to the island. Most of these lovely hills were quite literally pushed into the sea to form the reclaimed base for the airport.

Chek Lap Kok is now a vast complex of airport buildings, runways and taxi ways, aircraft support services, hangars, housing and road and rail links to Kowloon. Huge new suspension bridges for the road and rail links now run across to the mainland and hotels and housing for the airport staff are dotted along the coast. Years later, I was to be involved in selling some of the fire detection and airfield security systems for it, but on that warm afternoon on a quiet hillside it all seemed impossibly far-off in the future.

After that fortnight, we began to develop the Hong Kong market and used it as a stepping stone into China. About a year after the demonstrations I was pleased to get promoted to be the Far East Area Manager, so I then spent a lot of time there.

While Racal Decca was looking for a new agent, we met an expat called Vince Hall. Vince had been in Hong Kong for years with Marconi and then set up his own marine electronics service company in Hong Kong. We learnt that Vince actually wanted to sell his company; so Racal Decca ended up buying Vince's company and investing in new facilities and service workshops. Vince then ran the company as the resident director with his team of service engineers. Racal Decca wanted to use Hong Kong as a base from which to develop the new mainland China market and other parts of the region.

The phone call

On the not-so-happy side, I have some bad memories too. One year, when we were going to have a stand at the Far East's biggest marine equipment exhibition which was to be held in Hong Kong, I sought out my new boss in the UK, Commercial Director Dave Rodriques, who even looked like a Spanish pirate. He was a swarthy character, always well tanned; a tubby soul with a little goatee beard. He was cheerful but had never worked in the marine industry before and seemed unaware of what international selling was about. He was really one of those who thought that all you had to do was fly in, buy the agent a beer, fly home and the orders would follow. I asked him if it would be OK, if I paid, for my wife, Doreen, to fly out and join me for three or four day holiday in Hong Kong after the exhibition finished and if I could take some leave out there. "Yes, great idea," he said.

We planned accordingly. This was in the days before budget airlines and cheap flights, so we bought an advance booking, "not very cheap and not very flexible" ticket and she duly arrived the day after the exhibition finished. I collected her at the airport and took her back to the hotel. Once she was settled in the room, I had to go back to the exhibition site to help with the dismantling of the stand, but made sure that she understood my orders before she had a sleep. "Whatever you do, do NOT touch the Mini Bar – especially the Toblerone!"

Our plan was to spend four days in Hong Kong together on leave and then fly home together. Doreen had arrived on a Wednesday. After having been in Hong Kong for the exhibition a few days earlier, Dave had flown up to Korea for meetings with the Korean company with whom we had started working. At 0730 on the Thursday morning, the phone rang in our hotel room and woke us up. It was Dave.

"Gordon, I am having breakfast with Mr Kim of our partner company here. I want you to fly up here today and talk to them about setting up a marine radar service network for the radars that they will be making for us for the Korean fishing industry. What time flight can you get?"

I could not believe this. "Dave, have you forgotten that you agreed that my wife could join me out here? She arrived yesterday and I am now supposed to be on leave with her until next week."

"Oh never mind that, this is more important. I want you to come to Korea today and sort this out."

I felt I had been punched. Never mind that my wife would be left in Hong Kong when we were supposed to be on leave together. Never mind that she was now meant to go home on her own. Never mind that you, Mr Director, had agreed to this months ago.

"Dave, I think you must have forgotten our agreement!"

"No, I haven't, but this is work. Holidays can wait."

I was really angry now as I knew it should have been a senior service division manager that went up to Korea to talk to them, not a radar salesman. "Should not someone from service division be doing this?"

"You are already here," he said. "It will save money if you do it."

"Dave, I am not a service manager, I am a salesman!"

Doreen was listening to this exchange with her face dropping by the second. Either I capitulated to this idiot and felt the fury of my wife, quite rightly, for just meekly saying yes; or I took a stand and risked upsetting a boss who I had no real regard for anyway. He clearly had no regard for me or his agreement with me. Since Racal had bought the Decca Company, no one who had been a Decca employee had been promoted and indeed a number of good Decca senior managers had been made redundant almost overnight. The new senior positions had all been filled by Racal men from somewhere outside our division. I felt I had little to lose.

"Dave, even if I could get a flight today, which I won't know until the airline offices open, I will not get to Seoul until late tonight. Tomorrow is Friday so nothing will happen anyway, then I will have to wait around all weekend until Monday before they can start to get their guys together. I have not got anything prepared to present or discuss and to be done properly, this needs a service division person to do it. Can't this wait?"

"I have promised Mr Kim that as you are only in Hong Kong, you will come up today."

"David, I am not prepared to just leave my wife on her own for four days after this leave has all been agreed, just to spend a weekend in Seoul on my own." Then, I took my neck back off the block a little. "Look, what I will do is this. We are due to fly home on Monday night. If you insist on me making this visit, then I will just have to put Doreen on the flight home on Monday. Then I will come to Korea on Tuesday after my leave is over." Dave weakened. He realised that two days was not going to make any difference and agreed.

However, the spell had been broken and the holiday spoiled, all for want of a director who could not stop and think before he picked up a telephone. I did wonder if the gushing bravado and parade ground orders were because he was sitting with Mr Kim at the time. Doreen was naturally very upset as she felt it was her fault somehow. She never, ever came with me, or joined me on a trip, again. No way was I going to put her through that sort of nonsense again and no way was she going to put herself in the position to have that sort of nonsense happen to her.

We managed a pleasant, but spoiled, weekend in Hong Kong while the shadow of Dave's phone call hung like a black cloud over it all. Both of us knew there were no winners in the argument. Doreen flew home on the Monday night as planned. As she left to go through security, she looked at me and said, "Never mind, if you can't take a joke!" and winked. All was well again. I flew up to Seoul on the following day. I spent three days with the Koreans discussing the needs of electronic servicing support for the fishing industry, then flew home. The whole episode was a needless upset caused by someone who was obviously trying to impress the Koreans by "whistling in an 'expert'".

THE ODD LUNCH

I had a curious experience in Hong Kong with a customer that I have never had before. It was generated by a lateral thinking shipowner. We were following up on the earlier radar demonstrations and one of the marine superintendants from a large shipping company called and invited me to meet him for lunch at a well known restaurant in Kowloon called Jimmy's Kitchen. When I got there, I saw that the host was sitting at a large table and sitting round it were about six other men. *Who were all these people?* Then I recognised some, but not all, of the faces. I joined the group and was introduced to all my competitors!

When the last two guys had arrived, the host said simply, "Right you guys. Over the past few months, you have all been telling me why I should buy your radars. Now is your chance to convince me. I want you all to debate whose radar is better, then I can choose which one I will buy."

I was amazed. Decca was an old and honourable company and I had been taught by Ernie Cast that in Decca we never knocked the competition in front of the customer. This lunch set-up, for that was what it was, was a nonsense. There were four or five competitor companies sitting round a table and this marine super expected us all to 'debate' the merits and shortcomings of our product with each other so he could listen and then choose the winner. Two or three of us exchanged glances and obviously thought the same way. Then, the salesman for an American company jumped in and started going on about his radar and why ours and someone else's was no good. He clearly knew little about our system.

The superintendent looked at the man who represented the German system. "Willy, don't you want to respond?"

"Yes, I do," he said, "but I would rather respond in your office in a one to one meeting and not here, if you don't mind, as we do not like to criticise our competitors in public. I will happily discuss any points at all with you in your office, but I do not want to be involved in an open public debate." I nodded and a couple of other guys agreed and the discussion died. The American, thinking that we were chickening out, tried to make a few snide hits but no one responded and they fell flat. Then the beer arrived and things relaxed a little, the food came and we all had a friendly and good-natured lunch with little mention of radar! The marine super had actually thought that we were going to do his job for him with one manufacturer slanging off another until, by the time the deserts arrived and after winning a beer-fuelled debate, one company would emerge as the undisputed winner with all the others accepting the outcome and thus a fleet fit order to the winner. He must have realised he had got that one wrong.

CONSULTANTS

Our new Racal masters wanted to ensure that the Hong Kong and Korean markets were going well. One day I was called into the boss's office and Dave Rodrigues told me that on my next trip to Hong Kong and Korea I would be accompanied by a certain Mr Eric Tyler. He was a 'personal consultant' to the chairman. I was suitably impressed and smiled gratefully, but at the same time thinking, "Oh hell, why me?"

A few days later, Eric appeared in our office and introduced himself. He was large and loud with a ruddy complexion and a clearly well-fed stomach. There was no doubting his enthusiasm for the task. For half an hour, he name-dropped about his close friendships with the chairman and senior Racal guys – all of whom were invisible from my level – and what we were going to do in Hong Kong, China and Korea over the next few months. After half an hour of non-stop talking, he finished with the words, "Dont worry, it's all going to be jolly good fun." He then got up and vanished out of the office. I don't think I had said two words the whole time.

We flew out to Hong Kong together a few days later on what was to be the first of a number of trips. On the flight, Eric showed that he could eat and drink for Britain. There was nothing offered on the flight that he did not have, be it food or drink. Eric ate while I tried to sleep.

On one flight out there, not long after take-off from Bahrain for the last leg to Hong Kong, we had just settled down with another drink when Eric said to me, "I was talking to the chairman. We need one of our own men permanently in Hong Kong to oversee things here and in the region. What do you think about doing it?"

"What, as an expat? You want me to move to Hong Kong?"

"Yes, but think about it and give me your answer tomorrow morning, after we arrive." My mind, though jet lagged and alcohol fuelled, was racing. I had never seen myself as an expat and Doreen was very happy and did not want to give up her flying career. Had we ever had any interest in living abroad, then I was sure that we would have done something about by now. On the other hand, an expat tax-free salary, together with accommodation, car, local expenses, regular golf at the RHK Golf Club at Fanling, dinners at the Hong Kong Yacht Club etc would all be very nice and would mean we could let our UK house for a few years and maybe make a few shillings. Then, after a couple of years of the good times, we could go home with a very healthy bank balance. Also, Doreen would love the shopping. But I realised there were downsides to such a move. I was also aware that once I left the UK to work abroad, getting a job back in the UK, even in the same company, would be increasingly difficult. Would Doreen be able to get back into the airlines at the same level as she had left? Doubtful.

I got used to meeting with the British expats and one evening some of the true feelings about their lives came out. Tony, an old friend from school days, who I met by chance at an exhibition in Hong Kong, had been working overseas for about ten years in different countries. He explained his views about expat life: "You see, Gordon, the trouble with taking an expat job is that it's a one way ticket. Our salaries are high by UK standards and tax-free so when we arrive out here, or anywhere, we think we can save most of the money and retire early. In fact, it rarely works like that. You soon find that the money goes just as fast out here as it does at home. Maids, drivers, almost daily dinners at the golf club, holidays, air fares back to the UK three times a year, or to get Granny or the kids out here for school holidays. It all soon makes a big hole in any savings pot; so we all end up staying on 'for just one more year then, just one more year again'.

"It's not so great for my wife either. While I am at work, she gets bored in the flat as she cannot work out here and the endless round of expat wives' bloody coffee mornings, all for one charity or another; and where she is expected to take her turn and host them at home and dig deep into her purse at all of them on the basis that 'It's all in aid of charity, you know'. Some of the people here are dreadful and not the sort of person you would socialise with at home, but once you are here you are stuck with them whether it's at a dinner party or by the pool. Dinners at the yacht club every other night get boring as we all know the menu inside out and the food is not that good anyway. Golf in 100 degree heat is not golf; its torture, so I have given it up. The first few weeks in a new place are great fun, but then the routine and boredom set in. Then you discover that you really do not know how the place works. What do you do for a doctor in an emergency with the kids? Are the hospitals OK? Is the International School any good? Who do we call to fix the ancient and totally unreliable air conditioning? All the little petty things, things that at home we take for granted as we have grown up with it.

"Out here, once you have done the tourist bit, there isn't much to do. We have an Amah, but Julie, my wife, suspects she is nicking stuff – though we cannot prove it. We all miss the UK, of course, especially the good supermarkets – Lakeland and Marks and Spencer. I miss the changing of the seasons and though it sounds stupid, I really miss the cold of a frosty UK winter's day. We all really look forward to going home but realise that the days of maids, drivers and dinners out four times a week will be over. Also, UK salaries seem pitiful and even finding a job in the UK after any length of time overseas gets increasingly difficult".

I almost felt sorry for Tony as what he described was not quite the glittering non-stop fun and five-star living that expat life is painted as being.

On the wider front, Hong Kong at that time was a mess for Racal. We had decided to break with our long-time agents Swires, but had not yet finally broken with them and were still in the process of buying Vince's service company, so we had not got the new Racal company set up with its new service centre and offices. In any event, Vince would be staying on to run it as the resident director and would see himself still as the boss. He certainly knew the marine people in Hong Kong. He also had a small office in Taiwan and claimed to have 'excellent contacts' in

Korea and mainland China. I had already seen how Vince ingratiated himself to any visiting director by taking them to the "girlie bars" in Taipei and Macau. I tried to work out what my role would be. I could already see problems ahead as Vince seemed to have a rose-tinted view of future sales prospects that Louis and I did not share and Vince had already made it clear that he did not want any direct UK involvement in the running of 'his company' or 'his area'. Nor was he afraid to pick up the phone to the managing director and bypass the existing sales structure. Slowly, I began to see some order from the jumbled thoughts and reactions. From where I sat, any job I was expected to do there would be a loser. If the new company did well, then Vince would claim all the credit. If it failed then he would say that I was interfering and it was all my fault, or I did not pull my weight, or he would find some other reason that it was not his fault. As far as the other countries in the region were concerned, unless I accepted all his contacts then we would be in a constant state of conflict. I had already met a couple of them in Taiwan and was less than impressed. As the other passengers, including Eric, slept, I mulled all this through in my mind.

We arrived in Hong Kong and the next morning at breakfast, sure enough Eric barged straight in. "Well, have you decided? We can't hang about, you know, as we need to get this sorted."

"Eric, please explain what you think my role will be, exactly?"

Eric blustered on, "We need a good man who will oversee and report back to the UK, and will keep an eye on Vince."

"A spy, you mean!"

"No, no, not exactly," he said hesitantly. But that was exactly what they wanted: a tame man in Hong Kong to report back on what Vince was up to. "Eric, I am flattered at the offer but as I see it, it is a loser of a job and I don't want it. Thank you."

To my amazement and horror, Eric, without finishing his mouthful, said, "Quite right. You would have been an utter fool to take it. It is a non job but the chairman wants someone to do it."

I was appalled at the stitch-up I had avoided without even the time to talk to my wife about such a life-changing decision. However, that was Eric, charging along at full speed.

Although I was based in the UK, I now spent half my time in Hong Kong on my way to other parts of the region. Over the next few years, I used Hong Kong as a base while I travelled to China, Korea, Malaysia and Singapore, with occasional trips to Taiwan, Japan, Indonesia and the Philippines. It was a big region to cover and I needed to try to get to know the customers and agents personally and understand them, at least as far as the local culture allows. To do this, I needed to spend 100 to 120 days a year in the area. That meant spending half the working year in the territory. In Racal Decca, if a salesman did not spend that amount of time in territory, he was accused of not doing the job properly. Racal believed, quite rightly, that a salesman's place was in his area and that no one has ever won an export order by sitting behind a desk in London. So I got used to long flights, jet lag and long trips, and spent about 120 days a year travelling in the Far East.

Although I always loved going on trips and was excited by the prospect, I still never really enjoyed leaving home for a long trip, especially at the weekends with a night flight ahead of me. I would spend the day just hanging around, not able to totally relax and constantly checking that I had not forgotten anything, then leaving home just as everyone else was relaxing and looking forward to a lazy evening at home. Doreen and I had been used to separations all our working lives, so it was not a problem – just something else to work through. After the first few days of the trip and knowing everything at home was OK, then it was fine and a couple of phone calls home during the week were enough to keep my mind at ease. I was always pleased to be heading for home at the end of a trip and counted down the days. I found that on five and six-week trips during the last week or ten days I was not really as interested in work as the prospect of home began to loom larger. Then, once I was home, it all started again; following up on the actions arising from the last trip and preparing for the next one.

Cathay Jumbo

Chaotic Kowloon

Mr G, Tony Brookes and Louis Foy in
Hong Kong

Star ferry

The team relax. Doreen is on the right.

CHAPTER 3

China. (People's Republic of China)

Guangzhou

China – land of mysterious, misty mountains; the fabled "Far Cathay" sought out by Marco Polo. It is a land of floods and vast rivers, home to china tea and the destination for the magical Tea Clippers in the 19th century for the first teas of the harvest. Home of bright-coloured silk, fabulous palaces, emperors and the Great Wall of China. These were my early thoughts of China formed from childhood books. In one prep school geography exam, the question was: "What do the Chinese people grow?" My two-word answer, which surprisingly received a severe rebuke was: "Pig tails". (The correct answer was rice apparently, but I felt the question could have been phrased better). Now I was to see for myself what China was really like in the 1980s, after the Cultural Revolution and Chairman Mao and now as home to over one billion people.

In those days, I was dubious about flying on China Airlines and was less than happy at the state of the plane in which we now found ourselves. The BAC Trident aircraft was probably as old as I was, the paintwork was faded and dirty, the inside looked grey and drab, and the padding in the seats had long ago lost its spring. The flight to Canton from Hong Kong was full, the luggage lockers above our heads were just open shelves and crammed with briefcases, coats and paper carrier bags full of the red boxes of Camus brandy that all Chinese seem to take home from Hong Kong. The in-flight service was one small tub of ice cream. Tony found a piece of metal in his. We landed solidly, but safely, in Canton, but checked our rattled teeth as we taxied to the terminal building. We cleared immigration and customs in a crowded, high-ceilinged room that seemed to serve as Immigration and Customs, Baggage Reclaim and Arrivals hall all in one. We found our bags and walked out into the night air.

One of our main Chinese customer contacts in Hong Kong was the resident director of the China Ocean Shipping Corporation or COSCO. COSCO was the government-owned, deep-sea merchant fleet of China (PRC). They ran literally hundreds of ships all over the world. The fleet was so big, it was divided into regions of China for management purposes and the southern fleet was run from their Hong Kong offices.

During the Hong Kong radar demonstrations, we were invited by COSCO to give the same demonstration to their technical and operational staff in Canton – or Guangzhou, as it was now called. We were asked to stay for three days as they wanted the electronics technical people from the local institute to attend as well and the institute kindly offered to host the presentations in their main hall. This was a big opportunity, so we asked Tony Tuthill, our R & D director, to come out and join Louis and I. COSCO arranged our visas locally and we set off for Canton. Immediately after the Hong Kong demonstrations in the Furama Hotel, I had packed up the radar in its crate and we nervously left it in Swires' hands and they promised to ship it to Guangzhou. The best way to get the radar to Canton was to put in on a junk and sail it up the Pearl River – and that was what they did. They took it by lorry to the junk harbour at Causeway Bay for a Canton-bound junk that afternoon. The three of us, plus Ted and Mr Leung, were to fly up to Guangzhou on the following Tuesday. In spite of his past performance, we were forced to take Mr Leung as he spoke Cantonese and we definitely knew we would need an interpreter.

By the time we came out of the Guangzhou airport building, it was dark, but we were met outside by a senior representative of

IF YOU CAN'T TAKE A JOKE...

COSCO and by senior members of the Guangzhou Electronics Institute. Guangzhou is an ancient city – having been here since 200 BC – but outside the minibus window, all was darkness. There were few lights and those that we could see were weak and dim. The city is one of the five or six major cities of China and has a long history as a trading port. The Japanese took the city in 1939 and the Portuguese and British both have long associations with the city and the Pearl River.

We arrived at the hotel, which we were pleased to see was modern and looked pleasant enough. The rooms were functional, if not luxurious, and it was clean. The next morning we went down and met Mr Leung in the lobby as arranged. According to the information in the room, there was both a Chinese and a Western breakfast room. Our Mr Leung ignored this and said we must all eat in the Chinese room. Louis, Tony and I declined firmly as the Chinese breakfast seemed to consist mainly of fish congee. That was certainly not what I needed to set myself up for the day. We found the 'Western' breakfast room, where there were boiled eggs, toast, coffee and fruit.

On the way to the institute, it was clear that Guangzhou was not a rich place. A pall of black smoke seemed to hang over the town; the trees looked tired, dusty and grey, their leaves dull. The tarmac roads merged into the surrounding land through vast areas of grey mud and beaten earth. We saw few houses and those we did see seemed to be basic to say the least. None of the buildings we passed seemed to be more that two storeys high. There were very few cars, but a lot of bikes and the odd agricultural motor tricycle pulling trailers of various sorts.

We finally pulled up at the institute. It was a magnificent building with tall columns and a high stone portico. A flight of steps led up from the mud and scrubby forecourt to the front doors. Inside, we were taken into a large hall; half of it set out as a lecture room the other clear of furniture other than two trestle tables. We were all amazed to find that the wooden packing case containing the radar and the other boxes had arrived and had been placed in the hall. Mr Leung had obviously got something right. I left Louis and Tony chatting to the Chinese while I set to work unpacking the radar and setting it up. We had been expecting about a dozen people at each of two or three separate formal sessions, but the hall in which we were to give the talks had chairs and desks for fifty or sixty people. I set up the equipment, checked it out and soon we were ready to roll.

An hour later, about fifty serious-faced Chinese in their 'Chairman Mao' suits filed in. They all carried notepads or briefcases. They all solemnly came up to us and shook our hands, then sat down. The room was soon full and silent as they all waited to see what these foreign people had to say. During the introductions by their director, it became clear that this group of fifty were with us for the whole three-day period. This called for a strategy review, so we called a break while we decided how best to fill the time over the three days with one audience, rather than three days with three or four different audiences.

Tony gave a technical paper on the history of the development of the ARPA radar and the computer tracking system and then I gave a product talk, showed the film we had made for the radar and then demonstrated the radar itself to groups of about six or eight at a time. They all pushed and shoved to get themselves clustered and crowded round the radar and I found that the only way I could demonstrate anything was to stand behind the radar and work it upside down. I was assaulted by a variety of Chinese breath scents that made me wonder what they had had for lunch. I decided I did not really want to know.

We finished at around 6 o'clock. The translation and questions more than trebled the time it would normally take to go through the presentation, so we had not got very far. The senior Chinese delegate made a short speech in good English. He was a tall, distinguished-looking gentleman with a shock of white hair who clearly had the respect of the audience:

"Normally we would like to entertain our honoured guests on arrival to a special banquet as gesture of welcome to China. However, we are so sorry that due to lateness of your aeroplane arrival, we could not do that yesterday. Also, so sorry, today is the late Madam Sun Yat Sen's birthday and banquet room is not open. So, tomorrow we would very much like for you to join us for special lunch."

Dr Sun Yat Sen was a revolutionary nationalist who brought about the end of the reign of the Chinese emperors and set up the Chinese Nationalist Party or KMT. In 1912, the Republic of China was set up with the overthrow of the Qing Dynasty and Sun Yat Sen became the first president. He and his wife came from a small village near Guangzhou, so their anniversaries are still honoured in the area. Sun Yat Sen died in 1926 but is remembered by a mausoleum in Nanjing, the former capital of China.

The Banquets

The next day after the morning session, the Chinese announced that there was no more sessions that day due to the lunch and we were now to proceed to the minibus. We were taken to an old Chinese building that Ted told us was a recognised formal Chinese Banquet restaurant. It was built of wood which was all richly decorated and painted in bright green and reds, and set amid lush tropical gardens.

Chinese Banquets are very special. They are only held to mark special events like New Year, weddings etc, so for us to have one in our honour was a good sign. Whereas at normal Chinese meals all the dishes arrive at once, at a banquet each dish is served separately in a succession of dishes. Banquets consist of 'special' dishes; no sweet and sour pork here. Each dish is made up of individual items like meat or fish. Rice is the very last dish served. Also wine, beer or liquor can be served and often in generous portions as glasses are refilled at each course, and there can be about twelve courses.

As we arrived at the banquet rooms, it seemed that the whole of COSCO and the Institute was there standing round the tables and chattering and laughing away to each other. There were six big tables, each seating about ten or twelve people. The Chinese all thought this was great. A formal banquet like this was the equivalent of a business dinner at The Ritz for us at home, so they were in good spirits. We three were split up and each seated at a different table. The meal began and the courses started arriving. At the same time beer was provided, then, what I thought were water glasses were half filled with neat brandy. So the meal progressed, with course after course and glass refill after glass refill. Luckily I could just about handle chopsticks, but had some way to go to match the speed of our hosts. I cannot even begin to remember what we ate as for most of the courses I had no idea what we were eating.

I know we started with cold meats, then there was soup, then meat and a shellfish course – abalone, I think – then pork. There was something whitish brown and slimy. It looked revolting, but the Chinese all seemed to think it was fantastic and lifted it to their mouths and let it slide down their throats. I could hardly get it to my mouth and when I did, there was no way I could get it down my throat without my stomach trying to come and meet it. Then there were other meats, small crunchy brown things that no one could find an English name for; as well as a few courses that I was rather glad I did not know what they were. Some I managed to eat, others I gave up on. I kept drinking the beer and sipping the brandy, but the brandy in larger sips as the meal went on. During the meal I was watching Louis, who seemed to be struggling as much as I was with all the dishes, but we both made it. Tony was sitting with his back towards me so I could not see how he was doing. Finally, a rice dish arrived and fruit appeared. The end was in sight, surely? After twelve courses, I was not sure whether my legs would work. Certainly my bottom was dead.

It seemed to be the end. Our tall director friend rose a little unsteadily to his feet and made a short speech. Then, there were a series of toasts and many "Gam Beis". We all got up, goodbyes and thank yous were exchanged, and we boarded the minibus to go back to the hotel. It was getting on for 4 o'clock when we got off the bus and we looked forward to being able to relax for the rest of the day. Certainly no need for any dinner tonight!

As we staggered into the lobby, Mr Leung called us together and made an announcement: "We must all be back in the lobby at 5.30pm for our banquet."

Louis glared at him. "What do you mean, 'Our Banquet?'"

Mr Leung explained, "Yesterday, due to Madame Sun's birthday, the welcome banquet not possible. Tomorrow night you go back to Hong Kong, so no banquet possible. Therefore, we must give return banquet tonight. It is arranged. It is at 5.30."

"Why did you not tell us this before," demanded Louis, "and why can we not do it at lunch time tomorrow?"

"Not possible," said Mr Leung. Louis now was experiencing Mr Leung for himself and was not liking it one bit. Mr Leung continued, "It is arranged. You must be here in one hour and a half." With that, he turned and walked away. We stared at each other. Not only were we angry at the bad planning and total lack of notice, but also wondering how on earth could we eat another twelve-course banquet? Mr Leung had obviously arranged this days before without consulting us at all. We went to our rooms for an hour, then groaning inwardly, we set off for Round 2. Back we went to the same restaurant and there were the same crowd all standing around waiting and still babbling away merrily to each other. I settled in for an ordeal of how to look as though I am eating lots but actually eating nothing.

As with the lunchtime banquet, Louis, as our senior man, was sitting next to the director of the Institute. He was a jolly, talkative man with a loud laugh who kept Louis engaged in conversation. As the courses progressed, I kept looking at Louis. He seemed to be suffering. His face was not a happy one and his movements were definitely slowing. Louis was normally the soberest of men with a bearing of a naval officer, and the manners and behaviour of a diplomat. I could see that the host was piling more food on Louis's plate as soon as he had finished what was there. I was having a similar problem, but the guy next to me was fairly quiet and thankfully did not force food onto my plate. I also noticed, though, that the waiters kept the beer and brandy glasses well filled so we had plenty of drink with which to try and wash it down. I began to lose count of the courses and tried to ask my neighbour how many more there were, but was met with big smiles of stained teeth encrusted with meat or fish. The next time I looked over at Louis, he was smiling. What is happening? A course or two later when I looked, he was laughing. Now that was odd in itself, for although he was a really good guy, wild laughter was not Louis's forte. Finally, after what seemed an eternity, the rice and fruit courses arrived and we had finished. We staggered out. Tony and I made a bee-line for Louis. As we got to him, it was clear what had happened. He was drunk. We got him on the minibus and asked what had happened.

"Well," slurred Louis, "the old man kept piling food on my plate and not letting me leave anything. Then, when I had finished that he piled it up again. I thought 'God I am going to be sick', but then I noticed that the waiter kept filling the brandy, so I started drinking the brandy to help my stomach and then all of a sudden it's over and I am here with you nice boys!" He smiled as his eyes rolled pleadingly from Tony to me.

It was still only 8 o'clock as Tony and I laid Louis flat out on his bed. He was asleep before we left the room and we hoped all would be well. The next morning, after a cautious phone call to check he was actually alive, Tony and I were pleased to see him come down the stairs. Louis was fine again for the final day's sessions before we, thankfully, flew back to Hong Kong. It was not all in vain as the reports issued by the Institute and sent to COSCO were positive and COSCO ordered a large number of systems over the next few years.

Shanghai

Shanghai is the main commercial centre and port in eastern China. It is situated near the mouth of the Huangpu River where it meets the mighty

Yangtze. Shanghai became of interest to the UK after the first Opium War in 1839-1842 when it was named as one of five Chinese ports with which the British could trade. It was not a totally peaceful time and British troops actually held the city for a while. However, it continued to develop and an area was conceded to the British by the Chinese. The British sector was formed near the mouth of the Suzhou Creek and an American sector grew in an area to the north of it. Later, both were joined, becoming known as the 'International Settlement'. It was here over the years that the vibrant and cosmopolitan centre of Shanghai grew and developed with many large and grand colonial buildings, banks and hotels. The waterfront along the Huangpu River, where ocean-going ships could moor and handle their cargoes, was called 'The Bund'. It was the centre of town, along with the Nanjing Road that leads from The Bund deep into modern Shanghai. What is now called 'Old Shanghai' is in this area and small parts of it have been preserved as a time capsule from earlier days. Across the Huangpu River in 1981, in an area called Pudong, there was nothing; just marshes and the flat lands of the estuary and a few farms, a village or two. Down towards the Yangze River, some of the new shipyards were springing up. Today, the whole area is a major city in its own right with fantastic skyscrapers and futuristic-looking buildings that dwarf the original Shanghai buildings on The Bund; and it is home to the new financial centre for Shanghai.

By the 1930s, Shanghai was 'the place to be' in the Far East. It was a major financial centre and was known as the 'Athens of China'; an exciting city with wealthy foreign traders and overseas companies setting up offices and warehouses in the area – all making money and spending it on the delights that Shanghai offered. The French now had their own concession to the south of the International Settlement.

In 1942, the Japanese invaded the International Settlement and life there stopped. Most of the foreigners left and things were never to be the same again. Following Japan's defeat and the end of the War, there followed, in 1949, Mao's Revolution and communism. Again, the world changed and many of the international companies still remaining in Shanghai moved to Hong Kong and ran their China operations from there. Until the early 80s, Shanghai remained virtually unchanged, and when I first arrived in 1981 I thought that I had gone through a time warp. However, with China opening up to the West for trade and investment, Shanghai entered a new phase of rapid development and growth.

Our next event in China was a big marine exhibition hosted by China for the first time in December 1981 and called "Marintec". It was aimed at the rapidly growing Chinese shipbuilding and marine industry and held in Shanghai,

We landed at Shanghai Airport from Hong Kong. In the early 80s, it had a single, but imposing, terminal building built in the early part of the 20th century. We walked to it across the tarmac from the aircraft. The road into town was a pleasant, tree-lined, two-way country road. It was busy with bikes and ox carts heading into the city loaded with watermelons and other fresh fruit and vegetables. We were booked into a hotel called the "Jin Jiang". At the time, it was one of the biggest hotels in Shanghai. It was built in the 1920s as Shanghai grew and was situated in the old French quarter, and consisted of a large main building of about ten or twelve storeys and another large accommodation multi-storey building as well – all set in its own walled grounds. It towered above all other buildings in the area and was the hotel that Richard Nixon, then President of the USA, stayed in during his breakthrough talks with China.

To enter the main building, there was a flight of stone steps up to a brick portico. On entering the hotel, it was as if we had entered a 1920s time capsule. The carpets, the furniture, the pictures on the walls were all as they had been in the 1920s and 30s. Nothing had changed. The lift with its sliding iron cage doors, the faded, worn carpets and the upholstery on the aged settees and chairs all could have been from a film set for a Hollywood silent movie. The Jin Jiang was to be our home over the next few trips to Shanghai and we grew fond of it in spite of its non-updated shortcomings.

As I recall, the bedrooms were fairly well-sized but the furnishings and fittings were basic and from the 1920s and 30s. I recall lots of wood panelling, wooden floors, old rugs, big light fittings and baths, but no showers. Some people said they heard rats or mice rattling along behind the panelling but I never did. TVs, radios, Internet, DVD, CD players, trouser presses, mini bars and all the other standard trappings of today's five-star hotels were still far-off in the future for the Jin Jiang.

At night, we would walk across the road to the Jin Jiang Hotel's own club. In the 1920s and 30s, it had been the 'French Club'. In this complex was a large swimming pool, a snooker room with about four full-sized tables as well as billiard tables. There was a restaurant where we sometimes ate. The club put on a dinner cabaret every night with a young female violinist and a middle-aged male singer. Neither of them were 'to our taste' but given that they were Chinese playing western and singing western songs in English, it was not a bad effort. However, little did we know on that first trip that when we returned to the Jin Jiang Club three years later, we would find the same two performers playing the same songs in the same order every night just as they had done every night since our first visit. We found much the same atmosphere when we visited the old 'Cathay Hotel', now called the 'Peace', down on The Bund. This hotel had been the decadent centre in the 1930s and had a world-famous jazz bar at the rear of the ground floor and an equally famous Chinese restaurant on the top floor where the speciality of the house was boiled crabs. Both were still there and the jazz bar looked as though the 1930's musicians had just left for a break and the restaurant was thriving.

Surrounding the Jin Jiang were streets of single or two-storey houses, or villas – many built for the French expats and a few shops at the street corners. These, like the rest of the city, were pretty much unchanged in decades. It was hard to see who lived in the larger villas as they had tall garden walls. Some of the smaller houses that fronted onto the street were home to large families, often of two or even three generations. Nearby, there was a French restaurant called the 'Red House'. It was just that, a red painted house. Inside it had very simple decor, but it served good French food and made a welcome change from the hotel's continual Chinese style food. The speciality at the Red House was a marvellous lemon soufflé. That this place had been here since the 1930s was remarkable, but how it had survived the War, the Mao years and the Cultural Revolution, and could still provide good French food in the 1980s was incredible. We had to book days in advance and the latest time that a table could be booked was 1900.

Marintec 1 & No 4 Radio Factory

Initially, our main interest was with a Chinese electronics company who made marine radars. It was called No 4 Radio Factory, Shanghai. During the first Marintec exhibition, we were invited to see the factory and open discussions with them. So it was that on a bitterly cold December day we found ourselves in Shanghai on a visit to the factory. During the tour, we were shown into one of the work areas where girls sat at rows of work benches making printed circuit boards. It was freezing cold in the room. All the windows were open on both sides of the room and an icy north wind from Mongolia blew straight through the factory. The women workers sat huddled at their benches with coats and hats on, faces frowning as they tried to solder the boards. They all looked as if they were shivering.

"Why are all the windows open?" I asked.

"Solder fume," explained the interpreter.

Sure enough, the PCBs were being made using soldering irons held in shivering hands.

"But why can you not have fume extractor fans and then heat the factory?"

The interpreter slowly told us that in China if your factory is north of the Yangtze River you can have heating in winter. If it is south, then you cannot have heating. No 4 Radio Factory was five miles to the south of the Yangtze.

We also were taken on a tour of some of the shipyards. These were situated some distance away from the city. It gave us a chance to see life in the countryside. It was not pretty. We saw people in poverty – living in holes in the ground, almost. Tiny mud brick shelters half dug into the ground with rubbish and waste piled against the walls, while all around filthy, ragged peasants scratched a life out of the cold mud and dirt that encased them.

The shipyards were mostly new and China's infant industry was beginning to find success with their low prices. They seemed to have many new technology machines and equipments to help them, but were still building basic, simple ships such as bulk carriers or small general cargo ships. Many of their naval ships were either bought from the Russians or built under licence with lots of Russian help. On arrival in the yard, we were all given safety hats to wear. These were all made of woven cane. We did not see any workers wearing them but we did see them using their washroom. This consisted of one outside tap on a stand pipe over an old bath, in an area of mud and weeds between two piles of rusting sheets of steel.

Exhibitions, Chinese style

The exhibition was chaotic. When we first arrived, a couple of days before it opened, we noticed that there were small, but robust, fences round all the stands. We had not seen this before and wondered why they were there. Then, came the first day of the show; it was not like any exhibition that any of us had ever been to before. Every day, all day, it was not just crowded, it was jammed from opening to closing. Once we were on the stand in the morning, there was no way we could get off and go for a stroll round the other stands as we normally might do. The crowds were just too solid. Going to the loo had to be planned well in advance. Hundreds of milling people, all dressed the same, were gathering up everything they could. Brochures that were put out vanished in seconds, and any one daft enough to put down a sandwich, well, that went too. The Chinese took everything in arm's reach. We now realised why there were fences up. If they had not been there, the crowd would have flooded across the whole stand probably taking us with them. They were, however, very good and did not try and get inside the fence, but anything within arm's reach of the fence was fair game. Their thirst for knowledge was immense. We had already seen from our discussions with No 4 radio factory that they had books covering modern electronics theory, but they had no way to put it into practice as there were no R&D labs as we have.

At closing time, the security guards walked round the halls shouting into loud hailers telling everyone to leave. If they did not move, then they literally pushed people out of the building. If you were talking to someone, you could find that they suddenly vanished from in front of you as a grim-faced security guard pushed them out. One of the problems we had was the fact that they all dressed and looked exactly the same. You could be talking to a cleaner or an admiral, and you had no way of knowing which until the interpreter told you. Any conversation that you had with a visitor instantly created a crowd of other people all listening in intently to see what you were talking about. We quickly learnt to take anyone who appeared important or genuinely interested inside our tiny back room on the stand where you could, with the interpreter's help, have a reasonably private conversation.

The show ran for six days and closed at lunchtime on the last day. We all felt totally drained as the continual crowds, noise and endless questions never slackened once. That afternoon, the show's organisers had arranged a river trip for some of the exhibitors. So as we sat down to a relaxing lunch back in the Jin Jiang, we enjoyed a beer and started to think of a leisurely afternoon boat ride down the Huangpu before flying home tomorrow in time for Christmas. Some of us had been away from the UK for about three weeks and were ready for home.

Negotiations

I was sitting with a few others finishing my lunch when one of our guys came over. "Gordon, there is a group of Chinese downstairs asking for you. I think they are from the show."

"Go away, I have finished now and am off on my boat ride." I thought it was a leg pull.

"I am serious. They are the guys who were on the stand yesterday." *Oh Lord*, I thought, *what do they want?* I went downstairs to the main lobby where sure enough there was a group of Chinese gentlemen. Instantly I saw our interpreter, Mr Wang. He saw me and smiled broadly as he came across.

"Mr Gordon, No 4 Radio Factory want to discuss contract," he said.

"Well, that is great news! Please tell them that we are very pleased. As you know we are returning to the UK tomorrow, but will come back in early January with our commercial team," I said.

"No, no, Mr Gordon, you do not understand. They must do it now!"

"But we fly home tomorrow!" I tried to stall as I could see what was coming.

"There is no problem," said Mr Wang. "Please give me air tickets and we can change flights." This is where strong wills and diplomacy really came into the job. There was no way that I or Tony were about to hand our flight tickets over to No 4 Radio Factory. British Airways flights to the UK had been fully booked since early December and any chance of changing from the 22nd December to a flight nearer Christmas was a non-starter. As Tony and I had no intention of spending Christmas in Shanghai, there was no way we were going to miss tomorrow's flight. I was also concerned that as Alan Carnell, our commercial director, had already left Shanghai for the UK, leaving just Tony and I still here, we were a bit weak on the commercial side to form a strong negotiating team – especially as we did not have our own interpreter and would have to depend on Mr Wang, who worked for them.

We seemed to have an impasse. "Look, Mr Wang, it will be much better if we arrange to come back in January with our full commercial team and more technical experts. Mr Tuthill and I are the wrong people to discuss commercial contracts but we can start work on an MOU, a Memorandum of Understanding." He interpreted all this to the No 4 Team. They frowned heavily and talked amongst themselves for a while. Mr Wang then turned and, with a serious face, said, "Mr Gray, No 4 Radio factory wish to discuss Memorandum of Understanding leading to a contract now. Our director understands that it will not be possible to complete all the official details but we must start now."

"A good idea!" I relented, perhaps there was a way out here. "Please let me find Mr Tuthill." I dashed back to the restaurant and caught Tony as he headed for his boat ride. I explained to him what was going on and what I thought we should do: "We need to sit down with them now Tony and find out what they have in mind. You and I cannot sign anything, but we can get a clear idea of their plans. We can then say we must discuss it all in the UK with the directors and can return in January. I am afraid the boat trip will have to go without us though. This could be a long afternoon!"

Tony was great and agreed, and we took the team up to Tony's room as it was bigger than mine. By some sitting on the bed and with the three chairs in the room, we found seats for them all. We discussed radar, computing power and answered all sorts of questions that we had been over with them before. It became clear that they were looking for guidance from us to formulate a Memorandum of Understanding (MOU), or a Chinese equivalent.

After a couple of hours, we still seemed to be getting nowhere. They clearly wanted to make our radars in Shanghai and buy the bits from us, but seemed to recognise that it was one huge jump in manufacturing skills from where they were now. We had seen their factory. There was no way it was equipped either mechanically or in people knowledge or skill terms to build such a radar, but we could not say that to their faces. Tony and I went out into the corridor for a chat. After a few minutes, we had our thoughts in tune and we went back in. Tony took the lead.

"Look, what we think is that we should initially sell you a number of radars complete. We will teach you how to test and install them on the ships and then service them with a set of training courses both in the UK and here. You will not need any special manufacturing equipment for that. Then later, we will sell you the next batch of radars, but in a kit form so you can assemble them, then test and install them. Once that is complete, we will sell you the components and the special machines and test equipment you need to build the whole thing. After that, you just buy the parts from us. I suggest that if you agree to that idea we can sign an initial MOU now that we can take back to London and you can show to your directors."

Once this had been explained a few times and the idea understood there were lots of smiling faces.

We continued with discussions on delivery timescales and very rough orders of magnitude prices for the first batch of completed radars. This seemed to fit their expectations and the atmosphere quickly lightened. We all relaxed a little once we had found the right road to go down and they started to look around the room. We ordered some tea and biscuits. I was watching Mr Wang. It seemed that he had never been in a room like this before. He did not know I was watching but he put out his hand and felt the faded, worn candlewick bedspread with admiration. Then, he looked at me.

"How many people are living in here?" he demanded.

"This is Mr Tuthill's room, so just him," I said.

"Just one person!" Mr Wang seemed incredulous. We knew he lived in a small two-room flat with his wife, his baby daughter and his mother. Then, he said, "How much money does Mr Tuthill get each month?"

I burbled on about wages in the UK being different from China as things are very expensive in England. Thankfully the tea arrived and I got up to open the door. Our efforts that day resulted in a further visit in the January and a contract initially worth over £6 million. This was followed a year or so later by another one of similar size.

Summer in Shanghai

The second Marintec Exhibition was in the late summer of 1983. The trip did not start well. Most of the British exhibitors arrived on the same flight from Hong Kong and coaches had been organised to get all the British exhibitors to our nominated hotel, which was in a different part of the city from the Jing Jiang. It took ages for everyone to get checked in, but eventually I got my key and headed for the room.

As I opened the door, the first thing to hit me was the stifling heat. Then, I was attacked again. This time I was assailed by the most awful smell. I could not place it at first but as I advanced gingerly into the room, I placed it as a stench from something very rotten. The heavy curtains were closed so the room was dark. I found the light and looked around, thinking there must be a dead cat or a rat in the room somewhere. Maybe even the last occupant? The smell was very bad and I was trying not to gag as I looked under the bed. Nothing there. I checked the wardrobe. Empty! What was causing this smell? I opened the curtains to see the room better and as I did so, the smell got even more powerful. The room was at the back of the hotel and overlooked a courtyard. I opened the window and looked out. A couple of Chinese in white kitchen overalls were standing chatting and smoking below me. Then, I saw it. In the corner of the courtyard directly under the window by some rusty dustbins were 5ft high piles of rotting vegetables, meat and bone food scraps. I closed the window and left the room, taking my case with me.

I went back down to reception. "So sorry, hotel full. That is only room," was their opening statement when I explained that I wanted to change my room. As the guy had limited English and my Mandarin was not that good, I tried a different tack.

"Please bring me manager," I responded. He duly appeared.

Before I could say anything, he apologised. "Hotel sorry for room," he said. *Oh good I thought, he is going to change my room without any bother.* "We very busy today. Big Exhibition, you know. Hotel full. Please accept apologies and hope room soon OK. Try open windows."

"I know about the exhibition as I am part of it. I too am very sorry, but that room is not habitable because of the rotten food and kitchen waste outside the window. I will not sleep there. Please either find me another room or another hotel."

He and the receptionist busied themselves with their register and after a few minutes, they found me another room on the other side of the building – actually a rather nice one.

We were told that breakfast was from 0730 until 0900. On the first morning, we did not need to leave the hotel until 0900. So at about 8 o'clock, we started to wander down to the dining room. As we stood at the dining room door, we were greeted with a wonderful sight. The room was large and empty, but the long tables were set. On every place setting, there was a white plate with one fried egg sitting in the middle. The hotel had decided that the British like fried eggs. So at 0730 a fried egg was put on every place, even though no one had yet come down to eat – let alone ordered one.

The exhibition hall was huge. It had been built for the Chinese by the Russians. We had read about it before we came. 'Air Conditioned' they had boasted in their particulars. Air conditioned, my aunt fanny. It was stiflingly hot. The windows were set high up in the walls and the opening mechanisms were jammed. Our stand was in a corner and the sun shone through and down onto us as we sweated away setting up the stand, ready for the opening on the next day. Promises were made by the organisers: "No problem, tomorrow air condition work." Why do we believe what we want to believe when every other sense and all logic is telling us this is nonsense?

The next day in our warm western suits, it was a case of "the air condition, she no work". By 1000, we were all drenched in sweat. Jackets had long been shoved in the back room but our shirts stuck to us like wet rags. Sweat ran down our faces and backs and still the sun shone down through the closed windows. After two days, we were beginning to feel the effects.

Fortunately, the show closed at lunchtime and we were bussed back to the hotel for lunch. We soon developed a lunchtime routine. Into the room, run a cool to warm bath, peel off wet clothes, lie in bath until cold, get dressed in fresh clothes. Go and grab light lunch and drink lots of mineral water with a handful of salt added, then back onto bus. I felt sorry for the PR lady of one of the UK companies. She had brought thin white blouses with her, but by 1030 each day she may as well have just worn her bra – that was all anyone could see, as her thin blouse went instantly transparent. A wet T-shirt day twice a day, every day!

During the hot summer months, the streets outside the hotel filled with people at night. These were not people out walking or going anywhere, just the people who lived there, sitting outside in the street to escape the enclosed, airless heat of their tiny houses and apartments. They sat with their children and babies on their door steps, or in chairs carried outside, or just sat on the curbsides. Whole families made the pavements into a communal sitting room. The round, beaming faces of the locals looked up as we passed. "Hello!" "You Blitishers?" "Where you flom?" It was all very happy, in spite of the difference between our hotel and their life on the curbside.

Along the road sides and pavements and under the grey sad trees were small areas covered with pieces of drying orange skins that the locals dried and then used in their cooking. There were no streetlights and the whole community socialised in the dim night light. The few cars or taxis in those days ran without lights until they saw another car, then they flashed their lights onto full beam and carried on, hoping to miss each other as both drivers were now blinded and without night vision.

The Navy is here

On the third day I was setting up the radar display as the show opened, when an attractive young Chinese lady approached me.

"Excuse me Mr Gary?" she asked.

"Yes, I am Gordon Gray," I replied.

"I am Miss Ling, I am official interpreter for PLA Navy." She then turned and I saw a group of men standing on the edge of the stand. Most were middle-aged and clearly the one now standing nearest to me was their leader. "These gentlemen are Chinese Navy," she explained. "Please demonstrate radar to Captain Chang." Captain Chang bowed, smiled and shook my hand.

Slowly and deliberately, I explained and demonstrated the radar and each and all of its features; letting the young interpreter absorb the technical points and question me to be sure she had it right before she translated it into Mandarin. It took well over an hour to go through it all and there was then about another hour of discussions and questions; all done through the interpreter. Eventually, they all seemed satisfied. They all shook hands with me and left. "That's probably the last we will see of them," I said. "I seemed to be talking too much and must have bored them silly!"

The next morning at the same time, I was bending down to adjust some cables when I saw a shapely pair of ankles approaching. I knew instantly who they belonged to and stood up.

"Ah, Mr Gary. Sorry, Mr Gray, Captain Chang and Chinese Navy would like to negotiate contract for radar."

"Oh, that is fantastic," I said. "When would they like to do that?"

"Now, please. Can we discuss here?"

I was stunned. I had imagined that to reach this stage we would have need a number of separate visits to China and possibly even a visit to the UK for the Chinese Navy to see the factory.

"Er, yes," I stammered. "Why not? Let's go in here," and I led the party into our small, hot back office-cum-storeroom. I asked one of our stand interpreters to arrange cold drinks for the visitors and collared Alan Carnell, who was leading the Racal Decca team at the the show.

"Alan, I have got the Chinese Navy in there, they want to negotiate an ARPA deal."

"Well done," said Alan. "Do you want me in there too?"

"Can you come in now and meet them and then let me try and find out exactly what they want first, but if I need help will you be around?"

"Yes, of course, just shout."

I introduced Alan to Captain Chang, Miss Ling and their team. They all seemed very happy to meet a director. We settled down in the hot and stuffy room and began. The Chinese had come with a draft contract and pages of notes. Slowly, we worked our way through the details. I tried my best to be as nice as I could be to the lady interpreter as I knew if she decided she did not like me, she could scupper everything without me even knowing. So I was super nice, I think. I was forever making sure she had a full glass of coke. She certainly smiled at me a lot so I think she realised that I was struggling with this arrangement as much as she was. We spent the morning going through the technical specifications, discussed delivery time scales and quantities for any initial order, as well as some interface questions about other equipments. I gave them rough prices and agreed that we would send a full quotation within two weeks of our return to the UK.

At lunchtime, I briefed Alan on where we had got to. He seemed happy with the outcome. Alan was always helpful. He had spent years in the export market place, especially in the Far East, when he had been with Plessey. We all felt very comfortable to have him around. In the afternoon, they returned with more questions until, finally, they all seemed satisfied. We all stood up nearly falling over the chairs in the cramped room, shook hands, and they said goodbye to Alan and departed. We had promised to send a full quotation with a few weeks of our return to the UK for a significant quantity of ARPA radars. Happily, this later led to a full contract linked to the work we were doing with the No 4 Radio Factory.

Chinese Doctor

On one trip to the Far East, I had been in India for about ten days and then flew on to Beijing to join colleagues there for a defence exhibition. The second night there, I was ill. At first I thought it was just a bad bout of Delhi Belly with sickness thrown in, but it got worse and carried on all through the next day. My usual remedy, Imodium, had no effect at all. My colleague got back from the exhibition and gave me his supply of Kaolin and Morphine, but that had no effect either – even when combined with Imodium. Now, I was getting a bit worried. Had I picked up some Indian bug or some odd tropical disease? There are enough of them in India. Would the Chinese recognise it? Was it serious? How could I stop things happening? It continued for four days and I was now feeling really bad and visibly losing weight. On the fifth day, I rang reception and asked if they had a doctor. No, but they would arrange for me to see one at the International Hospital. I dosed myself up, got dressed and staggered down to reception where they had arranged a taxi to take me to the hospital.

After about thirty minutes, I was called in to see the doctor. The doctor was standing up as I went into the surgery. I was met by a tall Chinese lady called Dr Tang. She was well dressed in a smart dark skirt and white blouse under her crisp white coat, and she was smiling at me. She had glistening, raven black hair, cut in a neat bob and when she spoke it was with an American accent. She was lovely. I felt better immediately and even in my weakened state, I fell instantly in love. I described my situation to her and she then asked me to describe, in some lurid detail, what was happening with my body. (I shall spare you that bit).

Then, she said, "Oh, that's fine. You just have a bad dose of the Gastro Enteritis. There is a lot of it in Beijing at the moment. I was off with it last week." (She was so lovely I could not imagine that anything nasty ever affected her). "Take these pills and you will be OK in a day or two." I floated out of her surgery on a cloud of love and gratitude, and two days later, I was better. Just in time for the last two days of the exhibition.

The Cake

It so happened that my birthday fell during one of the periods we were in Shanghai. I was sure that no one knew it was my birthday and certainly did not advertise the fact. However, someone, perhaps the secretary back in the office, had alerted one of the guys about it. On the day when we got back to the hotel, I was told we were all meeting in the dining room as our training manager wanted a chat with us all. The guys from the stand and the two local Chinese girls, who were acting as interpreters for us, all filed into the dining room. I meekly and naively followed. Once there, we found that the dining room was empty. The eight of us then sat at a large, round table and Tony, the training manager from the training school, called over the waitress and ordered tea for everyone and then asked for the 'Cake' to be brought out. He looked at me and chuckled as he said it.

"Oh no," I cried. "Who told you lot?" General laughter but I did get a hint as to who was behind it. One young lady in the office would receive a ticking off when I got back! Out came the girl carrying a very large and very pink cake. The pink icing had a glossy sheen to it and it had my name on the top in lime green icing. Where the green met the pink, the colours had run, but never mind – it was a big cake! After the usual 'Happy Birthday' song and a small thank you speech from yours truly, a large carving knife was produced and I cut the cake.

The cake itself was a smallish sponge cake covered by about an inch of this thick, pink, shiny, slightly oily icing. The icing stuck to the knife, but I managed to separate them, served everyone up with a slice and we all tucked in. Well, that is until we tasted the icing. It was awful. It tasted of oil. However, as 'guest of honour', I could say nothing. The others could say nothing either as our two local Chinese interpreter girls would be offended at our poor respect for the Chinese bakery. We struggled on, trying to drown the taste with more Chinese tea. Several of the guys were shuffling icing around their plates and making polite and diplomatic noises about how nice it all was. We were all very conscious that it was in the very early days of westerners going into China and that these girls did not live in luxury. I was sure that a big iced cake like this was not something they would have at home very often, if at all. China had just come through the years of deprivation during the Cultural Revolution and we were the first westerners that they had met; so we did not want to insult them by giving them the impression that we thought their idea of a beautiful big iced cake was horrible.

Finally, after we had drunk the tea, everyone said that they did not want any more cake. Now as I am not an expert cake cutter, there was about a quarter of the cake left over.

"Oh, Mr Gray, you must take it home," the girls said.

"No, I cannot do that as it will be squashed in my suitcase! But you two must take it home now and share it with your families tonight while it is fresh." *Problem solved,* I thought.

"Oh, we could not do that" said the older one. "We would not give that to our family. They could not eat that."

"Why not?" I asked.

"Because the topping on that cake tastes horrible."

Beijing: Forbidden City

Marintec China. Alan Carnell, Tony Brookes and Mr G

Seminar for the Electronics Institute in Guangchou

The Racal Team in Marintec

The Great Wall

CHAPTER 4

Korea

Curfew 1981

Outside the train windows it had been dark for a couple of hours, but I knew we must be on the outskirts of Seoul as the train had slowed down and some passengers were beginning to get their things together ready to get off. The train rumbled slowly over another set of points on the approaches to Seoul Station. Mr K.Y. Lee, our agent, who was sitting beside me, kept muttering that the time was getting on. We had missed our planned train from Ulsan as we had been held up in meetings in Hyundai Shipyard for much longer than we had wanted. However, this train was on time, as nearly all Korean trains are, and we would be in Seoul by 11.00pm.

I detected a strong air of nervousness in the carriage as we slowed right down again and then we saw that the train was gliding slowly into Seoul station. It stopped without a jolt and everyone was on their feet and making for the exit. Once the train doors opened, there was a stampede along the platform. I was blissfully unaware of the cause for this panic that had suddenly gripped my fellow passengers. I assumed it was because they all wanted to get home to their families for the weekend.

KY pushed me out. "We must run!" he shouted and left me as he set off with the rest of the stampede.

I grabbed my bag and followed as best I could. Then, I remembered. The curfew began at midnight and this train full of passengers all had to be home in the next sixty minutes. When we got outside the station, I realised what the real panic was about. Taxis were few and far between.

It was 1981 and Korea was still under a curfew from midnight. It had been under a curfew since the end of the Korean War. We had to be off the streets by midnight or run the risk of being arrested as possible North Korean spies. That included me, being obviously foreign – probably especially me.

Queuing for a taxi was out of the question. It was hijack time. As each taxi pulled up, it was besieged by a mass of jabbering Koreans. They fought each other to get into the taxi, then pulled their friends in while trying to keep others out. Gradually, we fought our way to the front of the battle. KY yelled at a driver and tried to push me into the taxi, but a briefcase in the ribs from a Korean sumo wrestler slowed me down a little and the taxi had gone. Then, after a while, KY saw his chance: three women were fending off two men as they tried to commandeer a taxi. KY pushed me headfirst into the back of the taxi behind one of the women. He pushed on the door until most of me was inside, stuffed my bag in as well, then he yelled something at the driver.

The car accelerated away from the chaos with people jumping out of the way. I managed to settle into a part of the seat and wondered what was going to happen next. The women were clearly not at all happy that this tall foreigner had been forced on them, but said nothing and totally ignored me. I was staying at the Lotte Hotel near the centre of town and hoped that the taxi was going in that direction. The streets were dark, as in those days Seoul had very few bright lights. The curfew killed any idea of nightlife, so it was a depressingly dark and dull city. This was reflected in its residents. Most Koreans I had seen had a very glum look about them. After a few minutes, the taxi pulled up outside the Lotte Hotel and we all scrambled out. I tried to pay but the ladies in the front had paid already and they disappeared quickly into the hotel, not wanting to have anything to do with this strange creature. I stood still and took a deep breath of the crisp cold air, picked up my bag and went inside. Welcome to Korea.

On the Saturday morning in the office, I asked KY what it had all been about and had he got home OK? He had. He saw someone he knew and they grabbed a taxi home together. He said that he had heard the women shouting at drivers that they wanted to get to the Lotte, so he waited until they had got a taxi and then pushed me in too.

After a busy week with a lot of travelling and as I had never been to Seoul before, I was at a loss as to what to do with myself but not exactly bursting with energy as jet lag was still affecting me. I spent a quiet weekend in the hotel. I wandered through the underground shopping arcades and looked in the many small shops selling colourful silk ties and scarves, ginseng in all forms, and Korean ornaments, then looked round the vast Lotte department store with its huge food section that sold types of fish that I had never seen before. The Lotte is Seoul's equivalent to Selfridges or Harrods.

I relaxed in my room snoozing, reading or watching a little TV. The only English language TV at that time seemed to be the American Forces AFKN TV and that showed an endless list of troop flight arrivals and departures to the USA for the American Forces or 'family/community bulletins'. If you were lucky, you might catch an episode of *MASH*. Everything else was in Korean. After a few trips, I got braver and did some sightseeing if I had a spare half day. I have always been lucky in that I am very happy to be on my own for long periods and enjoy the freedom it gives me; so, a weekend on my own in Seoul or anywhere else is not a problem in terms of feeling lonely.

A Typical Week in Korea

That was my first visit to Korea in 1981. The arrival in Seoul station being the culmination of a week's trip to the south. Decca Radar supplied marine radars that had been ordered by shipowners for installation onboard new ships being built in the many Korean shipyards. It was part of my job to visit these Korean yards three or four times a year and make sure that they were happy with the deliveries, installation kits, manuals and operation of the radars.

We had an agent in Seoul, an old UK trading house with a long history in Korea. Mr KY Lee was one of their local managers who specialised in the marine products that they represented and he accompanied me down to the shipyards. In Korea, an agent was essential. Firstly, to officially introduce overseas companies to Korean businesses; secondly, to act as an interpreter and guide when travelling about the country; and thirdly, because in the early eighties the local companies did not like dealing directly with overseas foreign representatives. They did not speak English and we certainly did not speak Korean. The Korean shipbuilding industry was in full swing by the early 80s and new yards were being built. The Korean Government had declared that its industrialisation policy would be spearheaded by shipbuilding and so being a shipbuilder was a great source of national pride as they were competing head on with their historic arch-enemy, Japan. Their unashamed aim was to overtake the Japanese and go on to be the biggest shipbuilder in the world. They overtook Japan in 2003 and now build over half the world's commercial tonnage.

The shipyards were owned by the major Korean companies or 'Chaebols'. Hyundai, Daewoo, Samsung and KSEC were the main yards in the early 80s, with a number of smaller private yards building specialist ships such as naval vessels. Since then, they have been joined by Sundong and STX. Over recent years, many of the smaller Korean yards have been bought up by these big Chaebols and they are now buying overseas yards as well. They had long ago overtaken the UK as a major shipbuilder and the UK was seen as a spent force. Korean shipyard employees saw themselves as the 'crème de la crème' and treated all others accordingly. Due to the geography of Korea, the yards had been built in deep sheltered bays round the southern coast in, or near, Pusan and Ulsan – the major ports in the south – with some yards near Inchon in the northwest.

The routine that we adopted for these trips was that I would arrive in Seoul from Hong Kong on a Sunday afternoon. I would stay in Seoul overnight and early on the Monday morning, KY Lee would meet me at about 0600 out at the domestic terminal of Kimpo Airport for the hour and a half flight down to Pusan. Even at that time of the morning, Kimpo airport was a mass of people all trying to get somewhere. I used to try and get there early so I could at least get a coffee at one of the stalls before KY arrived. As I sat with my first cup of coffee of the day, waiting for KY, I would be surrounded by slurping, sucking, chomping Koreans, all eating noodles, kimchi or rice for their breakfasts. Above the din of their conversations and yelling orders for more tea, a TV up on a shelf blared out the daily local news. The Koreans ate from plastic bowls with a dedication and an intensity that worried me. If they were this serious about food, what were they like about work?

In those days, Korean Air flew Boeing 707s on the Seoul to Pusan route. The pilots all seemed to have just left the Korean Air Force and thought that they were still in their jets and threw these poor old 707s around like fighter planes. I tried to chat to KY on the flight. He was a shy man, probably in his early 40s, but spoke good English. He was small and had been a schoolboy during the Korean War. He had had his home destroyed and close family members killed in the war. He said he never had a pair of shoes until he was in his teens. He taught himself as best he could and had realised that learning English was as good a skill as any to learn. Even so, he certainly had never travelled outside the country, but had done well to have got where he had. Speaking English and working for an international company was a fine achievement given his start in life.

Unfortunately, KY hated flying. The only reason he flew down to Pusan was because the alternative was to give up his Sunday, the one day of the week that the office was closed, and go down to Pusan by train. Landing in Pusan was always a bit nervy as it was prone to fog and early morning mists. The airport is in a flat river valley but the surrounding countryside was all hills and mountains. The plane revved and banked, throttled back and we sank from the skies; then it revved up again and climbed steeply. Sometimes you would get a glimpse of hillside and trees below you, before it was gone as the plane banked the other way or climbed back into the cloud. Then, a break in the clouds revealed white-topped waves as we swung out over the sea.

Once we had landed and passed through the modern terminal, we got in line for one of the bright green taxis. Hyundai were now producing the first Korean cars: a simple four-seat saloon called the 'Pony'. It was a good name because like any beast of burden, the Koreans used them for everything and the suspension was rubbish. The Korean taxi companies bought vast quantities and they were all painted bright lime green. The taxi took us down through a wet morning, into the grey industrial city of Pusan and on to the ferry terminal.

By 9.30, we had joined the crowds in the terminal. KY dashed off to buy a sandwich before we boarded a hovercraft for the one-hour journey across to the island of Koje Do where Daewoo and Samsung had their shipyards. It was still raining and a brisk wind whipped up the waves and white horses stretched away into the gloom. The hovercraft was full of shipyard workers and a few young guys in suits who looked like me – sales reps. A TV set was mounted on the bulkhead at the front of the cabin. It was showing Korean cartoons with the volume turned right up to deafening levels to drown out the noise of the engines, but no one seemed to mind or attempted to turn it down. Many people slept, or tried to, as the noisy hovercraft rattled and rolled its way across the bay, with waves and rain sloshing past the windows, towards Daewoo.

Work started on Daewoo Shipyard in 1973 in Okpo Bay and was only completed in 1981, but by then they were already building merchant ships. It had two vast building docks, where a number of ships could be built at the same time and the yard was dominated by a huge bright yellow Goliath gantry crane, capable of lifting 900-ton ship sections. As we approached Okpo, all we could see beyond the harbour wall was this yellow gantry crane with DAEWOO painted on it in blue.

In Britain and Europe, shipyards always seemed to be cramped places, hemmed in on three sides by houses and other industrial works right alongside them. Here, it was different. Daewoo had taken the small fishing village of Okpo which lay by a quiet bay and started from scratch. They had built a sea wall across the bay for extra shelter, moved the entire village and everyone in it over the hill to the next bay, reclaimed a vast area of land and built a shipyard. It spread for miles in all directions. Fabrication sheds, welding shops, commercial offices, stores, training centres, steel storage yards, fitting out wharves and dry docks were all scattered about the bay. At the northern end lay the massive assembly docks and the yellow goliath crane. In fact, when we visited it first, there were three different shipyard bus services to take workers and visitors to different parts of the yard.

Our first meeting was with the purchasing department. Their offices were well away from the ship building area so we were nowhere near any ships. We got a bus from the main gate to the offices; then when we had finished in purchasing, having been berated for our harsh standard contract terms, we took another bus to the electronics technical department which was in a different part of the yard. After that, and a lecture on how to build radars from the assistant manager, it was off by bus again to the installation department. Apart from a few words of greeting, the Korean shipyard managers did not speak English, so KY acted as the interpreter. This did, of course, mean that what would be a half-hour meeting in the UK became an hour and a half or more in Korea. The Korean shipyard staff, all in company uniform of blue overalls regardless of position, seemed to feel that they had to find as much fault as possible with our products, methods, contracts, installation kits and anything else they could think of. I got the feeling that this was partly to impress their juniors who were often within earshot and partly because they were Daewoo Shipbuilding and the customer – therefore you, Mr Foreigner, must be in the wrong.

Finally, we took another bus back to the main gate. By this time, it was after 5 o'clock and thankfully it had stopped raining as we now had to walk. Breakfast had been the salad sandwich at Pusan ferry terminal that KY had bought and lunch had not existed. KY had booked us into the Daewoo company guesthouse for the night. This was a small boarding house-cum-hotel within walking distance of the main gate for people visiting the yard. There were a number of British guys living there and working in the shipyard on long-term contracts. To make life more bearable, the guesthouse restaurant also had a short, but welcome, Western menu. However, at KY's insistence, we went to a small single-storey Korean restaurant along the road, where we sat cross-legged on the floor for a bulgogi meal and a welcome OB (Orient Breweries) beer.

The next day dawned sunny and still. I stood outside and took in the scene. The tree-covered hills around the bay were like folds of green velvet as the low sun caught the sides, then they turned purply blue as they stretched peacefully away across the island. The paddy fields were bright emerald green with the new rice crop and a clear blue sky arched overhead. I could hear the shipyard noises of thumps, clanks, bangs and revving engines as the day's work started. The yellow Goliath crane gleamed and beyond the harbour wall, the calm sea glistened in the sun. The frustrations of yesterday were soon forgotten. The shipyard spread out below me in the sun, a new developing shipyard – which was set to become one of the world's biggest, progressing to build high-tech oil production rigs, chemical and gas ships, and eventually warships and submarines. It was for their submarine programme that I was to return to Okpo many years later.

We took a green pony taxi to the Samsung Shipyard, which was on the other side of the island. Samsung were building a series of oil tankers for European owners, which all had our radars being installed. We spent most of the day there, as again we had to see purchasing, electronics and installation departments to clear up and clarify all their various points. However, in Samsung, we stayed in a building by the main gate and the various members of staff came down to us. Again, lunch did not happen.

That night, we stayed in the Samsung Guesthouse. This was a new hotel and we arrived on the first day that it was officially open. It was built away from the yard, just above the shore on a beautiful deserted inlet of the sea. It was pure Scotland; a still, silent, black sea loch with dark brooding hills behind and the sun setting beyond them away to the west. The hotel was clean and smart. They had a restaurant with huge picture windows looking out over the loch and even a small bar area.

The rooms were simple but very clean and all had a peaceful sea view. As KY and I went for a stroll along the beach, I was able to appreciate the beauty of the southern part of Korea. Scotland with rice paddies was all I could think of to describe it. It was totally silent, apart from the sound of the wavelets lapping the pebble beach below the hotel.

On Wednesday, the weather had turned and a gale was blowing. We went to the hovercraft terminal but I was glad to find that it had been cancelled because of the weather. It was a really dirty day outside the bay and the sea was a mass of white horses. I have never been a fan of hovercraft, especially in any sort of a seaway. We were now forced to take a taxi back to Pusan – the green Hyundai Pony again. The taxi took us up through the hills and paddy fields and back onto the mainland, which is linked to Koje Do by a bridge. It took over three hours for the drive back to the nearest town of Masan. The back seat of the Pony was certainly not built for 6-foot Europeans. The road for the most part was narrow and bumpy, but the scenery more than made up for it. It was stunning with the hills and valleys, small picturesque villages and emerald green terraced rice fields. As we neared Masan, we joined a smooth, flat dual carriageway for the last few miles into town. In Masan, we took an express bus for an hour's ride back to Pusan, then another taxi to the KSEC shipyard.

KSEC, or Korean Shipbuilding and Engineering co, was one of the oldest shipyards in Korea and was situated in the town of Pusan itself. The west side of Pusan is built on a number of islands, so deep water for shipbuilding is available quite close to the town. This yard had a much more traditional appearance. A grey, featureless administration building fronted the busy main road with the yard and the slipways behind it. Our meetings were all held in one of a number of basic meeting rooms by the main entrance to the offices. These rooms all seemed to have just one large table and some metal chairs. My role was essentially to cover any topics that the shipyards wanted to discuss, as well as keeping them updated on new radars that we might be launching. These topics included all aspects of radar; from errors on installation drawings to commissioning queries;

from commercial terms and conditions to radar radiation levels. However, sometimes I felt that we were not really showing a heavy commitment to the Korean shipyard market with just one person coming to the shipyards three or four times a year, but my role in Korea was essentially supporting both the sales and service divisions as the main radar selling had already been done to the shipowners elsewhere in the world. It was therefore reasonable that one man should be able to do it.

We were supposed to meet the procurement manager in KSEC but were told on arrival that he was not available, so we met with a young purchasing assistant. We had been in discussion for a good while when there was a commotion in the next meeting room. The noise was such that we had to stop talking and wait while things settled down. Chairs were scraped on the floor, people shuffled about and lots of loud greetings exchanged. The purchasing assistant turned round to see what was going on. Through the dividing window, we could see that six Japanese businessmen in suits had come in and were being hosted by a similar number of shipyard officials, including the procurement manager. Like all shipyard employees in Korea, they all wore company uniform. Through KY Lee, the young purchasing assistant told us that, "This is the JRC (Japan Radio Company) monthly meeting. They come most weeks and we have a big meeting each month." JRC was a major Japanese marine electronics company and our main competitor in the Far East, and the fact that they could fly from their Tokyo HQ to Pusan with a team of six in a couple of hours did not help my mood. With customer focus like this they couldn't fail. It was, of course, out of the question for Racal Decca to send such a team anywhere.

After two further visits that afternoon to other smaller yards in Pusan, we spent the night in the Commodore Hotel. Here, on one of my later visits, I had the delight of a local visitor. Korean ladies of the night used to watch people going up in the lifts and then, after a while, follow them up and knock on the door. When you opened the door, you were greeted by a sweet smile and a demure voice in practised English saying, "Hello, sir, you want company?" A firm but polite "No, thank you" was all that was needed and the lady would disappear. Over the next few years, the hotel security was stepped up and this charming, but naughty and very high risk, offer of company became a thing of the past.

On Thursday morning, we visited two more yards in Pusan where we were supplying radars for naval patrol boats. Again, lunch was nonexistent and by mid afternoon we were back 'on the Pony'. This time we were heading for the biggest yard in Korea, possibly the world: Hyundai. Hyundai's yard is at Ulsan, some two to three hours' drive to the east. We arrived at their guesthouse called the Diamond Hotel. It was, again, fairly new, but this one actually looked like a proper hotel. They even had a coffee shop and a western menu displayed in the lobby. I whetted my appetite by reading it while we waited to check in. They had omelettes, burgers, even steak.

After a short rest, KY called me in my room. "We should eat now. Please meet me in lobby."

Great, I thought, as I was starving too.

As I came down the stairs, KY was already heading out of the door. I caught up with him. "Where are we going?" I asked, already dreading the answer.

"A little restaurant I know. Not far," he said and headed off.

After three days of no food or sitting on the floor with Korean rice or bulgogi bar BQ style food, I had just spent a couple of hours in my room planning a steak and chips and sitting up at a normal table. Now, I was confronted with more Korean food with, of course, more kimchi. I shrugged, 'If you can't take a joke...' KY led me through some alleys and narrow lanes near the shipyard and we entered a small low-fronted stone building, which was a local restaurant he had clearly visited many times. We settled into a small room and I tried to jam my long legs under the table as best I could. At least it was warm with underfloor heating and they had beer. The Bulgogi was actually quite good but my knees were not! I was not really in the mood for fiddling about with chopsticks and eating radish salad and kimchi. However, after a glass or two of OB beer, I began to relax and feel better.

Our meeting in Hyundai the next day did not go well. The first person we were due to see, the purchasing manager, was in a meeting so we went in search of the next person on our list. He was in the special ships division in another part of the yard. He was a serious but courteous man and we spent a long time with him discussing naval radars. He was actually quite reasonable and keen to learn about the new radars that Decca were bringing out. We then went back to find Mr Park, the purchasing manager, and after a long wait, he appeared.

He wore the Hyundai uniform, was young, probably in his early thirties, tall and glared at us through thick glasses. He said he had some problems with our radars and opened his thick file. We settled down while he read the notes in the file and then went through a list of complaints with KY in Korean. KY explained, "Hyundai are very unhappy as some telexes had not been answered and Mr Park says that telexes that have been answered, he does not understand or cannot read. His main complaint is about the installation kits that had been supplied with the radars. He says that the wrong bolts had been sent and that the instructions for installing the scanner unit are not clear and the packing note is different from the kit."

"Is that it KY?"

We then sat and went through with him the approved installation diagrams in the manual, but he still claimed that these were insufficient. As far as the wrong bolts were concerned, I apologised for the inconvenience, but it was clear that someone at our end had typed a five on the packing note instead of a four. The four bolts fitted the four holes on the radar scanner base. This was not good enough for Hyundai.

"Decca say there are five; bolts where is fifth bolt? You must supply one more bolt," he raged. He had the right bolts and the right quantity, but one clerical error allowed him to go on a thirty-minute tirade about our slack standards.

"We apologise for the typing mistake, but if you feel so strongly, why did you not contact our agent here in Korea or our service dept in the UK?" I asked.

"I do not have time for that. You must get it right; these errors will make the ship late and it will be your responsibility."

I refused to accept any responsibility for that or for any delay in completing the ship.

"Please wait, I need to discuss with my director" and he left the room.

The purchasing manager returned and began again, but was just repeating his earlier complaints. After a frosty half hour, we were told to wait. I told KY that there was no more we could do, we had answered all their questions and that we were leaving.

KY was upset. "You cannot do that," he said.

"I can," I said. "Anyway, we have a train to catch. Hyundai have not contacted either your office as our local agent, nor our service HQ about this – and just because we have come all this way, they think they can throw ship delays at our door. No way."

I was cross. Afterwards I recognised that I was wrong to get cross and I had lost face to the Koreans, but this was my first experience of Korean yards and I was a bit raw. Over the next few years in Korea, I learned to smile when I really wanted to scream. This always alarmed the Koreans as you were not meant to smile in meetings. I learnt quickly that in Korea there is no place in the workplace for friendly discussion or general conversation, let alone banter, jokes and a smile. The rule in the shipyards seemed to be that: "Work is war and the supplier is the enemy; treat him like an enemy and then make everything his fault."

We collected our passports from the main gate and looked for a taxi. We headed for the station but KY realised that we had already missed our fast train back to Seoul. The next Seoul train was a slow, stopping one. At Ulsan station, we relaxed and spent a pleasant couple of hours sitting in the warm sunshine sipping tea and waiting for the train to arrive. Hence the mad panic at Seoul some hours later at Seoul station when KY bundled me into the ladies' taxi.

The return of Eric (The Chairman's Personal Consultant)

Just before one trip, Eric Tyler, who I had met on Hong Kong trips, entered our office. "The Chairman wants me to come to Korea with you," he announced.

Inwardly, I groaned. "Oh good, that will be great Eric," I managed to reply with a smile.

We arrived in Seoul and were due to have a meeting with KY Lee's boss, Duncan, the managing director of the agency company. They had been Decca's agent for many years and we had always found them to be efficient and communicative. They were a lot more communicative than most agents, in fact.

On the way to the office, Eric briefed me on his plan for the meeting. "Look, I think these people need shaking up. Now, your role is to be the nice guy and I will be the bad guy. Just go along with my role play, it will all be jolly good fun."

I was bemused by this, but said, "Sure, fine, Eric, why not?"

We had settled in the managing director's office. Duncan was a very pleasant, helpful chap from Selkirk in the Scottish borders and ran a smooth and efficient office from what I had seen. With a coffee in his hand, he was describing his company and his perceived responsibilities to his principals, including us, when all of a sudden, Eric launches into the poor guy.

"Duncan, this is all very interesting, but you have just not performed. How are you increasing our sales? You have failed to do this. You are not representing us properly; you have no proper contacts at high level. Who are your contacts in the Chaebols? Do you know the president of Daewoo?"

Duncan, a gentle Scot from the Borders was totally taken aback. "I have met him, but I don't deal with him on a daily basis if that's what you mean" and so it went on.

He turned to me for support, which I offered as best I could by emphasising the value of KY's continued visits to the yards where our work was done.

Eric continued, "You should be operating at a much higher level if you want to keep our business. Racal Decca is going places and we must have the right people in places like Korea."

The message was clear: "Do as I say or lose the agency." I was as taken aback by the ferocity of Eric's attack as Duncan clearly was. Finally things calmed down and as we left some time later, Duncan even invited us to his home for dinner on the following Saturday night. It became clear from Eric later that Racal wanted to target Korea for future major defence business and the chairman needed a top level agent with contacts high in the government and the National Ministry of Defence (NMD) to help set up a major Racal presence in Korea. Decca's old agent, while excellent for what Decca needed in the commercial marine market, was not what Racal wanted. Hence the barrage from Eric, so he could report back that our agent was not up to the job. It appeared to me that I had not been briefed before in case I warned the agent.

The downside was that Eric was a workaholic, as many successful men are. Luckily, I have never suffered from this ailment. After a good dinner and a pleasant evening with Duncan and his wife in their home on the Saturday night, we got back to the hotel at about half past midnight. I was ready for bed, but Eric wanted to sit down then and there and debrief each other on what we thought of the evening and what had been said. All I thought was that I wanted to go to bed, but Eric wanted to go through the whole night in fine detail. I finally got to bed at about two thirty in the morning after agreeing to meet up again at eleven o'clock on the Sunday morning to discuss it all again.

I went to bed and fell sound asleep. In my dream, a phone was ringing somewhere. I came to and realised that it was my bedside phone. My first jet-lagged reaction was: "Oh hell, I am late, where should I be?" I picked it up and tried to work out what day it was and who would be calling me, but knew instantly it was Eric. Eric started without introduction or hello, "Now, about last night; what did you make of his comment about the Japanese competition?"

I looked at the clock. It was 7 a.m on Sunday. "Eric," I said, "what is wrong? I thought we were meeting at eleven to discuss all this?"

"Oh, I will see you later then," was all he said, and with a sigh and a 'humph' he rang off. I had probably just killed off any vague promotion chances I might have had.

Unknown to me, a Pusan-based company had contacted Racal head office directly and their details had been passed straight on to Eric. They wanted to represent Racal Decca for marine sales and servicing and they said that they represented other marine companies. Eric had not passed the information to me, nor had he asked the UK Embassy in Seoul what they knew about the company. Eric had agreed to go and visit them on a day trip from Seoul. Eric told me just a day or so before the trip, but as I had never heard of the company, I had not had a chance to check them out myself. I am sure I did remind Eric the night before to take his passport, but, unfortunately, he forgot it. In those days, as a foreigner, you had to have your passport with you to travel internally in Korea.

At the airport, we were asked for them by the security guard. He did not have his. He then tried to bluster his way through: "Look, this is only a domestic flight"; "It is in my hotel"; "I will show you tomorrow"; "I have some important meetings that I must attend." I was waiting for the "Do you know who I am?" but even Eric could not use that one in Korea. The guard was totally unmoved. He called his superiors.

We were both then marched off to the airport police offices and for thirty minutes Eric was questioned as to who he was and why he was in Korea, who he worked for, where his passport was. Finally they seemed content, but certainly not happy, that his story checked out. They quizzed me too, but as I had my passport, a couple of phone calls cleared me of any suspicion or risk. I then had to vouch for Eric in writing and even the UK Embassy may have been called. Eventually, Eric was given a slip of paper with police stamps all over it and we were allowed to travel, but only if Eric swore that he would not leave my side. I had to promise to look after him and we had to report to the police in Pusan airport. This did not go down well with Eric, who was bridling with rage and embarrassment but did manage to keep his temper (Eric, if you can't take a joke!) – while I enjoyed a private, but very silent, giggle. Still all jolly good fun, Eric?

The trip was a total waste of time anyway as the company who wanted to see us actually made car seat belts and knew as much about marine radars as I did about particle physics. Why Eric had not checked them out I have no idea, but at least there was no egg on my face. Anyhow, on the return flight at Pusan Airport, we had the same problem again and more policemen were called, the slip of paper issued by Seoul police was examined and checked, phone calls made and stern warnings issued before we were allowed through security.

Eric seemed doomed with Korean Air as on the next trip, even though he had his passport, as we arrived at the domestic terminal at Kimpo Airport to check in, the airline computers all went down. The crowd of shouting Koreans round the check-in desk grew. The delays grew. The Korean passengers grew noisier and more agitated and they were now pushing round the check-in desks, but nothing was happening. I worked my way to the front in Korean style and tried to find out what was going on. Then, Eric appeared at my shoulder. He was clearly getting edgy. The flight was due to go in thirty minutes and Eric was not where he thought he should be.

In his best English he shouted across at the poor girl, "Look, I know it's not your fault my dear, but I MUST get this flight and you do not seem to be doing anything about it. Why have you not given out the boarding passes? Please get on with it now and give us our boarding passes?" He waved his hand expectantly across the desk.

"So sorry," was the smooth, unconcerned reply. "Computer down. Must do manual check-in. Please wait."

Eric withdrew, defeated. Over his shoulder, he called, "Oh, you sort it out. You know this place." He gave a dismissive wave of his wrist and moved out of the crush. After that, Eric's saying of "I know it's not your fault, my dear, but," became a family saying normally heralding a bollocking for the poor unfortunate whose fault it clearly was.

When she finally handed out the boarding passes to everyone, I started to push my way out of the crowd. Eric called across to me, "You did get two seats together, didn't you?" I said nothing until I was clear of the crowd. I handed him his pass. "Eric, just be grateful we are on the flight. Now, let's go."

It all worked out well in the end because I had a peaceful flight as Eric was sitting ten rows in front of me and I could see that he was stuck in the middle seat of three, with two very large Korean men on either side for company. Eric was right. It is all jolly good fun!

In spite of his minor tribulations when travelling, Eric was always good company as he liked to tell a tale and he was naturally cheerful, except when he felt that the world was not doing what he thought it ought to. "Isn't this all jolly good fun" was the catchphrase he would often use as he briefed me on my role for another meeting. He was bombastic and dogmatic, but I just tried to duck all that and enjoy the ride. It was all a new learning curve for me.

One evening after we had got back into the Lotte Hotel in Seoul from another visit, we agreed to meet up in the coffee shop for a late meal. I was there first and I sat and watched as Eric came puffing round the corner with a really flushed face and a big smile. He could not wait to tell me his news.

"Do you know what has just happened to me?" he asked excitedly.

"No Eric, what has just happened?"

"I have just been propositioned, dear boy, in the lobby! And she was a beautiful girl, too!"

He was delighted. One of the Seoul ladies had collared him in the lobby as he came out of the lift. I think he thought that he had been selected for his good looks and physical potential and not the size of his wallet, but I did not disillusion him. In those days the ladies were able to wander relatively freely around the Lotte Lobby, which must have been one of the biggest lobbys in any hotel anywhere. Sometimes, the girls would hang around near the reception desk and find out which room you were given. On more than one occasion, I had no sooner got into the room than the phone would ring and the singsong call of "Hello, Mr Gary, you like companee tonight?" would trill down the phone.

One of the good things about travelling with Eric was that you always ate well. He insisted on the à la Carte restaurants rather than my usual coffee shops. We would enter a restaurant and as we were shown to our table, Eric would say to the Maitre D', "Bring us a chilled bottle of Chablis now and then bring the wine list and then bring the menu." He worked his way through the menus with a studious devotion that was obviously done so as not to upset the chefs by ignoring a course or leaving any food on his plate. A 'quick meal' was a two-hour affair.

During his involvement, Eric and I met many people, and at the end of the day, we started a solid relationship with one of the five major Korean companies which led to a major manufacturing deal for marine radars. However, it was one that was not to run smoothly and got me into more trouble later on.

Jet Lag and company changes

Jet lag is always a problem on trips to the Far East. On one trip, I flew all the way through to Tokyo – via Bahrain and Hong Kong – and it knocked me for six. For the first couple of nights in Tokyo, I was really suffering and hardly sleeping at all and then having to battle to stay awake all day. I felt as though my head was full of cotton wool and treacle, so meetings were a real struggle. I was there for just a few days and then flew on to Korea. The bad sleep continued as KY and I did our rounds of the shipyards. I ended up feeling really fed up with it and barely able to think straight.

With our meetings in the yards over, I was going back to Hong Kong on a Saturday morning. The Cathay Pacific flight left Seoul in the morning, getting to Hong Kong around lunchtime. At Seoul Kimpo Airport, I spotted a pharmacy stall in the departures hall. "Do you sell sleeping pills?" I asked the man.

"You want little sleep? You want big sleep?"

"Oh, I want little to middle sleep, maybe?"

"I sell you these small one. You take one for small sleep, two for big sleep." I paid him a few won, perhaps about a pound, for the box of twelve tablets. I dozed on the flight and got to Hong Kong and checked into the Harbour View Holiday Inn. I had a lunchtime beer and a sandwich at the bar, then at about 2.30 headed for bed and a quiet afternoon. I took two tablets and turned off the light.

When I woke up, I felt great. I was relaxed, knew I had had a great sleep and felt that I could now take on the world again. I stretched, put on the light and looked at the clock. It said 13.45. *No, that cannot be right*, but the sunlight filtering round the curtains told me it was daytime. But I had not gone to bed until after 1400. How can it still be early afternoon now? Then I realised. It was lunchtime on Sunday. I had slept for almost twenty-four hours! What great pills. I kept them with me after that.

Korea was a regular destination for me with Decca, Racal and occasionally with Plessey; but after I joined Thorn EMI, it became my main focus. I was working for Plessey when, after a hostile takeover, Marconi bought Plessey and we all became Marconi employees. A few months later, I was then lucky enough to be offered an export sales job with Thorn by a friend and former colleague in Plessey, John Hancock. John was one of the world's 'Good Guys' and had been on the Plessey defence team fighting the takeover, so he left fairly soon after the takeover to be the general manager of one of Thorn EMI's defence divisions, specialising in naval acoustic systems.

Things had been pretty depressing in Marconi. It was the only time in my working life when I questioned seriously why I was bothering to get out of bed in the mornings. We all felt that Marconi treated us all like misbehaving children and no one would or could ever make a decision. Everything had to be referred upwards to head office. If you were not a director, then you were a nothing. Regular overseas travel was virtually stopped unless it was to collect an order, so the incentive to try and cultivate a customer that you knew you were not allowed to go and talk to was diminished. The boss of the sales team even had a section from the company rules on expenses taped to the outside of his office door. This set the tone and attitude for the team. It basically said that no one was allowed to claim for any sort of alcoholic drinks for themselves on expenses. If we ate in our hotels, we had to provide a copy of the waiter's order sheet along with the hotel receipt, so that the company would know we did not order any alcohol. Basically, they were saying to us, "We don't trust you but we do trust a teenage trainee waiter we have never seen." The only time we could have alcohol was if we were entertaining. So when John rang me up with a job offer, I was receptive to it – to put it mildly.

On my first day at Thorn, John handed me a file. "We have just lost a bid for a naval underwater acoustics system in Korea," he said. "It was pivotal as it would have led directly to at least one and maybe two larger orders. Can you please see if you can work out what went wrong from what is in the file and whether we can get back in there?"

"Well, I will have a look and let you know." *Great!* I thought, *Day one and I am clearing up someone else's mess; thanks John*, but then I thought of my new salary and the shiny new company car outside and happily sat down to read the correspondence.

The more I read, the more fascinating it became. It soon was apparent that the person handling the prospect had been trying to win an export contract by playing telex ping-pong and asking the customer questions. In almost two years, not one visit had been made to Korea in spite of the agent repeatedly saying that this was what was needed. They had even submitted a bid without even talking to the customer face to face. Promises were made by telex, then not followed up, in fact. By early afternoon, I had read enough. I went in to see John.

"Well?" he said.

"John, someone has tried to win business by playing telex ping-pong with the agent and that will never work in Korea. In fact, I am surprised that the agent has not sacked us."

"I thought so," said John. "Do you think we could recover the situation for the next project?"

"I don't know, but I will tell you this. If you do not get someone out there soon to start to mend some fences, you certainly won't." I found myself on Thursday's flight to Seoul.

There was a view held by some senior managers with non sales backgrounds, that anyone with a sales title must have the gift of the gab and should be able to sell fridges to the Eskimos. They should therefore be able to go out and 'hard sell' a multi million pound sonar system to a customer over dinner, aided only by a two-page brochure. Of course, it never happens and John understood that well. Defence system selling is never a simple one-hit 'hard Sell'. It is a soft sell, over many months and years, with many visits in that time as confidence and trust grow.

I arrived in Seoul and started to dig. Meetings with the British Embassy commercial and defence sections, one or two old Plessey contacts and discussions with the agent himself, a Mr J.S. Yu, painted a fairly good picture. Thorn had been using an agent who was, on the face of it, ideally placed to win this type of business. If you are trying to sell a submarine or a ship, you need an agent with contacts at high level as well as a large office staff to assist in bid work. If you are selling a piece of equipment that fits onto a submarine or ship, then you need an agent with the right contacts at a slightly lower level. At my first meeting with Mr Yu, he was guarded, which, after the way he had been treated, was not unexpected. I explained that John and I had reviewed everything and we did not hold Mr Yu or his company responsible for the lost order. It was all our fault as we had not followed up on his requests. Mr Yu relaxed. I think he thought I was coming out to sack him.

"Look, Mr Yu, let's try and start again and see if we can win the next contract. We will do all we can to ensure that we can win it and will follow your advice."

This was for a different piece of equipment but was also needed on the same project. It was an expensive piece of acoustic equipment used for testing and calibrating sonars. Thorn made it and it was used by the Royal Navy, and we knew it would meet the needs of the Korean Navy. Our competitor was the French with a similar piece of equipment. Mr Yu's company should be ideal to help us with this. Mr Yu agreed it was still winnable, but the Korean Navy had not been impressed with Thorn's performance and we needed to do a lot of work to catch up. We got to work on the strategy that afternoon.

1991 Student demonstrations

When I arrived for a visit a few weeks later, student demonstrations had been going on in other cities in Korea for over a week, sparked by the death of a student, supposedly at the hands of the police. The papers and local TV were full of pictures of masked students hurling bricks and stones, in some cases even firebombs, at the police cordons. Photos of white smoking tear gas canisters rolling along shopping streets and riot police grabbing students and taking them away filled the papers. Tonight, it was Seoul's turn. The demonstration had been well publicised and there were warnings posted in the hotel lobby area about it. I was staying at the Chosun Hotel in the centre of Seoul, which faces onto the City Square. This was where the demonstration was due to take place, so it would be taking place outside the door.

I had arranged to meet Mr Yu and a customer for dinner that night. I rang him and suggested we meet at another place. "Yes, I agree, I suggest you take early taxi to Hyatt Hotel. We will meet you in lobby area. There will be no trouble there."

In the Chosun lobby that evening, people were asking the hotel staff if they would be OK to go out. The answer seemed to be "Not sure". I heard a couple of large Americans saying "To hell with this, let's get a pizza on room service" and they retreated into the lift. The student demonstration was due to start at about 8 o'clock, so by 7.30 the lobby was almost empty. The coffee shop, just off the lobby, and the cocktail bar nearby were deserted and the few people around seemed a little distracted. Even though it was May it seemed to be a chilly night and as I left the Chosun in a taxi, we passed rows of dark blue police buses parked in the roads that entered the main City Square. The buses had grills over all their windows and were full of riot police in black, padded combat suits and black helmets with visors. I gave a shiver at the thought of getting in the way of one of those guys.

The taxi moved rapidly away from City Square and climbed the hill, up past the Hilton and on to the Hyatt. The world outside seemed to return to normal. The Hyatt is a built on the top of a hill and overlooks a big bend in the River Han and a large part of Seoul city. It is one of the best hotels in Seoul, often used by international VIPs. I paid the taxi and entered the vast lobby. The place was busy and had a relaxed feel about it. A live band was playing in the lobby lounge and smartly-dressed people were standing in groups or sitting on the settees enjoying their cocktails as they looked out through the huge windows over the city lights spread out below. It seemed a world away from the siege atmosphere down in the Chosun. Waiters and waitresses were busy dashing around the groups of business people with trays of drinks. Mr Yu and his colleague, Mr Kim, were waiting to one side of the main doors. Mr Yu is a tall, slim man; much taller than most Koreans. He has the bearing of the naval officer that he once was and is a fine and gentle man. By this time, I had known him for a little while and felt that I was getting to know and like him. His colleague, Mr Kim, was short, stocky and always smiling, which worried me a bit as it was not like Koreans to smile so much.

"Why you not stay here instead of Chosun downtown?" asked Mr Kim. "Here is better hotel and away from trouble. We can get you good rate here." I could see his point. "I think I will," I said.

We set off together in another taxi down to a different part of town where Mr Yu knew of a good local restaurant. We stopped outside a restaurant on a busy street. It was, of course, Korean and it was his favourite one. From the outside, it seemed more like a workers' canteen than a posh eatery as the noise of loud chattering and crashing dishes carried out onto the street. The ground floor was lit by fluorescent lights and was very bright. The place was full and very noisy with

Koreans yelling instructions across the sound of dishes and glasses being placed or collected. Mr Yu headed to the left towards a flight of stairs. As he got near the foot of the stairs, a lady stepped out of a door and greeted him with a slight bow. He was obviously an honoured regular. We were taken upstairs where the lady escorting us knelt down on the floor, slid open a thin door and ushered us into a small quiet private room. There already was another of Mr Yu's team and a gentleman from the navy who we had met earlier. It was gloriously warm. We left our shoes at the door and the warmth of the underfloor heating instantly made my feet feel warm as I slid on the polished pine wood floor and settled down around the low table that filled the middle of the room. While Mr Yu and Mr Kim slipped easily onto the floor, their legs somehow vanishing beneath them, mine would not go where I wanted them to and I could not get comfortable. I never mastered the technique of 'losing' your legs in these places and always ended up with sore knees and a twisted back. Mr Yu issued a string of orders to the lady, and very soon, beer arrived. She then brought in a heavy black stone bucket of glowing hot coals and it was placed in a hole in the middle of the table, and a big 3-foot wide griddle placed on top of it.

Then, as we chatted and drank the 'OB' beer, the waitress arrived and crawled into the room on her knees pushing a tray of small dishes in front of her. These had radish salad, rice, a bowl of sliced garlic, small bowls of a whitish soup and, of course, the ubiquitous "kimchi". She slid silently backwards out of the door. Then she reappeared with a big plate of marinated, shredded beef, which she proceeded to further shred with a pair of kitchen scissors. We were then left to ourselves to divide out a few pieces of beef with our chopsticks and cook the beef, garlic and vegetables on the griddle, which by now was getting very hot. As more beef sizzled and the beer flowed, the smells of soy sauce, garlic and chilli rose from the griddle. The temperature rose, jackets were removed and a general feeling of warm camaraderie began to envelope the room. The Koreans have a fantastic work ethic and life is very serious during working hours. However, after work finishes, they also have a very strong 'let's enjoy life' ethic too.

A bottle of Soju was called for. This is a Korean spirit, a clear drink that is drunk neat. So, the events going on in the City Square fell into the backs of our minds. The beer and the Soju seemed to help my knees too as I was soon feeling more comfortable. The Koreans have a custom at these dinners that when one of the guests or hosts, it does not seem to matter, notices that someone else's glass is empty, they finish their own glass and pass it to the other person with both hands. He then takes it with both hands and the first person fills it for him from the bottle. Someone else will then do the same to the one who started as they have now lost their glass. And so it goes on! As the evening continues, you will undoubtedly have drunk out of everyone else's glass!

Eventually, plates of fruit, mainly apple and Japanese pear – beautiful juicy things – were passed in. However, with the fruit came a warning from the manageress that students and police were in a nearby street. Mr Yu decided we should leave right away, so we left and headed out into the chill night. We walked briskly for a few streets, then turned into a narrow alley. After a few yards, Mr Yu knocked on a plain door in a dark, old, single-storey building. It was opened by a Korean lady who invited us inside. My mind was now a little clearer after the walk and I was wondering what sort of place this was. It was dark inside, lighting was at a minimum, but it was warm and I could see it had a low ceiling. I ducked my head and followed Mr Yu's back as he led us into a booth at the back of the room. The five of us nestled into the cosy booth. As my eyes became accustomed to the gloom, I saw that there were three or four other booths, all with three or four guys sitting in them talking quietly and drinking beer or spirits. The only light was from heavily shaded lamps hanging low over the tables. There were a few small paraffin heaters on the floor. The booth seats were comfortable and well cushioned and the table was a normal height, so I enjoyed stretching my legs out. Soon the beer arrived and then a plate of sliced apples. It was not long before a tall and smiling Korean girl joined us. She was called

Anna and was there to act as our hostess in the best sense. She made sure we had beer and got more fruit when needed. She, of course, joined in the Korean chit-chat and banter, but her presence lightened the monastic atmosphere of 5 guys in business suits.

I was suddenly aware that there was a low humming mumble coming from Mr Yu's side of the table. Mr Yu had started singing. He sang a song called 'Arirang' – a traditional Korean folk song. Mr Kim whispered to me that Mr Yu always sang Arirang. Mr Kim had a go with another well known Korean song, but regrettably one unknown to me. He actually had a very good voice and sang well. Then it was my turn and 'Flower of Scotland' got an airing. As I finished the second verse, I caught a whiff of sharp acrid fumes. Mr Kim caught it too.

"Tear Gas," said Mr Kim. "We must go."

Mr Yu quickly paid the ladies and with hankerchiefs over our faces, he led us out into the alley. We turned right away from the main street and quickly headed further down the alley. We emerged into a brightly lit shopping street where we gathered together and decided enough was enough for one night. We all shook hands and went our separate ways.

I took a taxi back to the Chosun. We had not gone far though before we came across the police barriers and their buses. Bricks and stones littered the street and the driver slowly weaved his way through the rubble-strewn streets. Riot police stopped us at a checkpoint and peered inside. The driver shouted something to them and we were waved through. I assumed he was saying "A drunken westerner for the Chosun." We drove on. I had no idea where we were and just hoped that City Square was still open. The big blue buses seemed to be everywhere. Some were empty, some had riot police sitting inside. The police waved us off the main road and the driver went round some back streets until suddenly I realised that we were near City Square. Looking down a cross street, I had a quick glimpse of running students with scarves across their faces and white tear gas hung in the air. More buses were parked here and bricks, rubble, broken bottles and general debris lay across the road. The taxi had to weave its way through the debris which got worse the nearer we got to City Square. Finally the taxi pulled up in front of the Chosun. I paid the driver and added a decent tip as there was no way I could have got back otherwise. A slight mist of tear gas lay across the Square as I hurried inside to safety. "Oh well, if you can't take a joke," I said to myself.

The next day, I moved up to the Hyatt and always stayed there after that. Perched high up on the hill just below the Namsam Park, the Hyatt overlooks all of southern Seoul as it spreads up the wide valley of the Han Gang River. In winter, when the long, cold, dry weather gripped Korea, the Hyatt's gardens were turned into an ice rink and all plants everywhere were wrapped in sacking and straw. The sun, slowly rising into the clear skies above the hills, beyond bends in the Han River, heralded another day's work in Korea. Below my window, one of the largest cities in the world came to life and threads of smoke began to rise from the houses clustered round nearby Itaewon shopping area. Far below and across the valley, down near the river, where the sun had not yet reached, the fluorescent lights of shops and offices slowly flickered on while the lights of thousands of cars, buses and commuter trains streamed to work in the city across the many road and rail bridges over the river.

Daewoo

Although the end user for the equipment that we were now trying to sell was the Korean Navy, we were selling it to the prime contractor and procurement agent which was Daewoo Shipyard down in Okpo. This was the same place where I had been initiated into Korean shipyards over ten years earlier. Mr Yu had already set up the meetings with the shipyard and we discussed these in Seoul before travelling down a day or so later. After the first introductory presentation and meeting in Daewoo head office in Seoul, they had agreed to open a dialogue with us.

This was the start of a long road. I travelled to Okpo a total of thirteen times in twelve months and on many of those trips, I took our technical director, Jim Wardale, with me. Jim was a sonar and acoustics expert who was a sincere person with a wide and deep knowledge of his subject. He had an honest and open demeanour, which immediately impressed the Koreans and they accepted what he said. During the many trips to Okpo, we gradually built up their confidence in our technology and convinced Daewoo that we knew what we were talking about, or, rather, we convinced them that Jim knew what he was talking about.

Many emerging economies, as Korea was then, have developed their own local electronics industries. Daewoo had its own. The armed forces wanted to have the latest technology in their systems and had a good understanding of the technologies we were using. We often found that once we had presented our system, the customers always wanted a bigger one or a smaller one, one with XYZ software not ABC, or they wanted the S/W written in a different protocol.

The Koreans were very good at shooting you down after a sales pitch. If he is offered the latest technology light years ahead of the Americans, then he will say that it is untried and he does not want to be our guinea pig. If he is offered a well proven product, one that was used by the UK and US Forces in combat in the Gulf Wars, then he will say it is old technology. "We must have the latest." If it is something that was designed primarily for use by the UK Armed Forces, then it will probably be too expensive as the UK MOD are renowned for always wanting and buying sophisticated solutions with bells and whistles. If it is not used by the Royal Navy, then the salesman will be told: "It cannot be any good if your own navy does not use it!"

I was often asked "If your system is so good, why do you offer a spares kit with it?" One Korean captain said to me: "Mr Gary, please remove the guarantee costs from your quotation as if it is as good as you say, then it cannot breakdown – so I do not need guarantee." We embarked on what seemed to be an endless exercise of visits and questions, face to face technical meetings, followed by more fax exchanges once we had got back to the UK.

Over the intervening months when we were back in the UK, Jim and

I dealt with the daily faxes from Daewoo. Every morning at 0800, Jim and I picked up an overnight fax from the machine and got the technical or commercial team together so that we had an answer prepared and on its way back to Korea by close of play that day. The eight-hour time difference helped get us a little thinking time each day, until it was time to go out and go through all the questions and answers face to face to ensure that it was all clearly understood. Finally, Daewoo invited us out for one final meeting to finalise and conclude the technical discussions and agree the final specification of the system – or so we hoped.

On the last trip, Jim and I both felt that Daewoo had started to quiz Jim a little too deeply for a little too long, so we were determined to stick to our guns on this final session as we knew they had all the data they needed to properly assess our system. I had realised over the years visiting Korea that whenever you have an engineer with you, the locals will try and suck as much information from him as they can. They were quite blatant about it and did not care whether we gave away intellectual property data or broke MOD Classification rules of what we could say. A gang of Korean engineers would quite literally get an unsuspecting engineer in a corner and verbally pummel him until he had answered all their questions. We often had to wade in and physically pull the poor unfortunate engineer out of the room before he expired or gave away any secrets.

We asked Daewoo how long they expected these final discussions to last so we could plan our trip. They told us just two days to clear up a few remaining questions. Knowing Daewoo as we did by this time and based on our previous experiences, we allowed for three or four days in Okpo.

In Korea, it is important to establish a position in any discussions and keep to it. To shift position is seen as a sign of weakness and they will just push harder. On the other hand, we were the foreign seller so had to make sure we gave them enough information to enable them to make an informed decision to buy our system. This is not an easy tightrope to walk.

We arrived in Okpo on a Sunday night, spent a restless, jet-lagged night in the Daewoo guesthouse in the village and began discussions on the Monday morning. After the morning session of the second day,

I explained to the project manager, Mr Sunoo, who was our main point of contact, that we had to leave that evening so we trusted that we had now answered all their questions. He said there were still a few issues to be resolved. I said that was fine as long as they could be completed that afternoon. At 1600 that day, we said, "Thank you, we believe we have answered all your questions and you must now have all the information that we can give you and we must now leave."

Mr Sunoo asked for time to go and speak to his director, Mr Chang – the technical director. Director Chang joined us and said that there were still some issues to discuss and we must stay for a further day. I explained that before we came out, we had asked how long he expected the talks to last and he had said two days. Now, they wanted another day and we understood why and giving the information was not a problem, but the problem was time. We had to leave when we said we would leave as we had other meetings arranged in Seoul and flights booked back to the UK.

Director Chang pleaded their case and so we agreed that we would stay for one more half day at the most. It was equally important to show that we respected Mr Chang's request for us to stay as he had asked us in front of his team and we could not let him lose face by totally refusing. It was agreed with Director Chang that we would be finished by lunchtime the next day.

Jim and I discussed things that night. We knew they had all the product information they needed and we believed that they understood it too. The questions they were now asking were about basic acoustic theory, something we were not being paid to teach them. It was up to Daewoo to learn this themselves.

The next day I told Jim to be prepared to get up and leave when I said so, as I was not prepared to waste another day teaching Daewoo acoustics at our expense. We told Mr Sunoo in the morning that we had to leave after lunch. Lunch was a tense affair. We had it, as usual, in the shipyard canteen. It was the standard Korean shipyard lunch that everyone ate. We queued up with the yard workers and were handed a metal tray with 'lunch' already on it. On the tray was a bowl of seaweed soup, which was a clear soup with bits of seaweed in it, a bowl of rice and a bowl of kimchi. It was the same every day.

After lunch, I said to Director Chang that we had to catch the 1530 ferry from Okpo to allow us to catch our flight from Pusan to be in Seoul that night. He said that Mr Sunoo still needed more time to understand some the technicalities. I said that I was sorry but we had to leave as we had now stayed two days longer than they had requested. However, if it helped, then Mr Sunoo was welcome to see us in Seoul tomorrow. Mr Wardale and I would be in Seoul for a day as I had a couple of other meetings that I could not cancel, but I felt that Jim could stay in the hotel and he might be able to see Mr Sunoo during that time or in the evenings. There was a rapid exchange of conversation in Korean between Director Chang and Mr Sunoo who quickly left the room. Mr Chang explained that he understood our position, thanked us for staying and that Mr Sunoo would come back to Seoul with us so he could discuss acoustics tomorrow with Mr Wardale in the hotel. Mr Chang seemed happy with the compromise and then drove us to the ferry terminal.

We all flew back to Seoul. Mr Sunoo was happy as it enabled him to go and stay with his mother for the night and Jim and I returned to the Hyatt. The next morning at 0800, Mr Sunoo was in the lobby. I went to my meetings with Mr Yu and the embassy and left Jim to chat with Mr Sunoo. Mr Sunoo was happy as he said it was better to discuss things there than in the shipyard. That night, he flew back to Okpo a happy chap. Our agent had been working behind the scenes and confirmed that we were now in a very strong position as our main competitor, the French, had not responded as positively as we had and both Daewoo and the Korean Navy had a number of outstanding questions that the French had, so far, refused to answer. I told Jim and we gave a big sigh of relief.

A few weeks later, on a Thursday morning, we received a fax from Daewoo. "Would we please attend Okpo Shipyard next Monday morning for contract negotiations." I showed it to John. After twelve

IF YOU CAN'T TAKE A JOKE…

months and twelve trips, we had finally got to the contract negotiations.

Just when you think things are getting clearer, they get murky again! There was now another issue. We needed a commercial executive with the ability to negotiate and the authority to sign a contract and agree the final price. The executive offered by the commercial director was a lady. In Korea, females do not hold senior positions. They may be secretaries but at that time they were certainly not commercial executives. They tend to be no more than wallpaper in the offices and do not contribute to business discussions.

I had no idea how a female commercial executive would be viewed by the shipyard. Would they treat her badly and try to bully her? Would they feel offended that we had not taken a senior male director? I called an old friend from Plessey who had done a lot of negotiations in Korean shipyards. He said very simply if she is any good, take her, as a woman who knows her stuff will confuse and amaze them and we will get the better of the deal. I called John.

"Is she any good John?"

"Yes she is, she is good."

"OK, then we will take her."

Nina Barr was an attractive dark-haired woman of about forty with a reputation in the company for being a no-nonsense girl. She was certainly very intelligent, quick-witted and was pleased to come. I explained to her the Korean culture and their views of women as second-class citizens in male-dominated industries like shipbuilding. She was still happy to give it a go. I sent a fax to Daewoo on the Thursday night with the names of those coming, without highlighting that 'N. Barrs' was a female. *They will find that out on the day*, I thought. *It gives us an advantage and might catch them off balance.*

To be in Okpo for the Monday morning meant arriving in Okpo on the Sunday night. That meant leaving London on Friday and flying via Tokyo and Seoul, before a domestic flight down to Pusan and then getting ourselves out to Okpo. After a long flight to Tokyo, there was a delay until the flight to Seoul, where we met up with Mr Kim from the agents office. Then, we had to get over to the domestic terminal for the flight down to Pusan. From there it was a taxi for a one-hour ride to the port of Chinhae and then a two-hour ferry boat ride to Koje Do Island. By this time, we were exhausted, could only drink black coffee and were long past being hungry. Once on the ferry, Nina instantly found a corner seat and fell sound asleep with her mouth slightly open and her head lolling on one side. (I still have the photo somewhere). Jim and I tried to stay awake by standing on deck and enjoying the beautiful scenery as we sailed serenely through the islands and bays. Once on Koje Do Island, we took another taxi for the final short ride to Okpo village. We collapsed into the Daewoo guesthouse at about 7 o' clock on the Sunday night feeling totally shattered. But we had made it.

We presented ourselves at the shipyard on the Monday morning. We were taken to the meeting room and the Daewoo team arrived. We knew the technical team, led by Mr Sunoo, but the commercial man was a new face. He was a young procurement manager who had been brought in for today's negotiations. When we introduced Nina to him, his face was a picture. He was totally confused. He did not know whether she was a personal gift to him or a foreign devil woman who had been sent to show him up in front of his colleagues. We set to work and with the technical specification already agreed, Nina took Daewoo through all the commercial issues and conditions. Price was negotiated to both sides' satisfaction, but more so on our side as we had a slightly better deal than we had anticipated we would get.

By mid-morning the next day, we had a signed contract that would grow in time with extensions and additional systems to a value of over £5m. Nina had been brilliant and had all her facts and figures, percentages and deliveries and other negotiating factors locked in her head. The poor young procurement manager never had a chance against Nina's charms and brain, and Daewoo had not seen it coming. We walked away with a good deal in terms of price and delivery. That night we all met up in a local restaurant in Okpo for a Korean meal to seal the deal and Nina impressed the Koreans even more with her ability to sit cross-legged on the floor, eat kimchi, drink beer and use her chopsticks to cook bulgogi.

Nina was the only female to join me on a trip, which highlights the scarcity of them in the defence industry. This is directly due to so many defence sales guys coming from the Armed Forces. I only knew of one female salesperson, but she was a technical specialist turned salesman for a specific UK MOD project. In the early days, we always had young secretaries to do our typing and help us to organise our lives and make sure our expenses were signed. It was always good to ring the office and have a chat with the secretary and find out what mood the boss was in before she put you through to talk to him, as well as to give you the latest office gossip.

Regrettably, the advent of the now ubiquitous laptop changed all that. "You are your own secretary now!" they told us. "You must type up and print all your own stuff." Females rapidly left the building, redundant. We were left totally high and dry. We were all just handed laptops and if we were lucky, we might be in the country for the half-day course on Microsoft Office Word. Then it was, "Back to your desk and get on with it". As most of the others could not even type, let alone know how to use one, the complexities of typing, storing and printing a document using Microsoft Word and working it out for ourselves given the weird logic of the computer was stuff from another planet. It was a trying time. "Come back the girlies," we would say.

Now, a few years down the road, it is second nature to do everything ourselves. However, as everyone organises their laptop files and folders in their own way, if anyone else ever needed to get into someone else's laptop to find something they had written on it, then I am afraid there would be no hope. Central office paper filing systems fell into disuse and vanished. Few people bothered with hard copies of emails and even fewer actually keep paper files anymore. "It's all in here!" they cried triumphantly, pointing at their laptop. There can be very few companies today that have an efficient and complete paper record of all their transactions.

Kimchi

Much is made of the Korean national dish of kimchi in travel articles about Korea. It is, very simply, pickled cabbage. However, it is the other ingredients that the Koreans put into their own homemade kimchi that gives it its reputation. The very first time I had it I was in a small restaurant in Seoul having just arrived that morning from the UK. I felt fine eating it but the next morning I thought I must have eaten razor blades.

Traditionally, kimchi is made in late summer to preserve fresh vegetables and the vitamins in them so they can be eaten through the long cold Koran winters. In rural areas, the cabbage was placed in layers in earthenware pots. Between each layer, they would put a mixture of ingredients ranging through garlic, ginger, soy sauce, salt, water and hot chilli peppers in varying quantities and to their own family's taste. Some families preferred mild kimchi, some liked it hot. Indeed, there probably are as many variations as there are families that make it. The pots when full were sealed and buried in the ground to ferment slowly until they are ready to eat in the winter. Kimchi is served everywhere and with every meal, including breakfast. It always pays to test a tiny amount before eating as this kimchi might not be a mild as the one we had yesterday!

After we had won the acoustics contract, our managing director, Bob, came out to say a personal thanks to Mr Yu and his team and Mr Chang, the Daewoo director. He had heard all about kimchi and on the day he arrived, as we sat down for dinner in the Hyatt coffee shop, he said, "OK, you guys, what's with this kimchi stuff that everyone goes on about? Do they do it here?" It duly arrived and Bob sampled it carefully. Then, he chewed with a little more vigour and tried a larger amount. "Not too bad," he said. "I really cannot see what people make all the fuss about."

The following night we were out for dinner with Mr Yu. As usual, we went to his favourite Korean restaurant. Once we were all seated on the floor and the beer had arrived, the small dishes were served including the kimchi.

Mr Yu said to Bob, "Mr Bob, have you heard of kimchi?"

Bob was on solid ground here. "Oh yes," he said proudly "and what's more I had some last night when I arrived."

"Oh good," said Mr Yu. "Would you like some now?"

"Yes, of course."

Bob boldly took a large scoop of kimchi with his chopsticks. Bob ate half of his mouthful, then stopped. Now, I know it was warm in the room, but his face turned bright red and perspiration stood out on his balding scalp. He stared straight ahead, his eyes reflecting an inner panic. He tried to swallow, but could not; he tried to drink some beer, but found that it turned to steam in his mouth. He stood up and opened the window above him. The cold night air fell in on us as Bob took two or three deep gasps. After a while, he shut the window and sat down again. His face was still red and all he could say in a thin, strained and squeaky voice was, "Wow! That is different from what I had last night!"

"Yes, kimchi here very good," said Mr Yu innocently. "You like more?"

Charles and Di

Some time later, in 1992, HRH Prince Charles and Princess Diana visited Seoul. In the four years since the 1988 Seoul Olympics, Korea and Seoul had changed a lot. Not only had a lot of work been done on the transport systems and road networks in and around Seoul, but the whole place had brightened up. With the curfew abolished, there were neon lights, huge electronic advertising billboards and the whole city seemed a brighter, nicer, happier place to be. The Koreans themselves all seemed happier. The glum grim faces of the early 1980s had been replaced by, if not smiling, then at least helpful and acknowledging faces. The Koreans were now happy to help foreigners and tourism had arrived in the Republic. The Koreans instantly recognised that tourists equal money and their demeanour towards tourists was a helpful one.

It was to this new, brighter, happier Seoul that Princess Diana brought her trademark smile and the people loved her. A 'Korea-Britain' week was tied in with the royal visit with talks, a mini exhibition, dinners and a visit to the ballet. The royals and their entourage were all staying in the Hyatt. John Hancock and I were there too and watched the couple arrive. The hotel lobby was full of the biggest Korean men I had ever seen. They all stood with their hands clasped in front of them and with bendy plastic straws sticking up from their shirt collars and disappearing into their ears. Once the couple arrived, it was nearly impossible to see them for all these heavies in the way. We were trying to take photos but the heavies started shouting at people, "No photo, No photo!" We never knew why, but some local Koreans who took photos were bustled out of the way and their cameras pushed down in a far-from-friendly manner. The stories about their marriage and its breakup had been in the press and are better documented elsewhere, but we did observe that there seemed to be very little affection between them as they entered the hotel lobby. They were greeted by cheers from a crowd of British expats, including the ambassador. The royal party had taken over one of the top floors and one of the six lifts had been sectioned off for them. We always knew when they were about to leave or arrive as the lobby filled up with the heavies half an hour before.

It was, I confess, sad to think of the emotional turmoil that they must have been going through at the time and then having to cope with all the formal official engagements. Reports emerged that Princess Diana was suffering with jet lag and spent most nights watching TV.

One afternoon, I happened to come out of the lift as she and her escorts came round the corner heading for their lift. Our eyes met and I tried to smile naturally at her. She looked straight at me and gave me a nice smile back as we passed, but then she was gone as the lift doors shut and her heavies surrounded her. That was probably as near as I will ever get to meeting royalty.

John also suffered from jet lag that trip, but made it worse by making a cardinal error. We had been out quite late together on his second night there and had had a few OB beers. We were going back to our rooms and as John opened his door, he saw an incoming fax had been shoved under the door.

"Ah, a fax!" said John.

"John, leave it alone and read it tomorrow," I told him.

"But it might be important!" he replied.

"Not at one in the morning it's not," I said, but John had already closed the door.

The next morning John was late for breakfast and when he did appear, he looked dreadful. "I have not slept at all. I feel awful," he said.

"John, welcome to jet lag! I am sorry but I told you not to read the fax. You did read it last night, didn't you?" He nodded glumly. "It only triggered your brain back to work issues."

"You are right, Gordon. It was from Roger and I thought if I called him then, with the time difference, he would still be in the office. Then Dave Smith wanted to have a word with me. Do you know I was on the phone for over forty minutes."

"Well, it serves you right," I said teasingly. "Did any of it have to be done last night?"

"No, not really," replied a doleful John.

The trouble is you do not know whether a fax is important or not until you have read it. However, 99 times in 100, at that time of night, it is not that important – or if it is important, then it is not urgent. If it was, then someone would have rung up with a warning that it was coming or have left a message asking for an urgent return call. Once a jet-lagged brain is triggered at that time of night, it is impossible to go to sleep.

John had a great selection of sayings and general rules for survival in life. Among them, there are a few that stand out:

Rule 1. **"It is always easier to obtain forgiveness than permission."** If the boss is not contactable and something must be done that is clearly right, then go for it.

Rule 2. **"Never miss the opportunity to keep your mouth shut."** This is another life-saver. How often do people open their mouths and flap it to fill a silence and as they do so, dig themselves into huge holes.

Rule 3. **"If you don't think you will like the answer, do not ask the question."** This is also a very practical rule.

Chinese Lunch

Mr Yu always insisted that on my last day in town, we go to lunch together in his favourite Korean restaurant. After our contract success, I insisted that he lunched with me and I invited him up to the Hyatt for lunch in the excellent Chinese restaurant there. He happily accepted. I was pleased – no more seaweed soup on this trip. I was now looking forward to a Chinese lunch with sweet and sour pork, or crispy duck. Mr Yu arrived and we settled down for a chat while the menus were brought. I favoured the crispy duck or should I try the chicken with cashew nuts? After about ten minutes, Mr Yu had still not decided. Then he shut the menu sharply and waved the waitress over. He babbled away to her in Korean for a while and she nodded rapidly. Then, she took our menus and disappeared.

Oh! I thought, *he has ordered a set menu; a bit strange though as I am meant to be the host here.* But I let it pass. "Have you ordered for both of us?" I asked.

"Yes, but there was nothing on the menu," he said.

Now I was confused. What had he ordered? Then, after a few more minutes, the waitress reappeared with two big trays. She placed one in front of me and the other in front of a beaming Mr Yu. My heart sank. It was the typical Korean lunch, just as we had had in the shipyard! Seaweed soup, rice and kimchi. Mr Yu had got me again.

Turtle Ships

I have many lasting memories of Korea, and one of the nicest is of a pleasant afternoon I spent visiting a life-size replica of a turtle ship at the Korean Naval Academy in Chinhae. The turtle ship was first conceived by the Korean Admiral Yi Sun Sin for the war against Japan between 1592-1598. The ship actually looked like a turtle; it was relatively short and broad, with a fat rounded hull for a body. This body had an enclosed deck with a curved roof, or shell, over the top of it. It was made of wood with big, thick, pointed metal spikes mounted on top pointing upwards. This shell protected the sailors from incoming fire and the spikes deterred any would-be boarders.

One of the features was a dragon's head on the bow which was used either to send sulphur fumes and smoke towards the enemy like a smoke screen, or it could have a cannon mounted in it. The ship fired guns through gun ports in the sides and she could carry about twenty-four or twenty-five cannon. She was manoeuvred by sail and oars. For a ship with a worldwide reputation as the ultimate battleship of its day, it was surprisingly small. It was about 100 feet long by 30 wide and very manoeuvrable. She would have carried a crew of about 130 sailors and soldiers in the enclosed deck space. It was probably more akin to a medieval submarine in terms of closed-in living in a small space. It was, however, very solidly constructed. She seemed to sit low in the water and looking at her from a distance, all I was aware of was the turtle back covered in metal spikes and the gun ports. There was no open deck area at all. It seemed quite the reverse of the idea of fore and after castles built at the ends of European medieval ships. It did have a mast that carried sails but it was not clear to me how the sailors handled the sails or rigging. Anyone going up the mast would be more concerned with falling onto the spikes on the turtle back than anything else. Korea is very proud of the turtle ships and their part in its history, so the replica is a national treasure which I was lucky to be allowed to visit.

Ten Golden Rules

"Gordon, I want your body," the female on the other end of the phone demanded. Initially I was pleased and a little flattered, as it is not every day I got requests of that nature. Then I recognised the voice. It was Nicky, who I knew well. She was an executive officer who worked on the Korean desk in DESO (Defence Export Services Organisation) – the part of the MOD that covered defence export sales.

"Nicky, it's yours!" I replied instantly. Then she let me down, and not very gently either.

"Good, as I want you to speak at the MOD Symposium on 'Doing Defence Business in Korea'."

"Oh, thanks, Nicky, just what I need. Would you rather not have my body instead?"

"No," she said, a little too firmly I thought. Then she got to work with her charm again and after ten minutes, I had agreed to do it – but I had negotiated hard: "This will cost you a beer." "Done," she said – and I had been.

The theme she wanted me to speak on was 'How to succeed in Korea at defence business'. I let my mind wonder round the topic for a couple of days, then started to jot down ideas. After a while, a few ideas firmed up and to stop going off into a diatribe of waffle and endless bullet point slides, I tried to stick to just ten major elements of working in Korea. I came up with 'Ten good rules for doing business in Korea' and selected the following:

1. The need for a clear overall vision and a strategy. As someone once said, "Anyone working in Korea without a strategy is just a tourist."
2. Agents, their roles and importance.
3. The importance of regular visits.
4. Keeping things simple (written and verbal).
5. Getting things right the first time. The Koreans cannot understand how any professional can submit proposals or write letters with mistakes in them.
6. The importance of correct formal introductions and meetings.

7. The vital need for business cards.
8. How to manage technical meetings and not give away all your secrets.
9. Negotiations. The Koreans are professional warriors and see it as a battle they must win so it is important to have a very clear pricing and negotiation strategy
10. The need to visit Korea again and again if you want to succeed.

I then decided that I needed to illustrate the talk, otherwise it would be very boring. But with what? I looked around for ideas. Then I realised that I had a Korean calendar on my desk with fifty-two bright colour photos featuring 'Life in Korea'. These ranged from folk singing to shipbuilding and sumo wrestling to village dance scenes. After a bit of thought and help from the company photographer, I was able to use them to provide the background for bullet points or to make a point on its own.

The presentation was given in Northumberland House, an MOD building in London, to over 100 defence industry and MOD staff. It was a bit nerve-wracking as I was speaking to an audience of senior MOD officers, including the Military Head of Deso, Rear Admiral Sam Salt, as well as my industrial peers; many of whom knew Korea far better than I did and over a longer period of time. However, no one came up afterwards and said it was a load of rubbish, so I took it to be a case of: "I think that all went rather well, don't you?" Nicky kept her side of the deal and bought the beer the next week in the pub.

People can always let us down

On two separate occasions, I have taken company directors to meet customers to help deal with complaints and problems caused by poorly performing equipment. One visit was to a shipyard and one was to a shipowner. However, on both occasions, the directors managed to let me and themselves down.

On the first of these trips, the director in question was Dave Rodrigues – he who was mentioned earlier regarding my local leave in Hong Kong. He was going to be in Korea and I asked him if he could come along with me to meet a shipyard managing director. The shipyard had been having some continuing trouble setting our radars to work and had requested a meeting with a senior person. I had seen the shipyard director twice already, but in spite of my reports to the service division, the problems had persisted. I hoped that Dave would convince the yard that we were really trying to sort out their problems.

We arrived at the shipyard for the meeting but were kept waiting for some time. After a tense meeting, where the shipyard managing director made his complaints again most forcibly, Dave, having said little and having given a less than a robust apology and explanation, shifted nervously on his seat. As I watched, he plucked up his courage and said to the complaining customer, "Look, what I can do for you is this." I was expecting him to make a generous offer of some free servicing by a 'sea-rider' engineer or a visit to the yard by a senior engineer until things were resolved, but what he said was unbelievable. "I can leave you a brochure of our latest radar," and with that he made a great show of picking up and opening his briefcase, taking out the said brochure and handing it to the director. It did at least stop the shipyard director in his tracks. He could not believe it and nor could I. I wanted to crawl under my chair I was so embarrassed. He had just spent twenty minutes telling us he thought we were rubbish, so the boss gives him a brochure!

The other occasion involved another director called Mike. We had been struggling with the reliability of a couple of specific radars on two ships belonging to a major shipping company. One of our troubleshooting engineers had spent a number of days, at our expense, at sea 'seariding' on one of the ships trying to sort out the problems. However, the company was still not happy. The company was one of the biggest container ship operators in the world and their patronage was vital to our long-term success in the region. Mike had decided that he wanted to visit Hong Kong to see the new company and service centre that had just been set up. He called me before the trip and asked if there was anyone I wanted him to meet when he was out in the Far East. I said, "Yes, we need to get a director in front of this company's technical director as they have had a lot of service problems. Can you please talk to Fred in the service centre before you leave the UK; he has the full service reports of the ships in question." Mike said he would do that. I contacted the shipowner and explained that our director would be coming out from the UK and would like to see him. The shipowner agreed and we set a time and date for the meeting.

Mike duly arrived in Hong Kong, then after a couple of days, we flew on with Vince up to the shipyard. Vince and Mike had been out late the night we arrived but, I had agreed with Mike that we would meet in the hotel lobby at nine for the short walk to the shipowner's offices. At 0900, he was not there. I rang his room at 9.15. Eventually, he answered the phone.

"Mike, are you on your way down? It is 9.15 and we need to be there by 0945."

"Oh, look, I think I can skip this one, can't I? You don't really need me and you will be fine on your own, Gordon, as you know the background. Anyway, I do need to do some shopping this morning before I fly back to Hong Kong this afternoon."

I was speechless. He put the phone down and I was left staring at the receiver. The guy had come all the way to the Far East and he refused to keep an appointment with an unhappy customer. I then had to explain to the shipping company that our director had taken sick in Hong Kong and sent his apologies.

Daewoo Shipyard in the early days

Downtown Seoul circa 1990

Korean meal. Mr Yu, Jim Wardale, Mr Kim, Nina Barrs and Mr G

Okpo fish market

Seoul from the Hyatt

CHAPTER 5

Thailand

With all the noise, so many thousands of tourists and such manic traffic chaos in Bangkok, why are the Thais such kind, gentle and attractive people? Why don't they leave for the coast and never return? Arriving in Bangkok after the long flight from the UK, we are assaulted by the noise, the humid heat and the traffic. Before a new flyover expressway was built, the drive from the airport used to take two hours of bumper-to-bumper traffic and fumes. It was not always that easy, though. A friend of mine had arrived in Bangkok late one night from the UK. He was tired and just wanted to get to his hotel. He knew he still had a long taxi ride before he got to his hotel, so was pleased when he saw his case appear on the carousel and heaved a sigh of relief. He picked it up and headed for the taxis. Two hours later, he got to his hotel room and tried to open the case but couldn't. Then, he realised in horror that it was not his case at all. He was, luckily, still awake enough to ring the airline who told him that a young lady was still waiting in arrivals for her case and they had one bag left over with his name on the label. He then had to get back into a cab for the long drive back to the airport and do a swap. The young lady was not amused.

However, arrival at one of the downtown hotels was like entering another world. The "Sawasdi Kap" greeting from a lovely Thai lady who opens the huge glass door for you; the quiet, cool atmosphere of the lobby; gently splashing fountains and the helpful reception staff offering a cool fruit drink and a cold, damp flannel as I check in soon make the frustrations of getting there vanish. Everywhere in Thailand, it is the same – lovely gentle people who always seem happy to see you and make you welcome.

My early visits to Thailand, when I worked for Plessey, were aimed at trying to win the contract for the sonars, torpedo launchers, radars and the command systems for three small anti submarine corvettes that the RTN were planning to build. A couple of colleagues, Roger from the sonar division and Norman from radar, had already done most of the hard ground work and established themselves and the Plessey company to the RTN, and had given the introductory presentations of the sonars and radars that we wanted to offer. I was asked to join them on their next visit as the RTN now wanted to discuss the command systems.

We stayed in what was then called the Tewana Ramada Hotel in the Pat Pong area. Pat Pong was famous for its girlie bars, street markets and vibrant nightlife, all of which was compressed into a couple of city blocks. The Tewana was just across the road from all of this, so temptation lay easily to hand. The hotel was quiet, a bit dated and staid, but the rooms were big, clean and – if you were lucky enough to get one of the rooms at the back facing the garden and pool – very peaceful. The Tewana had a good coffee shop and a smarter buffet restaurant.

We met the captains and commanders at Naval Headquarters, a collection of old two-storey stone colonial style buildings down by the river. We presented our ideas for solutions for their new ships and answered their questions. One of the main benefits of our offer was that the RTN would get a fully integrated system where all the information from the sonar and the radar would be processed and presented to the command team on a single display of the command system, which would give them the ASW data they needed to know to fire their torpedoes. This was a novel solution in those days. Further visits followed and we exhibited the command system at a defence exhibition in Bangkok, so the navy could actually see it working and operate the consoles.

Our evenings in Bangkok were spent quietly with a meal in the hotel coffee shop or one of the many seafood or Thai restaurants nearby, or perhaps with the agent – a Thai called Suwit who was a lovely, peaceful chap who had very good connections in the navy. After dinner, if the mood so took us, we might wander across the road into Pat Pong itself and sample the beers in a bar or two. The cool, air-conditioned bars offered a respite from the overly warm and humid evening air. Mostly the bars and clubs were dark, dimly lit places with loud pop music playing. A traditional wooden bar round the central area served as the stage for the continual pole dancing that some bars offered. We would sit with our beers at the bar watching the scantily clad, gyrating girls and making sure that their stiletto heels did not end up in our beer. Roger and Norman had been coming here for ages and so some of the girls recognised them. I was the new boy. They knew that Roger and Norman were not out for anything more than beer and treated us all accordingly. The great thing about the bars was that there was no pressure to go any further with the girls.

After a couple of beers, it was time to go or move on. As we moved to the door, cries of "OK Mista, bye bye, see you tomollo" trailed behind us – always it seemed, followed by big winks and giggles from the girls as we stepped out into the humid, equally noisy street. On the way back to the hotel, we would join the tourists as they made their way round the side streets which were tightly packed with market stalls, often dodging the rain and the supports to the overhanging tarpaulin roofs. There seemed to be endless stalls of copy watches, silk scarves, T-shirts, copy handbags, ties, Thai ornaments, plastic toys and every other sort of merchandise from wooden elephants to radios. The stall owners would stand bargaining with tourists and yelling at their co-workers to get out more boxes of these rare Rolex watches. Bargaining was the fun activity of the night and was always done in good humour with much teasing and cries of "No, too cheap. You make me poor man. Wait! Wait! I give you better plice."

Eventually, the RTN signed a deal for their three new ships and our 'NAUTIS' combat systems were specified. We had won. Our French competition had not had the same technology as our system and Roger and Norman's prolonged efforts over many months of visits had paid off. Soon after that, however, Marconi bought Plessey. I left soon afterwards to join Thorn EMI and lost touch with the project. Little was I to know that it would come back round again. A few years later BAE bought Marconi.

Twelve years after the initial Nautis deal with Plessey, I was in BAE and the RTN were now planning to buy new frigates as well as fighter aircraft and army systems. A government-to-government deal was being discussed and BAE Systems were out in force. The project was being run by a BAE expat resident director called Clive, who was based in Bangkok. Clive was a go-getter and was under a lot of stress trying to run the whole project himself. He had three different BAE teams out in Bangkok at the same time and was charging round the office from one to the other trying to manage every detail. This was his project and it was going to work his way. Local Thai agents for different parts of the project drifted into meetings, then drifted out again with knowing smiles that seemed to signify that they had seen it all before.

"Nautis! You cannot be serious. No way. No one is going to wreck this deal by offering that load of junk. Take it out now or you won't be going to the navy tomorrow. I will offer them a French system rather than Nautis."

Clive did not seem happy. I was totally stunned by the outburst. I sat and looked at him. What on earth was going on here? Clearly, something was very wrong as this bolt out of the blue was heartfelt. We were in a small back office running through the presentations for the next day.

"Clive, what on earth is going on. We know nothing of any problems with the RTN Nautis."

Slowly, Clive calmed down and explained the history. It emerged that the original Nautis systems had not been properly supported by Marconi after they had bought Plessey. The ships were all based in the

South of Thailand and rumblings of the RTN dissatisfaction had reached Clive, but with Chinese whispers and a lack of any technical details, these had become exaggerated on the way. Clive was adamant that he had sent faxes to Marconi, but the information had not filtered down to our Nautis technical support team or the BAE support division. In all honesty, we should have checked more fully that all was well with the old systems before we left the UK, but our Nautis team just said they were not aware of any problems when we checked, which was true.

I argued with Clive and tried to convince him that this was the only system we could offer that was suitable for the new ships and if there was a problem with the old systems, then we needed to sort it out. We could get an engineer out to survey the systems and put a repair and upgrade programme in place so that they would be the same standard as any new ones. I failed. Clive was adamant. No way were we going to mention Nautis.

I went back to the hotel to calm down and think things through. Later that night in Clive's flat, we had a further discussion and Clive finally relented and agreed that we could address the issue head on with the admirals. The presentation was altered to explain the Plessey/Marconi/BAE changes in the company and the support responsibilities. We also now included an upgrade package. We waited for the admirals to react. I held my breath. Then, in true, polite Thai style, the admirals smiled, then expressed their concerns about support for the current Nautis and quietly, but thoroughly, probed us to establish the full story of the company changes. Then they had a private meeting, after which they expressed satisfaction that this route offered the most sensible way ahead.

We continued with specific meetings with the project team and further numerous BAE visits to Bangkok, and down to Sattahip to see the corvettes themselves. The RTN came to the UK to see our factories and Nautis fitted ships in the UK. Finally, Nautis C2 and our radars were specified for the new ships as well as the upgrades to the older systems. We heaved a sigh of relief. All we had to do now was wait for the shipbuilding contracts to be finalised, which always takes a while, and we would receive our order from the shipyard.

Then, on the news one morning, I heard the announcer say: "The Thai Prime Minister has left office." Politics had got in the way of the deal. The Thai Prime Minister was the main champion of the project and now he had gone. The services were ordered not to proceed by the new government. Then, after the tragedy of the Boxing Day tsunami, the perspective and priorities for the new Thai Government and Thai Armed Forces changed and the whole project was shelved.

Modern Bangkok

Senior RTN officers visit AMS

CHAPTER 6

Malaysia

Last out of three

Not long after the Plessey takeover by Marconi, we got a new boss. Sadly, Bill Hawley had retired and we found that a Marconi man, Jim McDuff, was our new boss. My early feelings towards Jim were positive, mainly because he promoted me to run the Middle East with a small team of two sales execs, both from the Marconi side.

One day Jim called me to a meeting in the Addlestone, where the naval command and control systems were designed and built. The meeting was chaired by Jim. Jim loved big meetings and this was no exception and there were about twelve or thirteen people gathered round the table. Reportedly, the Royal Malaysian Navy (RMN) was ordering new warships from the UK and the rush was on to sell our command systems to them. A salesman called John had been asked to run the Far East for command and control division. He was a pleasant and bright guy who had not been doing the job for more than a few weeks, but was still getting a hard time from Jim as to why our systems were not already specified. Jim felt that as John had been out there once, we should already have the order. Apparently, Jim had just been told by Marconi Corporate HQ that their intelligence suggested that one of our UK competitors was the favourite to win. John got the backlash from Jim. "Have you seen the C in C?" "Who is the navy's project manager there?" "Why is our competitor so well placed?" "Is the agent any good?"

We all know that it takes a while to get fully up to speed in these places and I knew that John had only been to Malaysia once and that was for a just a couple of days to meet the agent on his way back from Australia. I was sitting half enjoying the battle that was going on and half feeling sorry for John. But also I was wondering why I had been called to a meeting that was nothing at all to do with me or my area of the Middle East.

I was jerked out of my dream as Jim turned to me, "Gordon! What are you doing over the next couple of weeks?"

"Err, well, the usual, but I have a trip to Oman planned for next week."

"Cancel it. I want you to go out to Malaysia and sort this mess out. Stay behind after this and I will brief you."

Oh boy what have I been volunteered for now? Whatever it was, it sounded like a very wet and slippery rugby ball was being passed hard and fast at me and I was going to be told to catch it and score a try.

When the others had gone, Jim briefed me. "They have got it all wrong," he said. "I have been told that this is winnable but they don't know how to do it. You can go and sort it out, I am sure."

"Jim, I do not really know Malaysia, the agent or the customer. I have not been there for a few years. I can go and get a better picture for you but it could be difficult to turn it around if another company has already been specified."

"You must," said Jim firmly.

Oh well, that was easy. Jim was obviously looking to get lots of points by winning a big contract within a few months of taking over.

"Get cleared so you can go out there this weekend and go and see these guys when you get there." He gave me some names and phone numbers. Most of them seemed to be the Marconi corporate people in the Kuala Lumpur offices, but the list included a local businessman of whom I had heard. "I will tell them you are coming. And don't bother coming back until you have got the order."

I smiled. So, Jim had a sense of humour after all. Then I looked at him. He was not smiling. I was right all along; he did not have a sense of humour. He was serious.

"Jim, I will see what I can do." I got up and left.

IF YOU CAN'T TAKE A JOKE...

Once I had got to KL, I went first to the Marconi corporate offices. They should have a good view of things. They were pleasant enough but did not really want to concern themselves with little things like naval command systems at just £3m a time. They were busy trying to sell fleets of aircraft and ships for billions of pounds. There was a man based there from the UK shipyard, but he and the others seemed more interested in playing golf than anything else. The shipyard man should have been the key link into the navy who gave me a very short brief, but said he could not introduce me to the key players as it would not be appropriate – and anyway, he was busy that week. He was playing golf, I later discovered.

I went to see one or two of my own contacts from Plessey days to get the local view of the project. The Plessey agent, who I had met years before, was happy to have a chat and was both friendly and helpful. He filled in a lot of the gaps in my knowledge and explained a few of the relationships that the navy had with the other competitor companies of which we were unaware. He also told me that we were not being considered for this deal by the navy. The local Marconi office guys were not interested, because as our competitors were already specified, they believed it was all over. They also saw little point in helping me and risking upsetting the navy. The Plessey agent did know one or two other people in KL who provided me with some very useful information that proved important. I still felt that this was not going to go well, but at least I felt that I could see the picture more clearly.

I went to see the defence section in the British High Commission, and the picture was the same. Out of three potential suppliers, we were number three. Everyone said so. The question was why? Our system was in service, used the latest technology and our competitors were offering 'Paper Tigers' – ie: a system that was only at the design stage, not one with any proven service track record, and that they were telling the RMN that they would do whatever they wanted to make the new systems meet their precise requirements. Our main competitor had a local office in KL and an expat manager who had been in KL for years.

He obviously had very good relationships with the senior navy staff. On the other hand, we had not even visited KL, so the navy did not know us at all and would not see me at short notice.

We were definitely not in a good position. I decided it was time to try the phone number of a local businessman. I explained to his PA who I was and that I would like a meeting.

"Not possible this week, I am afraid, and after that he is out of town." End of conversation. End of interest.

I rang again the next morning, "Any chance today?"

"No, I am sorry, but where are you staying and if he has a cancellation, I will try and call you?"

I rang that afternoon, and the next morning, but always I got the same response. This was not good. I had tried again to get a meeting with the navy's project manager but he said he was 'busy' this week. I was clearly getting a big brush-off. I was not going to ring the UK until I had something positive to report and I ignored incoming phone calls in the hotel in case it was Jim wanting to know whether I had the signed contract yet.

Somewhere along the line, I had heard that someone in KL, who was indirectly involved in the project as a neutral and had some influence with the navy, was actually a lot closer to our competitor than he ought to have been. I rang him up and asked for a meeting on the basis that I was passing through and thought it would be a good opportunity to meet him and brief him on our systems. He reluctantly agreed to see me. I chatted informally about the company changes and new products, then explained my problem and asked for his help. In doing so, I may have mentioned to him that I had heard a rumour that 'some locals' were very close to the competitor. I had no idea who, but I would need to mention it in my reports back to the UK. His face registered the message.

Then, after about a week of waiting, my phone rang. "He can see you for just fifteen minutes at 15.30 today. Do not be late." It was my local businessman's PA. I went round early and waited. Finally, I saw the man in his surprisingly small, dark office. As I walked in, all I was conscious of was the vast amount of books in it. They were piled up on shelves, on the floor on his desk, everywhere. The businessman was a large man in his sixties with a serious face and hard eyes that peered at me over the top of his gold-rimmed glasses and over the top of the books.

"What do you want?" he asked.

I quickly explained my problem and told him some of the information that I had gathered since arriving. He listened but did not say anything.

Then, when he spoke, it was a series of rapid questions: "Tell me what is special about your system?" "Which navies has it fitted?" Do the British Royal Navy have it? Why is it better than the competitors? "What is wrong with the competitor's system?" "Tell me about this man". Finally, he said, "Hmmmm. Leave it with me. I will call you."

In the meantime I kept calling the navy. Early the following week, the navy project manager finally agreed to a short meeting. He was charming, but made it clear that his committee had already made up their minds. I said that I understood, but still asked if I could give his project team a thirty-minute presentation on our system and its benefits so I could have a chance to understand their concerns and so we could learn more about their actual requirements. He reluctantly said yes but added that he felt it would achieve little.

I gave the presentation to the navy a few days later. The navy were courteous and outlined what they liked about the competitor systems and told me what they felt our system did not have. I assured them that while the existing systems, which were already at sea in RN and overseas navies, did not have some of those new features promised by the other company, those systems now being built have better capabilities included. But they must remember that our competitor's whole system had not yet even been to sea. It essentially seemed to boil down to them wanting the latest 'sexy colour display systems'. I had already rung our technical team and they assured me that those improvements were already being included in all future systems.

I plucked up my courage and rang Jim and brought him up to date. He was not happy when I told him that the story was still the same even though we now had a much better picture of what was going on and I had found some chinks in our competitor's armour. He did not sound very happy. "You just stay there until it is sorted" were his final encouraging words.

Time passed and I waited in KL. One would think that staying in the Shangri La Hotel in KL with absolutely nothing to do while I waited for phone calls would be bliss. In fact, I found it frustrating and nerve-wracking as I spent my time going over everything we had done, or not done, again and again. Who should I call? What can I do? At the same time, I knew that there was little I could do about anything. I was totally dependent on others now. The weekend came and the businessman was now out of town. I went to the zoo, I read, I snoozed by the pool, I watched for the message light on my phone. There was not really anything more to report that Jim did not know already.

I went to see the Marconi guys again on the Monday morning. They told me that the UK shipyard team was arriving that night to make presentations of their designs for the warships and its systems to the navy on the Wednesday. That should include our systems as they were already being installed in the ships the yard was building. On the Tuesday morning, I contacted their technical manager at the hotel, a friendly guy called Bob, who I had met a couple of times before.

"Hi Bob, I gather you are here to make a presentation to the navy. If you would like me to be present and to contribute anything on the command system side, I am available to help."

"No thank you, that won't be necessary," was his brusque response.

What was going on here? Why was the shipyard being so dogmatic when our system was fitted in ships built in their yard, meaning they knew our system and that it worked? This was a positive card that the shipyard should have been playing hard on our behalf. It seemed clear that the navy had already decided which C2 to fit and

IF YOU CAN'T TAKE A JOKE...

told the shipyard to include it and it was not ours.

Later that morning, I got a phone call from the businessman's PA: "He is back in town and can see you today at 1.45. But just for ten minutes."

"Thank you. I'll be there." I forgot lunch and made sure I was in his outer office fifteen minutes early. The meeting was short: "Mr Gray, I have spoken to some people. Don't worry, it will be arranged. There is nothing more you can do here you should go back to the UK. It is done. The navy will be informed." I thanked him and left.

The navy had a major function at a big naval base in the north of the country and all the senior staff were going to that and would be away for a week. The businessman was also leaving town – this time for three weeks' holiday in Europe.

That night, I rang Jim McDuff and told him the situation. "There is nothing more I can do here, Jim, and even if there was, there is no one to talk to."

I waited for the "OK, come home" but instead he blew up. "I don't know what you are talking about. Are we specified yet?"

"Of course not Jim, you know it does not work like that."

"Then you have done nothing out there."

I was a little shocked. The man seemed to have totally lost it.

"I told you to stay there until it was all sorted, now stay there until I tell you to come home!"

"Jim, this is not the way we do things. We will be specified but we have to wait until things have worked through the system. I have been told by the locals there is nothing more for us to do for at least three weeks."

"Don't you ever listen to me? Stay there until I say you can come home!" he screamed. Then, he slammed the phone down on me.

Oh great! Now what do I do? That was an easy one. I went and had a beer. As I took my first mouthful, I reminded myself that: 'If you can't take a joke!'

The next morning, things did not seem quite so bad. I rang Dick, an old pal from the company who I had known well since Plessey days and who was currently in Indonesia so we were on the same time zone. I knew I would get a more considered and cautious approach to things from Dick. We discussed things in general terms.

"I think you should stay there, at least for one more week and see what happens after that. If Jim has not called you again, have a rethink!"

Good advice, I thought. I checked with the Marconi guys again on the Monday.

"The Navy HQ has basically shut down as all the key navy guys have left town for a couple of weeks. "It's a bloody nuisance," said one of them "My golf is buggered for the next few weeks now!"

I rang a few of the local contacts and the message was the same. Nothing will happen for about a month. I relaxed some more, then decided that this was crazy. By the Wednesday morning, I had still not heard any more from Jim, so I decided I would go home and take the consequences. If he sacks me, then I will go to a tribunal I boldly thought. I flew out of KL on the Thursday night for the UK.

After a nervous weekend, I went into the office on the following Monday morning braced for the bollocking I was due to get. I hoped John's rule about forgiveness being easier to get than permission was going to hold good. As I walked into the sales area, I looked anxiously towards Jim's office waiting for him to catch sight of me. Jim was not there yet. I walked on and saw Roger, a good friend, sitting at his desk.

"Hi Roger, Is Jim due in today?"

He looked at me blankly. "Haven't you heard?" he asked.

"Heard what?"

"Jim was sacked last week. He was told to clear his desk on Thursday."

I never did discover what he was sacked for and I didn't really care; but if I had not disobeyed his order, I would still be in KL.

The navy contacted us a few weeks later and discussions started in earnest. We won the command system order, but the navy insisted that the extra display features that they wanted were included in the system. Even though we won this contract, it does not change any of the basic principles of export business. It was the exception that proved the rule. If I had not gone out there, then our competitor would have won easily. He was doing all the right things in marketing terms and almost had it all sewn up. We came charging in at the last minute and upset the apple cart. Our last-minute intervention through local business and direct selling caused everyone to re-evaluate the situation. It worked for us that time, but it is really not the best way to win export business.

Derek's Fish Head Curry

Sometime, years later and with a different company, I returned to Malaysia. On this trip, we were talking to a department of the navy that was responsible for some of the larger shore-based test equipment and ship's signature assessment systems. This was run from the port of Lumut on the NW coast of Malaysia. I had with me one of our underwater acoustic technical experts, John. John was a dyed-in-the-wool sonar and acoustics man who had worked in the acoustic and sonar field all his life. He reminded me of an absent-minded professor in his looks and manner. John was well known around the world for his knowledge and well liked as a thoroughly honest guy. He and the customer in Lumut had known each other for years and were old pals. We also had with us an executive from central marketing called Derek. Derek was the Far East 'expert' and wanted to meet the navy guys in Lumut. He was a bit younger than me and a lot younger than John. He saw himself as a bit of a smoothy, with his cream lightweight suits and a straw hat. Even though he was the youngest, as he was from corporate marketing and the Far East manager, he saw himself as the senior figure of the group.

Before we went up to Lumut, we visited the agent in his offices in

Johor Bahru – or JB to the locals – just across the causeway from Singapore. Following our meeting, the agent kindly offered us lunch: "I have booked a table at the Royal JB Golf Club, if that's OK," he said.

You bet it's OK, I thought.

Then, Derek jumped in, "Oh no, we should show these people the real JB and go to Mrs Wong's." By 'these people', he was referring to me and John.

"Do you really think so?" queried the agent, who clearly did not want to go to wherever Mrs Wong's was.

I tried to step in. "No we can do Mrs Wong's another day, Derek, when we get back from Lumut. Our agent has already booked a table at the golf club."

"No, I want us to go to Mrs Wong's," said Derek.

As he was the senior company man there, the agent and I decided to let it go and we backed off. I did not want a row on day one of the trip.

It was raining cats and dogs as well, just to add to the fun. We ran for the cars, then drove down into old JB. We hunted around for a place to park and eventually found one not too far from Mrs Wong's. Derek led the way as we ran, leaping over puddles, dodging bikes and cars, squeezing past food stalls but not missing a couple of large puddles, so I got wet feet for my efforts. As I ducked into the door, I had noticed that I was entering an old brick building decorated with wrought iron grills and with weeds growing from the cracks in the brickwork. It had been painted yellow, but a long time ago.

As we entered, I saw the kitchens were downstairs and there were open food stalls and tables outside at the front. In spite of the rain, a few hardy locals sat there squeezing up to each other under the umbrellas to avoid the rain. Derek led us upstairs. We were shown to a round table in an open area of the room. The table was covered in coloured oil cloth and there were a number of hard chairs scattered round it. There were french windows at the front which opened out onto a balcony, so we could hear the rain as it lashed down outside.

Even before we had all sat down, Derek took charge. He called over the waitress. "Now, everyone, we are all having fish head curry. I always have it when I come here."

"How about some beer first?" asked John.

"Great idea, John. Derek is a bit slow on getting the priorities right," I said with a smile at Derek.

"OK, some beer then. Who wants beer?"

The waitress was a middle-aged lady with an apron who had done it all and seen it all before. She was not in the least impressed by Derek's posturing and stood looking bemused as she waited for some sense to emerge from his mouth.

When he had ordered the beer he said, "We will all have fish head curry."

"Not for me, thanks, Derek," I said.

He looked at me. "No, you must have it," he responded.

If there is one thing that annoys me, it is people telling me what I will eat. Long trips to Korea had taught me to eat what I want and not what someone else wants.

"Derek, you are probably not aware, but in an earlier life I worked on Hull Fish Market from 7 until 9 every morning. To me, fish heads are things that are scraped off the floor with the skins and bones and sent in tipper trucks to the fish meal factory where they are made into fertiliser and cat food. They are not what I have for my lunch. I will pass on it, thank you."

I then looked at the waitress, who was quietly smiling and holding her order pad and pencil poised to write, "Do you have any chicken satay?"

"Yes of course," she said.

"Thank you. I will have that."

Derek looked dumbfounded.

The fish head curry duly arrived. It came in a large, yellow, plastic washing-up bowl. The brown curry 'sauce' slopped around like old washing-up water and from time to time the boiled head of a large fish, minus its eyes and some skin, broke the surface. It looked revolting. Derek served those that were having it, slopping lumps of fish head meat and oily gravy into their plates and shirts. Needless to say, he was at pains to tell me what a fantastic dish this was and ladled another spoon into his bowl. My satays arrived and were excellent.

As we went downstairs, John whispered to me, "I wish I had had what you had. That fish head curry was bloody awful!"

The next day, we set off to drive up to Lumut – or rather, Derek drove us in the hire Volvo440 he had organised. The journey was going to be long and fascinating as it gave us a rare chance to see the countryside away from the city and enjoy a quiet day watching the world go by. However, Derek was one of those drivers who had road rage gushing out of his pores, and on the main highway North, no Malaysian was going to get past him – thank you very much. And if they did, they would be chased down for miles. It all became a bit stressed. John gave up and went to sleep in the back.

Eventually, however, we turned off the main highway and swung down onto some peaceful and relatively traffic-free country roads, passing through small villages and rubber plantations along the way. At one point, we rounded a bend and found ourselves faced with a long, low, single-track wooden bridge that spanned a wide and fast-flowing river. To me it looked secure enough, albeit there were no sides or guard rails to the bridge and the river was just a couple of feet below the wooden plank top of it. Derek stopped.

"I'm not going over that!" he declared.

"Fine by me," said John, stirring from his slumbers in the back "but you do realise, don't you Derek, that if we go back we have to go miles up to the north before we can turn and come back south again? This is the only road to Lumut."

Derek was unmoved. "No way is that safe," he said, pointing at the structure. "Gordon, get out and see if it is safe."

"Yes, Derek."

I got out, glad to be away from the car and walked safely out across the bridge for about 50 feet. Derek watched. What he would have done had I disappeared downstream on a chunk of timber was not clear. Anyhow, I felt that the bridge was secure. In spite of the river rushing just below the loose planks, there was no vibration or any sense that it might suddenly collapse.

"It's OK Derek," I called. He was still unmoved.

In the meantime, John had worked out that the detour to avoid this bridge was 150 miles and would take us about five hours. Then, just as we were beginning to despair of Derek deciding to risk it, a big yellow tipper truck appeared on the road on the opposite bank heading towards the bridge. Without even slowing down, it drove straight onto the bridge. Derek had to reverse from the entrance to the bridge to avoid getting crushed as the truck roared towards him. The planks rattled and dust flew up from the road surface, but the truck made it across and the bridge remained intact. After the truck had gone and the dust cloud and diesel exhaust fumes cleared, we looked at Derek.

"There you are, safe as houses!" John said.

Derek had no choice. Gingerly, he drove the car slowly out on the bridge and crawled across in first gear with me walking ahead like a red flag man.

Once in Lumut, Derek decided that we were going to eat at the Chinese food stalls and he started again, "I think we should all have the steamed crabs, they really are great here."

I lost it then. "Derek," I said, "if we are to get on for the rest of this trip, then you really must stop doing that. Why can I not choose what I want to eat myself? I am not three years old, I can choose food from a menu myself."

I had my sweet and sour pork with rice, John had a chilli beef, while Derek had his steamed crabs. To Derek's amazement, we all survived.

In later life, Derek ended up running a small hotel in Norfolk. I often wonder what he fed his guests.

CHAPTER 7

Singapore

I first visited it as a midshipman in the Royal Navy in 1971. I loved it then and have loved it ever since. It was green, lush and full of fragrant scents. Since then, Singapore has changed a lot, but the atmosphere, the buzz and the whole feel of the place has not. It is still an exciting oriental city. People sometimes complain that it is too sanitised, that the rules are too strict and that everything is too clinical. Well maybe, and those living there will feel it more than visitors, but it does make for a clean and safe city. The MRT railway system is clean, fast, efficient and safe. Changi Airport is one of the best in the world, and taxis and MRT can get you anywhere you want to go on the island.

Some of the old parts of the city have been kept or restored, like parts of Chinatown and other old institutions, such as Raffles Hotel, have undergone massive refurbishments to restore them to their former glory. Raffles is not like it was twenty or thirty years ago. Then, it was rundown, half full of hitchhikers and backpackers lounging on the floor; the long bar resembled a youth hostel lobby more than a fashionable cocktail bar and weeds grew from the outer walls. Today, Raffles is as good as any hotel in town, just as it was in its golden days.

Big duty-free shopping complexes with hundreds of shops in them – huge new developments such as Marina City and Raffles City – seem to have appeared out of nothing. Bugis Street that used to be a magnet for nightlife of all sorts back in the 1970s has now been restored, but to a clean, family-friendly environment. Today's Singapore retains the history in a modern climate. The vast harbour stretches right along the south side of the island where the many hundreds of anchored ships lie waiting to load or unload, or waiting for spare parts or repairs. On a hot tropical afternoon, there is nothing nicer than sitting on a pleasure boat under the awning, with a cold Tiger beer in your hand and a sea breeze blowing across the deck, just sailing past all these ships – large and small, new and old, smart and rusty – that have arrived from all over the world. It brings back the feeling of what a massive trading port Singaapore has been since Stamford Raffles first set up the trading post in the early 1800s. It is one of the busiest ports in the world with ships arriving and leaving every few minutes, twenty-four hours a day.

Much of the city centre is relatively new. The skyscrapers and office blocks of the financial area could be anywhere, but away from that Singapore is still Singapore. It is lush, green and jungly; it is an island no bigger than the Isle of Wight, but with a population of over five million. Eating out here is a delight. Food is everywhere – from the food stalls at Newton Circus and out on the East Coast Parkway to the seafood restaurants around the town and the smart 'fine dining' restaurants in the many new international hotels. Unlike many oriental countries, the food stalls are to be recommended. They serve fresh, hot and delicious food, big chicken satays and huge grilled prawns – to name but two – and both washed down with Tiger Beer. Without Singapore's strict hygiene rules, you would not dare eat in these places. But now you can and, indeed, you are encouraged to by the Government Tourist Department.

Singapore was first noted as a port in the 11th Century. In the 14th century, it was an important local port but was destroyed by the Portuguese in 1613. Following that, the Dutch challenged the Portuguese for supremacy in the region. They actively excluded the British from their areas, but as this was an important trading route for Opium from India to China, in 1819 Sir Stamford Raffles was sent out to investigate the possibility of setting up a trading post in the region to protect British interests. He quickly recognised that Singapore Island had all the attributes he was looking for with a deep-water harbour, fresh water and plenty of timber for ship repairs.

By means of some good local politics, he was able to secure the rights from the Malays, who nominally ruled the island, to use it as a British trading post. It was under British rule that it grew and developed into a major city port.

During WWII, Japan conquered and occupied Singapore by famously attacking it from the 'impenetrable' jungles of mainland Malaya. The British had expected a frontal assault from the sea and all their big fixed guns were in the wrong place.

After the war, Singapore reverted to UK rule, but with increasingly more local government. Singapore then merged with Malaya in 1963 to form Malaysia, but following strong demonstrations against Malayan favouritism and prejudice, Singapore was thrown out of Malaysia and became an independent sovereign state in 1965. Its new prime minister was Lee Kwan Yew. It was under his government that Singapore developed so rapidly over the recent years with major industrialisation programmes, housing development schemes and the implementation of a strong education system. By 1990, Singapore was one of the world's richest countries.

During my time with Decca and then Racal Decca, many of the local shipowners were good customers so it was an easy decision to take the computer radar (ARPA) to Singapore for a series of demonstrations to the shipping market there. The equipment was shipped down by air from Hong Kong and was due to arrive in Singapore Airport three days before the demonstrations were to begin. These were to be held over three days in the Marco Polo Hotel. I arrived two days before so that I would have time to check the function rooms, meet with our agent and get the radar set up.

When I arrived, the good news was that the equipment had arrived at the airport. The bad news was that customs had not released it. This should not have been a problem as we knew the paperwork was OK, but for some reason there was a query on it. I was told that there was nothing I could do but leave the agent to sort it out. I asked whether we should postpone the demonstrations. "No, it will be fine, please do not worry. We will get it to the hotel on time." I was dubious. They would call me if they wanted any information.

The day prior to the demonstrations, the agents salesman, Mr Woon, told me that he thought things were now OK. The query had been a simple question of where was the radar going to next. All was well and it would be released later that afternoon, they said.

The day of the demonstrations arrived. The conference room was set up, the coffees were organised and the invited guests had all confirmed that they were coming. The only problem was that there was still no radar. I went to panic mode. *How do I play this one?* I thought. Mr Woon was sorting it out. The problem was not customs this time but the lorry they needed to bring the radar from the airport had broken down.

As the guests started to arrive, I played for time as best I could. I explained that we were a bit delayed by customs and transport issues but expected to be OK later. "In the meantime, I will give you a presentation and show you a slide show on the technology of the system."

Mr Woon came in. "It has just left the airport," he whispered, "but it will be a good hour before it gets here."

Maybe if I drag the slide show out it will be OK. We proceeded with the film and then I started on the slide show, slowly. I was about three quarters of the way through when suddenly the doors swung open and four very sweaty Singaporeans in jeans and T-shirts appeared. They were sweating and grunting as they struggled with the radar in its packing case and the other cases that came with it.

"That's super," I said. "Can you just put the crate by the wall there," pointing at the electrical socket in the wall. They levered it in and then left. I finished the slides and called a coffee break. Everyone went into the adjoining room to have coffee.

I then took off my jacket and set to work with a screwdriver to undo the packing case. Once I had the top, sides and front off, I set to work on wiring it up with the tape player from the other box. I had no time to take it off the pallet or to remove the back of the case. Everyone could see the display as it was. It was a good job I had done this before!

After about twenty-five minutes, I had the whole system connected up. I switched it on and held my breath. I just prayed that it was OK. The picture came up and I relaxed. It worked and all the functions seemed OK. I went into the coffee room.

"Whenever you are ready, gentlemen, we are ready!"

I opened the connecting door and walked through leaving it open so they could all see that the radar was actually working. The guests came through and were all amazed that we had a full working system up and running in such a short time. The demonstrations and questions lasted another hour and a half, then the first morning's work was over. The guests started to leave, but three officers from the navy stayed behind and questioned me more.

A few days later, Mr Woon told me that the Singapore Navy had been in touch with him and were going to place an initial order for six radar systems. I was delighted and I think that the delay actually helped in establishing the resilience and reliability of the system, in that we could get it unpacked and running so quickly.

Downfall in Singapore

Never fiddle your expenses is an obvious and simple rule. Yet, it is amazing how many people fail to follow the basic rules and common sense when travelling overseas or putting in their expenses. Some people think that the company will happily fund *all* their activities including those well outside normal work activities. One of the worst examples of this was a technical guy called Robert. Robert was a bright and ambitious project engineer who had worked solely in the UK for many years, but suddenly found himself given the job of project manager for a joint venture project the company was running with its Singaporean partner. Robert was in his 30s, a well meaning guy, but had a reputation for a large mouth and an even larger opinion of himself. He knew everything and no one could ever tell or teach him anything. When he first went to Singapore, most people who knew him felt that there was a disaster waiting to happen. Before long, he was spending significant amounts of time out there.

A couple of months later, the finance director called me down to his office and started asking peculiar questions about how much I tipped when overseas. At the time, I was unaware of Robert's activities. "What sort of phone calls would I normally make?" "What is 'normal' entertaining?" " "Have I heard of such and such a restaurant or is this place a nightclub or a restaurant?" "Would I take my customer to such places?" I was confused as to what this was about but answered as best I could. Later, of course, I realised that Robert was being watched very closely.

A few weeks later, I went out to Bangkok for a defence exhibition and out of the blue Robert appeared at the Show. He was not meant to be there as he was not involved in Thailand or the Defence Show.

"What are you doing here, Robert?" I asked.

"Oh," he said nonchalantly, "I just decided to fly up from Singapore for a couple of nights as I have never been to Bangkok before. I have heard about it though, can you tell me the best places to go?"

His meaning was clear. I had actually had a call from the office that day saying they were trying to contact Robert and did I know where he was.

There is no question Singapore is a lovely and exciting place, but there are all sorts of temptations lying in wait for the naive and innocent. When he arrived in Singapore, this chump had decided he had landed in heaven. The local agent had taken him out for dinner, then to some nightclubs. The local girlies had turned their oriental charm on him and he was smitten. I subsequently learnt that he had rapidly progressed to the point where he actually had girls staying in his hotel room for days at a time. They were using his company mobile phone to call their family and friends in Thailand, Indonesia, Malaysia or wherever; calling for meals on room service while Robert was out at meetings; clearing the mini bar and generally taking the idiot for everything they could. Apparently, Robert was even buying the girls flowers from the hotel florist and charging those to his room bill. Then at night they were all off out to the restaurants and night clubs again, where, of course, Robert was paying. He thought he was 'It' and could fly around the region as he wished and do whatever he wanted and the company would pay for it all. When I saw him in Bangkok, I told him he should get back to his project in Singapore as he had no reason, or approval, to be in Bangkok: "You had better cut all this out because the accountants are studying your expense claims and if they find anything they don't like then it is 'instant dismissal' stuff."

"No, No, it's all OK, Gordon," he told me. "I know what I am doing and the project is going well!"

I have no idea whether he went back to Singapore or not, but he did vanish from the Bangkok Show. I learnt later that when he got home from that trip, the finance director was waiting. He called Robert down and presented a dossier to him which detailed all his expenses since he started his trips to Singapore and demanded explanations for every single item. Of course, Robert was not able to provide any. He had to put his car keys on the desk and was escorted out of the office in minutes.

As a direct consequence of this, every expense claim that anyone in sales submitted was dissected by the accountants to such an extent that we had to state who we called and why for every telephone call on our hotel and mobile phone bills.

Unfortunately, many years later and with a different company, expenses were the cause of the downfall of another colleague called Adrian. Adrian was well into middle age, a sensible, intelligent man with a fine military background. The financial director had caught him out on a couple of small expense claims in the past and was known to be gunning for him. Adrian had been on a overnight business trip in the UK. He was caught out after he falsified a receipt and that was that. The poor guy knew he was doomed. He resigned on the spot before anyone could fire him and he was home before lunch. He then had to explain to his wife why he was home early and without his company car. Not a lot of fun!

CHAPTER 8

Saudi Arabia

"Bismillah, Al Rahman, Al Raheem." The opening announcements in a deep baritone voice on the Saudi Airlines flight to Jeddah reverberated through the cabin. Translated, it means: "In the name of God, the compassionate, the merciful." The flight was long and dry and the last two hours were in the dark. There was nothing to see outside the aircraft windows; it was black, black desert. Even though I had spent many months in the Gulf on an RN Minesweeper, I was genuinely nervous about visiting Saudi itself for the first time. However, after the ten days, I found some parts of the trip very frustrating but some really fascinating. During the flight, I got chatting to the guy sitting next to me. He introduced himself as Sean; he was Irish but an old Saudi hand who worked in the heavy plant business – excavators, bulldozers and that type of thing. He visited Saudi often and so knew a lot about the place. As we sipped our orange juices, he began to explain things in his slow Irish drawl.

"You will get used to no alcohol," he began, "but you have to remember that Islam rules OK. Saudi Arabia is the birthplace of Mohammed and Mecca is the centre of Islam. Mecca is not far from Jeddah but non Muslims are not even allowed to go there. All the oil fields are on the East coast near Dharan. The oilfields and refineries are run by expats in the Arabian American Oil company, or ARAMCO. Saudi is still a closed and insular country and Jeddah is the commercial and diplomatic centre. All the foreign embassies are in Jeddah. Riyadh, the capital, is reserved for the royal family and government ministries. Foreigners need special permits to go there. I have been coming here for years but not yet been to Riyadh. Sheikh Yamani, a former Oil Minister, once said, "The Holy cities of Mecca and Medina are on the other side of Arabia from the oil fields but in our eyes they matter more than anything else." Nothing is more important to a Saudi than his religion. It is more important than his job and, often, his family. Islam comes first in everything they do. The one thing you must always remember in all your dealings in Saudi is that Islam is what drives every action there. The Muslim pilgrimage, the Haj, happens in Mecca and Medina every year when literally millions of Muslims follow the call of the Koran to visit the two holy cities and associated sites at least once in their lifetime – if they are able to."

"Do you like Saudi?" I asked.

"It's OK if you stick to the rules but I would not bring my wife here, or live here. Most of the expats hate it and tend to become pretty miserable and short-tempered. They are only here for the money, then find that they are trapped as they cannot afford to go back to the UK again and live on UK salaries. Today, Saudi is a well developed country with every modern technological facility at its disposal. However, well into the 20th century, it was little more than an empty desert inhabited by Bedouin tribes."

We landed in Jeddah and spent a seemingly endless time going through Immigration and Customs. I was tired and my mind drifted as I stood in the queue. Suddenly, I was brought back to reality. There was shouting at the front of the queue. A customs official in a sandy coloured uniform was waving a magazine in the air and berating one of the passengers in Arabic. His colleague wandered over and joined in. A young guy from our flight was having his briefcase searched and the official had obviously just found a *Playboy* magazine which was immediately confiscated. The poor guy looked very sheepish and embarrassed as the customs officers made a big play of it before sending him on his way.

I was cleared and emerged into the balmy night air. Geoff, the agent, an Englishman in his early forties, had a worried look on his face and was holding up a small board with my name on it. We introduced ourselves and he drove me to the hotel. On the way, he gave me, what must be, a standard lecture for all new arrivals into Saudi – all the dos and don'ts. "Do not to worry, stay in the hotel and you'll be fine. I will come and get you sometime tomorrow, but I cannot give you a time yet. This is Saudi and things don't really work to any sort of timetable."

The Jeddah Port Authority was interested in developing the port and extending the docks area and had asked for someone to visit them to discuss harbour radars and vessel traffic management systems. Geoff collected me early in the following afternoon and we drove to his office which seemed to be on the outskirts of town. The area was made up of single or two-storey sand-coloured buildings and it was hard to work out which were offices and which were homes. The thing that struck me was that there were no people on the streets. But it was not surprising really as the temperature was well into the high eighties.

It transpired that the meeting with the port officials had not yet been fixed but they thought it would be in the next couple of days. Clearly something was still being set up, so all I could do was wait. On the way to the office, in his air-conditioned Range Rover, Geoff explained that none of the roads in the newer parts of town had name signs so you had a hell of a job to find anywhere as there were no up-to-date maps of Jeddah. He was clearly far from enamoured with Saudi Arabia. He hated it, his wife hated it, he hated the Saudis and all he wanted to do was finish his contract and go home.

"Haven't you found those copier people yet, Geoff?" was his secretary's friendly greeting as we entered the office. "No I haven't, have you?" was his sharp retort. In the office, the major issue of the day was immediately apparent. An ordered delivery of copier paper had not appeared. Local office runners were sent all over town to try and find out what had happened. In the end, it seemed that the copier shop had moved but no one knew its new address. Finally, the following afternoon, they found it and collected the paper but only after ringing everyone they could think of to see if anyone else had found it. While this was going on, I was left to read magazines. It had taken the whole office of about five people nearly three days to find photocopier paper. Clearly, things worked differently here. Now, after two days kicking my heels, I hoped that Geoff would concentrate on fixing our meeting with the port authority.

This took place about two nights later in the office of the port director. It was a big office in a modern building near the entrance to the main port of Jeddah. We were ushered in by a male receptionist. The room seemed quiet, even though there were at least a dozen men sitting around it. There were about six long white sofas round three walls, while the port director himself sat behind a large mahogany desk that took up most of the fourth wall. The air conditioning purred quietly and the room was cool and brightly lit. The desk was covered with framed photographs and at least four telephones. The director was wearing a white goutra and thobe, as were all the others in the room except Geoff and I. The director appeared to be a tall man of middle age with gold-rimmed glasses and he sat, leaning back in his reclining office chair, watching and listening. He spoke softly and gently in Arabic to the others in the room.

Without any introductions, other than a slight nod of the director's head, Geoff and I were ushered to an empty sofa where we were then promptly ignored. We then sat for an hour while the others sitting round the majlis, discussed their business with the director. Sometimes, one of those sitting on the other sofas would stand up, bow slightly to the director and leave. Others seemed to discuss their business but then remain in the room. I sat listening to the Arabic chatter trying to work out what they might be talking about, but without much success. Finally, just when I was thinking that I should have to come back tomorrow, the port director spoke to me in perfect English and asked me curtly what was my company and what did I want. As he was the one who had asked us to come to Saudi, I thought this was a bit off. However, I outlined the company, what we did and why I was there. He seemed happy enough, spoke about increased traffic in the port and the need for vessel safety, then granted me permission to tour the docks and carry out an initial site survey. Then he asked me to submit a preliminary proposal and sent us on our way. We carried out the survey the following day and I made some initial observations, so that the technical guys back in the UK would be able to turn my report into more solid budgetary proposals.

I was then due to fly across to Dharan on the East coast, where the ports of Al Jubail and Al Dammam were reportedly interested in harbour radar systems. These were near to the huge oil terminal of Ras Tannurah where we already had a harbour radar system installed. On the East coast was an engineer called Steve, who worked for the Jeddah agent as his East Coast man. Steve met me at Dharan Airport and took me to the hotel, a small Holiday Inn in the little town of Al Khobar.

As we got into the car, Steve started chatting about the area. Steve was in his late thirties and was an open and easy-going guy. "I have been here for over fifteen years," he began. "The last four in Saudi. I was in the UAE before here. I love it. I love the country, its history and the people are great once you gain their trust and get to know them a bit."

He had read up on the history of Saudi and grown even more interested in it as a result. He carried on, "Saudi was not formed as a country until 1932 when King Abdul Aziz Al Saud conquered the last of the warring tribes and united the country. Since then, the Saudi has been run as an Islamic state under an Absolute Monarchy. King Abdul Aziz and his sons have run the country since then and still do today through the many sons and nephews of the Abdul Aziz" Steve chatted on as he drove, "You should also know that all the laws are based on the Sharia. That is the Code of Law taken directly from the Koran. The punishments handed out today are centuries old and beheadings are still carried out for murder and other serious crimes."

I asked about oil. "Oil was not discovered here until 1938 but today Saudi is one of the richest countries in the world as it has roughly 40% of the world's oil reserves. You should try and see Saudi as it once was, so if you ever get to Riyadh then try and go out to the old capital, a place called Diraiyah, which is not far from modern Riyadh. It is fascinating and gives you a good feel of what this place was like not that long ago."

In the space of twenty minutes my whole view of Saudi changed.

Over the next three days as we drove up and down the East coast between meetings, he chatted about the history of Saudi and the places we passed through. Steve knew what local tribal battles had been fought in the local areas and showed me a few of the sites. His enthusiasm was catching. I too found it fascinating after the gloom and attitude of the office in Jeddah. He recommended that I read a book called *The Kingdom* by Richard Lacey if I really wanted to start to understand about Saudi and how it works. When I got home, I bought a copy and Steve was right; it is a fascinating read.

Steve taught me that 'to have interest' in a place you have 'to take an interest' and learn about it. The more you learn, the more interesting it becomes. He understood the vital and central role that Islam and its history played in the country. To think that in the 1930s Saudi was a barren desert with a scattering of warring tribes, no real wealth and little obvious future; then Abdul Aziz al Saud finally united the tribes and led his people to form the Kingdom of Saudi Arabia. Once oil was discovered, the West could not wait to be friends. The rest, as they say, is history. I flew back to the UK from Dharan and left Saudi with a deepening interest that stayed with me during many later visits.

Steve and his interesting viewpoint of all things Saudi made the trip for me.

Travelling Alone

Over the years that I was travelling, on most trips I was on my own. The company of a colleague was a fairly rare event. "You must get lonely?" people would say to me. "No, not really. I enjoy being on my own" tended to be my answer. I was always comfortable in my own company and rarely yearned for someone else to talk to. I enjoyed the freedom of evenings to myself to catch up on writing reports or, latterly, emails, or reading. The only downside was that long trips could become a bit of a slog; so it was a nice change when the trip demanded that a technical or commercial colleague joined me for a few days. I sometimes wished that there was someone to discuss things with over a coffee or to offer advice over a presentation or perhaps how to put across a technical point in a meeting, but otherwise I just got on with it and dealt with any problems that arose; be they domestic or business related. I would meet an agent occasionally and the customers obviously, but there was no one with whom I could discuss company or business matters. As each salesman in the division had a different region or territory, then we rarely met each other at all. Even when I was back in the office, at least half the other guys would be overseas in their patches or on leave. A few of the guys did find the travelling tough, especially the younger ones and those with young families. It is not the lifestyle for someone in that situation. There are too many concerns about what may or may not be happening at home where a wife has been left to sort out everything; be it children's illnesses, school or domestic problems, be they a broken washing machine or a sick relation. It was a bit like being in the navy. The navy taught me a degree of self sufficiency and how to just get on with the job, so I was better prepared to cope with the separation and with working on my own than some people were.

On that first trip, the flight home from Saudi was on a Friday with Swiss Air via Geneva to Heathrow. We arrived late in Geneva and I knew I only had minutes to make my connection to the last London flight of the day. I dashed to the connecting gate where a pleasant lady told me that the other passengers had already been boarded and the flight was ready to go. I must hurry as I was the last. I knew my case would not make the connection but it was the last flight of the day to London. The plane was out on an open stand and a mini bus was quickly arranged to take me out to the plane. It was a dark winter's night and there was slush and ice on the tarmac. The minibus raced across the deserted aprons. We could see the plane, a small twin engine commuter jet standing with its orange lights flashing through the dark, but thankfully the door was open and the steps were still down. Light from the cabin spilled down onto the tarmac and the ice glinted in the snow piled nearby. The minibus skidded to a halt at the foot of the aircraft steps. I could see that the steps were the small lightweight ones that folded out and retracted back into the plane's fuselage when not in use.

"Off you go and have a good flight," called the driver. I could hear the plane's engines being run up as she was all ready to go, except for her one last passenger.

"Thanks a lot," I cried as I grabbed my briefcase and jumped out onto the tarmac and into the cold, noisy air. I was reminded of James Bond leaping onto moving aircraft to capture the baddies.

I ran the last few paces to the foot of the steps and out of the corner of my eye, I caught sight of a slim, blonde stewardess standing at the top inside the plane. I gauged the distance and the number of steps and made a leap for the middle step. As I did so, my foot slipped in the slush, then my other foot missed the middle step. I pedalled like mad and the next thing I knew I was sprawled in a heap on the cabin floor still clutching my briefcase. The stewardess looked down at me in a bewildered way and everyone at the front of the cabin seemed to be peering round their seats and staring at me as if I was a lunatic.

"Good evening, sir, welcome onboard!" she said. "You were late, but we would have waited while you walked up the steps."

So much for my James Bond impression. I staggered to my feet and blushingly found my way to my seat.

Minehunters

Some years, later I was the Middle East Area Sales Manager with Plessey Naval Systems. I worked for an ex-RN captain, and Fleet Air Arm pilot called Bill Hawley. Bill was in his late fifties, a stocky, bull terrier of a man and a Fleet Air Arm legend. He had flown every type of naval aircraft from Swordfishes to Phantoms and was still alive to tell the tale. He was firm and fair and as long as he knew what we were doing, he let us get on with the job. He was one of the best bosses I ever had. Bill also recognised that as we were selling naval systems. The old Plessey company made everything from sonobuoys to torpedoes, from radars to submarine sonars, as well as command and control systems. Bill believed that it was vital to have sales staff who were from a naval background and understood what they were talking about and could relate to their naval customers. All twenty of us in the Sales Department were ex-RN, either ex-senior rates who were experts in their field or former officers who had run sonar or command teams.

Bill ran the department like an RN ship. There were no office politics here. We all knew what we were meant to do and were trusted to get on and do it. Bill always wanted a face to face debrief before and after any trip, but apart from that left us to our own devices. I later discovered that many bosses never seemed to bother to ask how the trip went and I often wondered if they even bothered to read the visit reports. Bill always insisted that the very first thing we did after a trip was to complete our expense claims. As I have already described, there is more hassle and grief when expenses are either not done, done wrongly or receipts are lost, than any other issue. Once the accountants get hold of a dodgy expense claim, then heaven help you and everyone else. Bill, by making us do our claims before anything else, removed the pressure from us so we could get it done properly.

Part of the job involved talking to UK and European shipyards and persuading them to offer Plessey equipment as part of their ship's fit and then supporting them in their overseas sales campaigns. I was in close touch with Vosper Thorneycroft (VT), who were working hard to secure a minehunter contract with Saudi Arabia as a part of the Al Yamamah 2 contract. This was a complicated government-to-government contract based mainly around military aircraft and to be paid for in oil, but the UK defence industry was keen to try and meet other Saudi needs – one of which was to update its mine countermeasures capability as there had been a lot of trouble with mines in the Gulf. Unfortunately, the French were aware of this need and were trying hard to secure a separate deal for themselves.

I made many visits to Riyadh, which had now become a more open city that foreigners were allowed to visit on business and foreign embassies had been established there. Overseas companies could operate in Riyadh under the guidance of their local sponsors. The Saudi MOD was based there, along with the Royal Saudi Naval Forces (RSNF) HQ.

Plessey had their own sponsor and an expat resident man in Riyadh, Peter Buchanan. Peter was an ex-army officer, very professional, brisk and to the point. He was also keen as mustard. He had recently taken over and was as eager as I was to try and secure the minehunting deal. Over many months, we gave presentations to the operational, technical and senior levels of the Royal Saudi Navy, backed up by written briefs to answer specific questions or issues. Bill, however, was not convinced that we had any chance of winning against the French, who were our main competitor and notorious for somehow clinching the major deals. The French have a justified reputation of leaving no stone unturned to make sure they win any contract they feel they want.

On one of Peter's visits to the UK, Bill called us both into his office. "Look," he said, "I know that you both think you can win this Saudi thing, but I think that you are wasting your time. The minehunters will go to the French as a sop for the UK winning the aircraft deal, which will go to BAE. Vosper may even win the contract for the ship's hulls, but the French are fighting for those too and I think they will at least win the minehunting systems. The Saudis won't want to upset the French by cutting them out completely as they are currently trying to buy frigates from France too. However, if you both really think you have a chance, then I will back you to try and win it, but don't hold your breath!"

"Bill, you are wrong," countered Peter. "This is definitely winnable. We have done well so far and the locals are with us."

"OK," said Bill. "Then go for it!"

Peter and I left Bill's office even more determined to try and win. We continued our lobbying, writing briefing notes and giving presentations to the various staff in Naval HQ, BAE and VT staff in Riyadh. We visited the Saudi Naval bases where they had their existing minehunters, which were old ex-American mine sweepers with small, obsolete sonars fitted to them. The Saudis readily admitted that these were not of much use. The plan was to see if in addition to the six new ships we could propose that these ships could be upgraded with modern sonars and command systems.

One day, I returned to the office after a trip to another part of the Gulf and as I walked into the sales area, the lovely Alex, our blonde secretary, called out, "Oh, Gordon, the managing director wants to see you immediately when you get in. He says it's urgent."

Alex had a wicked sense of humour and I just thought she was joking, so said, "Well, Alex, when I have had a couple of coffees, caught up on all your scandals and done my expenses, I will go and see what the young lad wants."

Whereupon Bill called through his open office door in the corner. "Alex is serious, Gordon; it's OK, but you do need to go and see Derek right now."

"OK, Bill, fine," I said.

I left my briefcase by Alex's desk and walked nervously round to the managing director's office area. *What on earth have I done now?* I wondered. It was only Bill's "It's OK" that stopped me panicking there and then. As I walked in, Clare, the MD's PA said "Go straight in Gordon". What on earth was going on?

Derek Wilson, the managing director, was one of the nicest men I knew to have as an managing director. He had none of the usual bull and bluster you associate with some managing directors; he was just a normal, quiet and pleasant man.

"Gordon, welcome back, now sit down. What I am going to tell you is government classified information and is not to be repeated to anyone else, either here at the office or outside. Is that clear?"

"Yes, Derek."

"The Saudis have asked the UK Government to get VT to send their negotiation team out to Riyadh tomorrow to finalise the technical details and negotiate a deal on the minehunters. They have also asked for you to be on the team to cover the MCM systems. You have to go up to the Saudi Embassy today and get a visa, which is waiting for you to collect, and you will get the BA flight to Saudi in the morning. The VT team will also be on that flight. Clare has your ticket already. The reason for the secrecy and the urgency is that the Saudis do not want the French to know about the visit. So, I repeat, you must NOT tell anyone about this trip. I have spoken to Peter Buchanan this morning and he is expecting you. He assures me you have all the material you need out there already, but take anything else you need from here, just as long as you fly out tomorrow. Good luck."

"Thanks Derek," was all I could muster. I saw Bill, then grabbed a coffee and set off to drive back up the road to London and the Saudi Embassy.

My visa was added to my passport in the embassy and I was amazed to find it was a "Multi Entry, Indefinite Time" visa. For Saudi Arabia, these were as rare as hen's teeth. Normally we went in and out on single-entry, thirty-day visas as that was all they would issue to businessmen. This was going to be a special trip.

The next day found me in a club-class seat on the BA flight to Dharan where I met up with the Vosper guys. We cleared immigration there, then transferred onto a domestic flight down to Riyadh and settled into our hotel, the Intercontinental. The next day we started two weeks of negotiations with the Royal Saudi Navy concerning the final specifications for the minehunters. The VT team numbered well over ten as they had engine experts, glass reinforced plastic (GRP) experts, naval architects and electronics engineers on their team as well as a team from their ship logistics and support division. The UK team was led by the UK Naval Attache in Riyadh, commander Nick Carr RN, who acted as the UK Chairman.

The Royal Saudi Navy team was led by their director of operations, although the real decision-maker was the Vice Commander of the Navy – a rear admiral who was also a royal prince.

IF YOU CAN'T TAKE A JOKE...

The Saudi team was of a similar number to the Vosper team and I recognised a number of faces from previous meetings. Each team sat along opposite sides of a huge conference table in the boardroom on the top floor of Naval HQ and we had a number of offices behind our side of the room that were allocated to the VT team for private meetings during the negotiations. I sat at the back and listened in fascination as the negotiations commenced.

After two or three days of general discussions on the hull design, engines, construction technology, endurance, layout of the ships etc; various sub groups were formed to go off and discuss the final points of specific areas of the ship in more detail, all with a view to agreeing a final technical specification against which a contract could be placed. By this time, the fine details were being covered including the need to have special rice boilers fitted in the galleys.

On the fourth morning, I was then called on to present the Plessey Minehunting system proposal to the main group. The commodore said, "We must now decide on the sonar and command system. Commander W will lead that group once we have all heard from the Plessey Company."

Commander W, a friendly and kindly man who I knew from earlier visits, took over and simply said, "Gordon, please tell us why we should have your system rather than the French system."

That was clear enough, I thought. I nodded to Peter who had the carousel projector from the office in a box.

"No need to get your projector, please, use ours, it is already there" said Commander W.

"Thank you, sir," I said.

I stood up and made my way to the end of the table, where a 35 mm slide projector had been set up for me. I took a couple of deep breaths and prepared myself to give the final presentation that Peter and I had worked on and which covered all the requirements for the system. It covered all the key features and benefits and addressed all the concerns that we knew the Saudi had raised about our system and about minehunting in the Arabian Gulf and Red Sea areas. This was our final chance to get it right and take a giant step closer to an order worth many tens of millions of pounds for potentially six ship systems. "Better not blow it, Gray," I said to myself.

The course of true love never runs smooth and nor do some key presentations. The navy's projector was an old model with a very sensitive forward and reverse button and had a lovely habit of going backwards instead of forwards without warning, which, to say the least, was a little off-putting. In spite of the navy's dodgy slide projector, I felt that we had managed to get the key points across and answered all their questions.

Over the next few days, Peter and I spent many hours in separate meetings with the minehunting sub-committee clarifying points or describing some operational points in greater depth. Finally, the meetings were all over and the negotiations complete. All we could now do was wait. No one really knew for how long as the Saudis were not saying anything. On the final night, Commander Carr invited us all to an informal farewell reception that he hosted for both teams in the garden of his house in the Diplomatic Quarter.

As Peter and I arrived, Nick said, "I am sure that the commodore will come and I have also invited the rear admiral, but I think it is very unlikely that he will come as royals rarely visit private residences, especially those of a foreigner."

Peter and I relaxed and mingled with the VT guys and some of the Saudis. About an hour or so later, as we were chatting, we noticed that a small group of Saudis in Arab dress had just arrived and had begun circulating and being introduced to people by Commander Carr. It was the prince and his team. He got to Peter and I and Nick introduced me.

"Ah, Mr Gray," said the Prince. "My people tell me we should buy your minehunting system. Well done." He smiled and shook my hand.

"Thank you, your Highness," was all I could say and he and his party moved on. I looked at Peter, who was as open-mouthed as I was. "Does that mean what I think it means?" I said.

"I think so," said Peter. "We've done it!"

Anywhere else in the world and we would have gone down the

pub, but as we were in Saudi, more orange juice was called for. The next morning, Peter and I had great delight in sending a coded telex to Bill from Peter's office through the Plessey Head Office.

Some months later, after the contracts had all been finalised and the prince had been on a visit to our facilities in the UK, we took our marketing director, Giles, out to Saudi to make an official call on the prince in Riyadh. The prince was a charming man with a quiet sense of humour and spoke excellent English. In the general chit-chat at the start of the meeting, we were discussing the Iraq war and the scud missiles that had been fired at Riyadh by Iraq.

The prince recounted a story to us: "During that time, I had been tied to the Naval HQ for weeks and spent many hours at night in the air raid bunkers here underneath NHQ. However, one night I was at home with my family, when the air raid sirens sounded again. I hurriedly called the family together and I set off to go down to the cellar, but my two young daughters were already running upstairs. "Where are you going? We must go to the shelter!" I cried. "No, Daddy" they shouted back. "When the sirens go, we always go to the roof to watch the fireworks!"

Excess Baggage

In the 80s and early 90s, the standard format for official presentations was 35 mm slides. Laptops had not been invented and computers were just starting to appear as large desktops. Some fairly sexy computer-generated presentations were beginning to be seen, but they were still very much "non portable". The 35 mm slides, however, were easy to carry, and slide projectors were readily available anywhere in the world and you could chop and change the presentations to suit the occasion.

At the start of the 90s, I was working for Thorn EMI and we were working with other Thorn divisions on proposals for a major test range for the Royal Saudi Air Force. As our division would have the lion's share of any contract, I was selected to give the presentation of our capabilities and experience with the UK MOD and RAF in test range instrumentation monitoring and safety. We had been involved in the lead up for months with visits to Riyadh by myself and others from the company as we tried to build up relationships with the senior Air Force officers, so we could understand what they wanted and so they could understand what we could offer to meet their requirements.

It was now time to put together all that we had presented and discussed before and present the whole picture to the top layer of the RSAF and the Saudi MOD. In the weeks leading up to the trip, one of the senior directors from corporate HQ, Tom, was put in charge of the whole activity. Tom was an ever cheerful Welshman in the Max Boyce mould, who was well liked by all and seen as a 'good egg'. It was decided by head office that we needed to make this presentation a bit special with all the slides being specially customised for the Saudi Air Force and to make sure that every aspect was properly covered. Tom found a computer graphics company who then worked with us on creating the best visual effects for the presentation. They assured us that they could make a 'moving slide show' that could be projected from the computer onto a screen with seamless blending from slide to slide and some virtual graphic simulations to show special features in operation.

However, the computer, with the presentation stored in its hard drive, needed a large Barco three gun colour projector. This was about 2 foot square by 1 foot high. In those days, neither equipment was small. In fact, both were very large and very heavy. We spent quite a few afternoons at the graphic house looking at their initial attempts, correcting the slides and suggesting improvements. As our departure date drew closer, we found that a lot of the promised 'virtual' scenes and movie effects were no more than a series of still shots. It gradually dawned on us that the promises of moving 3D pictures and virtual scenes had been a little oversold! What we had was little more than a glorified slide set. At the same time, after a few computer crashes in the graphics house, Tom got more and more nervous about the reliability of the computer and projection system and how we could ensure that we could set it up correctly and that it worked when we got to Saudi.

The week before we left, Tom wisely decided that we needed one of the graphics company's engineers to come out with us to set it all up and make sure it worked. There was an internal debate and a young guy called Phil was volunteered to go. He just about had time to get his visa before we left. He seemed a good choice as he had been involved in the slides and seemed fairly calm and unflappable. Three days before we were due to go, we had gone over to their offices for a run-through on their final version of the presentation. It had not gone well. The computer had crashed again and Tom was not happy with the graphic effects and looked decidedly agitated about it all.

I was sitting at the back while a discussion about the computer's resilience was going on, so I said to Phil, "Can you please let me have a 35 mm slide of every one of the images on the computer?"

Tom turned round. "Why do you want that, we have it all on the computer?"

"Well, I agree Tom, if it all goes to plan, but if for any reason we have a problem with the computer or BA send it all to Hong Kong, then at least I will have the slides."

There was a moment's silence before Phil said, "Sure, no problem. They can be done tomorrow."

We all met at Heathrow for the flight out, together with a user expert from the MOD who we knew well. We all helped unload the three big wooden cases from the company van onto a big luggage trolley; the projector, the computer and a box full of "other stuff", which included a standard Kodak Carousel 35 mm slide projector. The check-in girl looked at it and demanded that it all got weighed. The excess baggage bill ran into thousands of pounds, which Tom charged to his company credit card.

Following our arrival in Riyadh, we were met by the local Thorn director, John, with a rented van. We got all the boxes into the van and it disappeared off to the office. The next day, we went down to the office and Phil, Tom and I set up the equipment in an empty office. After a few hours of fiddling, cursing and tweeking, the colour projector was deemed to be working OK! Then we tried the computer; that too, seemed OK. We were able to show the slides on the wall. Our local man, John, was then asked to call the Air Force HQ and ask if we could take the equipment into the HQ that evening and set it up the day before our meeting. This was not easy as the presentation room was booked to be in use all that day, but eventually they agreed that we could take the equipment in after 1800.

As we were loading it up, John took me to one side. "What the hell do we need all that stuff for? What if it doesn't work?"

"John, I am with you. It was Tom's idea and he is running it, but don't worry, I have a plan if it all goes pear-shaped!"

John looked at me, "What is that?"

"The 35 mm slide set in my briefcase" I answered. John visibly relaxed.

The four of us duly set off in the van to set it all up in the RSAF HQ. We carried all the boxes from the car park across a courtyard and then up two flights of stairs to get it to the conference room. Being Riyadh in the late summer it was hot work and we were all dripping by the time we started to unpack it all. We confidently set things up and ran cables and inserted plugs; with any luck, we would be out of here in under an hour and could go back to the hotel for a nice cold orange juice.

The graphics man, Phil, switched on the projector and a warm glow of colour grew on the screen. "Good, that's all OK," he sighed. Then he switched on the computer and... nothing! Not a sausage! Not a green light, not even a red light, let alone a humming noise. Dead!

"Check the power cable!" called Tom.

"It's in," said Phil.

Then the two of them started prodding and poking, as you do, hoping against hope that it was no more than a dodgy connection. It wasn't. To help things along, one of the Saudi Air Force contacts, a group captain, popped in to see how we were doing. His timing was not the best as a few choice Anglo Saxon words were beginning to be issued.

"We cannot do anything here; we must get it all back to the office!" decided Tom.

So off we all went, first disconnecting everything, repacking the computer in its crate, then the projector; then carrying it all back down the stairs, across the yard and into the van. When we got it sorted, it would mean an even earlier start tomorrow.

Back at the office, Phil and Tom set to. Their backsides were all I could see as the computer top came off, then the sides were opened and screwdrivers inserted into holes, with boards wiggled and pushed. "Try it now" Click! Nothing. "Again?" Click! Nothing. After about an hour of trying to get the thing to respond, the considered technical view was that the computer was dead! "Must be the power supply."

"Oh hell," said Tom, "what on earth do we do tomorrow? Can we hire a computer here?"

"Forget it, this is Saudi," said John helpfully. "Anyway, even if there was a computer hire shop and you could hire a similar model, how would you get the presentation from the memory of the dead one onto the hired one?"

By now it was after nine at night and we were all tired, hungry and more than a little thirsty, so tempers were a bit frayed.

"I have got all the slides," I bravely mentioned. "We can do it on the normal slide projector. All we will lose is the gradual fadings from slide to slide and the visual effects the computer gave us; but everything else is there on the slides!"

"But what are we going to use as a projector," said Tom.

"The carousel in the case."

"Oh, yes, I forgot we brought that."

It was finally agreed that that was what we would do. We called it a day and headed back to the hotel.

The next day, we duly arrived at the Air Force HQ. We were escorted up to the conference room and within a few minutes, we had the projector set up on the end of the table and the slides all loaded.

Tom was due to start the proceedings and I was to take over halfway through. The slide projector worked perfectly and our message was delivered, questions answered and everyone happy. Job done!

Diraiyah

During this time in Riyadh, I remembered the advice that Steve had given me years before in Dharan. "Go to the old capital at Diraiyah." I did. I took a taxi from the hotel and when I told the miserable, surly-looking driver where I wanted to go, his face lit up. He was delighted and he waved his hand over the front seat and we shook hands. "My name is Mohammed, you are most welcome," he said. He then took great pleasure in explaining all he knew of his country's history and its ancient capital. As we drove out of town, he explained the history:

"Diraiyah was an ancient settlement in the Oasis of Wadi Hanafi. It was settled by King Saud's ancestors over 600 years ago. They were just farmers and traders then, of course. The very old part of the town has gone but the later parts can still be seen and we are restoring it for future generations." He was clearly very proud of this chunk of history.

He explained, "In the 1700s, the leader of the Saud tribe made a pact with an Islamic reformer called Abdul Wahhaab. They agreed to spread the true version of Islam throughout the land and Wahhaab moved to Diraiyah which became a religious centre. Because of this, Diraiyah grew prosperous; it became a trading centre and pilgrims came here from the Haj. By the mid 1700s, the Al Saud and Wahaabb embarked on military campaigns across Arabia to enforce the Wahhaabi Islam. In the early 1800s, the Ottoman Turks sent an army into the area and after a long siege took the city. The Saud ruler surrendered but was put to death anyway by the Turks who destroyed much of Diraiyah. However, the Saud families remained in the area and set up a new town in what is now Riyadh."

Mohammed parked the taxi and took me on a walk through the

ruins. Much is being done to restore the mud walls and buildings to their former glory. We walked through the deserted ruins and he took me through a low narrow doorway into a watchtower in the walls. It was over 90 degrees outside, but in this simple mud tower, it was cool and refreshing. He showed me storerooms, houses, mosques, old ornate wooden doors and the remains of the old palaces which had been the homes of Al Saud families. Some of the restored palaces were, even just from a distance, fantastic buildings – massive sand-coloured fortresses, some rising maybe 100 feet into the air. All of this had been built with just mud bricks.

I left Diraiyah fascinated. I hope that the Saudis complete the restoration as it will be fantastic to see this city and citadel as it once must have been. I thanked Mohammed sincerely and we left as friends.

"It is not usual for foreigners to want to go there," he told me. "So I am pleased you did."

Moonshine

It was at about this time that I encountered the local hooch. Strictly illegal, but it was sometimes made within the expat communities. We were invited to someone's house and offered a little something special. "Yes, let's try it," we all said, like naughty schoolboys having a sip of cider. A bottle with a pale-coloured liquid in it was produced from a cupboard at the back of a cupboard. Half an inch was poured into glasses and we all took a glass.

"We find that some fizzy bitter lemon helps it," said our host.

So, we all added a small amount of bitter lemon. Then, with much ceremony, we raised our glasses to the skill and ingenuity of someone able to make such fine liquor in the middle of Saudi. We sipped the nectar. Never have so many men struggled to keep a straight face and not insult their host. The stuff was disgusting! We all accepted more bitter lemon. It did not help.

Slowly we finished this awful liquid in sips, but were thankful that no more was offered on the basis of the costs to make it. I am sure you could have fuelled a jumbo jet with it. As for drinking it, then I will stick to coke, thanks. You would really need to be desperate to drink that stuff.

Arms Dealers

In some parts of the media international defence salesmen are often referred to as "arms dealers". The media love the terms as it conjures an image of a decidedly dodgy fellow in a trilby hat sneaking through the dark back alleys with half a dozen Kalashnikovs hidden in his raincoat. They seem to have an idea that a salesman, or "arms dealer", simply flies into a foreign land, meets another dodgy man in a bar late that night, passes him a thick brown envelope and flies home with an multi-million pound order. The media's conclusion is that all defence sales people are at best immoral fortune hunters and at worst accessories to genocide. Unfortunately for their stories – and they never like the facts to get in the way of a good story – defence sales never happen like that. Some parts of the media choose to forget that defence of the realm is the first duty of government and to do that a defence industry is essential. To help fund the nation's defences, the overseas sales of defence equipment to friendly countries is a vital source of income. Overseas defence sales provide funds for research and development that help provides our own defence forces with the latest and best equipment. It is all totally legal and a key national industry that pays corporation taxes, provides work and employs taxpayers. All overseas defence sales must get the approval of the UK MOD before the salesman can even hand out a brochure. I am sure there are independent, lone operators who peddle arms to illegal groups and do get paid cash for them in bars late at night, but they are not employed by UK Defence companies.

IF YOU CAN'T TAKE A JOKE...

There are corrupt and tyrannical regimes, as well as politically unacceptable ones, around the world and we are barred from approaching these by the UK MOD. However sometimes today's 'good guy' can turn into next year's 'bad guy' due to coups, revolution or even elections. In those circumstances, companies can find that they have to cancel orders already placed on them and can end up with equipment ordered and built, but which cannot now be delivered and will never be paid for. These losses just have to be swallowed by the industry as part of the game.

The media also love to talk about overseas "agents" as if they are the very scourge of humanity. In some countries, it is a legal requirement to operate through an agent. The agent forms a vital link between the supplier and the government. The agent ensures that things are done correctly and is there to ensure that the company follows the correct legal practices. If they do not, then the agent can be held responsible. If operating in a country where an agent is required, then naturally the agent will need to be paid for his expertise, time and work.

In other countries, it is illegal to have an agent. In such countries, the government prefers to deal directly with the overseas supplier and will point out the legal requirements directly to them. Such countries feel that they can conduct their business without the help of an agent. Every country can choose how it buys its defence systems as dictated by its history, culture, customs, and its own laws. It is their country and they can buy whatever they want, from whoever they want, however they want. To succeed in defence sales, it is better to accept that and abide by the rules.

Often we read in the UK press about supposed goings-on behind some of the really big defence deals, with all sorts of accusations about slush funds and of arms dealers bribing overseas government officials, or offering 'inducements' to these officials, such as entertaining them to dinner in return for 'favours'. The press only look at one side of the picture so even if these incidents actually occur as reported, and few events ever happen exactly as reported in the press, what is never reported is the other side of the picture. The press never manage to learn about the work needed to win overseas contracts; the endless visits; the writing and rewriting and submission of proposals; technical evaluations, demonstrations, visits, debates with the customers about benefits and technology; and the efforts to counter what the foreign competitors are offering to try and win the order. We operate in overseas markets and must deal with what we find in front of us in those markets. We have to pursue our sales within the local laws and customs of the country, as well as within the UK laws on business ethics. All we can do is be aware that other countries do not follow UK laws on ethics. No country will change their culture, laws or procurement methods just to fit in with the views of a few misinformed people in the UK media.

On a few occasions over the years, I have been at meetings where the customer blatantly let it be known that if we did something personally for him, he could arrange a large order for us. In most cases it was so blatant as to be laughable and in all cases, all the 'offers' were sidestepped and no more was ever heard from the customer. In one case, we were asked to buy him a large riverside house on the Thames. He even showed us the estate agent's brochure. End of prospect.

We did have one colleague though who, much to everyone's amusement, liked to live the life of a clandestine arms dealer even though he was just a naval systems salesman who had been involved in the sale of radars to Middle East. He seemed to spend weeks in a couple of Middle Eastern cities, which we found odd as there was no imminent business in either town. We met him by chance in the Sheraton Hotel in one of these cities one evening. He insisted on sitting in one particular seat behind a large pillar in a dark corner at the back of the lobby.

"Why do we have to sit here?" we asked.

He leant forward towards us and glanced over our shoulders.

"Well," he said in a hushed tone. "From here I can see who comes in the front door, I can see who comes out of the lift and I can see who comes up from the underground garage, but they cannot see me!

I must never be seen, you see. You will never see me during the day as I really only work at night. I never know when the phone may ring in the night and I have to rush to a secret meeting somewhere. And, by the way, you have not seen me here no matter who asks you. Only my secretary ever knows where I am and how to contact me."

Incredible, but that was how he saw his life. We left him to it but he was always just 'double oh three and a half' to us after that.

Camels and BBQs

In the days after the first Gulf War, there were a number of defence sales opportunities in the region and so large companies were targeted by local businessmen offering to sponsor or represent them in the Kingdom. In Saudi, a local sponsor was a legal requirement. On one visit we had three different project teams in Saudi, so there were probably about a dozen of us, including three directors, all in Riyadh. One such businessman made a heavy play to our directors to represent us and invited us all to a BBQ out in the desert. He also invited the British Ambassador and a number of the families from the embassy. After discussing the invitation with embassy staff, it was decided that we should accept. We were picked up at the hotel by a fleet of big Toyota 4x4s and taken out into the desert. A camp had been set up on a sandy hill overlooking Riyadh.

There were large tents for cooking and as we arrived, the BBQ was already sizzling away. There was a tent for drinks, a tent draped in pink for the ladies, as well as one for children and a tent for the men. All the tents were furnished with rugs and cushions. The BBQ was on an industrial scale. A number of big metal troughs were pushed together to form a line about 20 feet long. Some were loaded with juicy steaks and chicken joints. Others had corn on the cobs and vegetable kebabs. An oven was warming breads and rolls and a table was laden with bowls of salads and fruit. The smells and smoke from the charcoal and sizzling beef drifted through the camp on the balmy night air. Appetites were awakened and the drinks went down well.

Just away from the camp, in a small paddock, were two camels and a horse. The horse, we were told, was a pure Arabian thoroughbred. The ambassador was a known horseman and was offered the chance to ride it. This he accepted, giving us a riding display across the sands. The camels were from a large herd owned by the businessman. We looked at the camels warily and stayed in a close group well out of their reach and then watched as a small boy climbed into the paddock and started to milk one of them. Shortly afterwards, as we were watching the ambassador galloping across the sands like Lawrence of Arabia, a servant appeared with cups and a bowl of fresh, warm camel milk.

"You try, mister," invited the servant, "it is very good."

We tried it. It was very nice and reminded me of skimmed milk. It was not in any way unpleasant. Another first for me.

The evening went well; the food was plentiful, delicious and well cooked. Our directors sat with the businessman chatting, the embassy families kept to themselves in the family tent, and a few of us sat on rugs laid on the sand and watched the lights of Riyadh twinkling in the distance.

Abiding Memories

I remember the peace of Saudi. It always seemed to be quiet even in the cities. As the heat of the day eased and the pink sun set across the vast desert, the calls to evening prayer faded from the minaret loudspeakers and Riyadh settled peacefully into a slumber. Even walking round the souk or the modern shopping malls after evening prayers, it seemed peaceful and non threatening. We also found that when we went there for two-week trips, the lack of alcohol did us all good and we felt better for it. We also spent more time exercising in the gym or swimming, rather than drinking in a bar somewhere. Because of the strict Sharia laws, many visitors feel intimidated and fearful of being arrested on some strange charge. While that certainly happens and executions still take place after Friday prayers, you must know what you can and cannot do – though I never found Saudi to be stressful. I recall the kindness and friendliness of the people and their total commitment to Islam. We often said that if in the West we were as committed to Christianity as the Saudis are to Islam, we would live better lives and be in a better place and perhaps politicians would be a bit more committed to preserving a Christian society.

Interior Ministry, Riyadh

Masmak Fort, Riyadh

Old city of Diraiyah

Old Palace Diraiyah

CHAPTER 9

Egypt

'URGENT' it said on the telex RFQ (Request for Quotation). I took it into Bill.

"Bill, we have got this urgent telex RFQ from the Egyptian Navy HQ for minehunting sonars."

"Don't be stupid Gordon. Urgent is not a word in the Egyptian dictionary. In fact," said Bill, reading it, "if you look in the file, I am sure you will find that they asked for the same thing about three years ago and we sent them a quote then."

I checked and they had and that RFQ said urgent too. Things move slowly in Egypt.

Considering that it is so near to Saudi Arabia, its history could not be more different. Egypt is a country whose history and civilisation goes back over 5000 years. It is a country that grew rich on the fertility provided by the waters of the Nile and was one of the great civilisations of its time. The Great Pyramids and temples built in those times are still wonders of the world and reflect the huge wealth and knowledge that Egypt possessed. Today it does not have the wealth that Saudi has and many parts appear to be neglected and rundown, but it still plays a major role in Middle East politics with its large population and strong ties to Islam – but with a western tolerance factor applied. It has a much more cosmopolitan feel about it than Saudi has, but it is still a Muslim country.

New Minehunters

Back in Egypt, Plessey had a fine agent. A former senior Egyptian naval officer called Adel Moustafa. Adel was a kind, intelligent and dedicated man. He was also highly respected within the Egyptian Navy. I had known Adel for years and we got on well. He was extremely enthusiastic about our work. Now that Plessey had been taken over by Marconi, Adel remained as our agent.

However, the Egyptian Navy did now want to buy new minehunters which would be built by an American shipyard. The deal involved a very low-cost loan from the US Government but with strings attached. These strings meant that the Egyptians had to buy US-made equipment for the ships and could not choose, for example, UK-made systems. We already had arrangements in place with a Plessey factory in the USA where we could make enough parts of the systems to qualify as 'US-Made'. In addition to the American companies that were bidding, the French were also bidding and had their arrangements in place for some of their naval equipment to be part-made in the USA so that they also 'qualified' for the deal.

Over a period of some months, we had been visiting the Egyptian Navy at their HQ in Ras Al Tin in Alexandria. Ras al Tin is a complex of building that used to form one of the palaces of King Farouk. It is situated out at the end of a promontory near the main port of Alexandria and is surrounded by the blue Mediterranean Sea. These visits had consisted of a combination of presentations and friendly, often informal, discussions with groups of officers, and then one to one discussions with the more senior naval staff. Whether it was the friendliness of the Egyptian Navy, or the seemingly endless warm sunshine and gentle sea breezes blowing in from the Mediterranean, I don't know, but these meetings out at Ras Al Tin were always a pleasant experience. Eventually, the navy selected two preferred bidders. Plessey was one and the French were the other. It would now be left to the shipbuilder to select the winner after commercial discussions. Things moved slowly in Egypt and as Easter approached, no one believed that the discussions were going to start again until later in the summer.

I arrived home from the office on the Thursday of Easter week and was looking forward to a long weekend at home, when the phone rang. It was Adel, our agent, calling from Alexandria.

"The American shipbuilder is starting final comparison discussions with the French in Cairo on Saturday," he said. "The French have engineered a meeting with them over Easter weekend to force their solution through. If we are to stay in the race, we must be there too so that there is a proper comparison made."

The comparison was to be based on a series of matrices where all the key operational, technical and commercial features and benefits, including prices, spares, support etc, were all graded and the best overall total score would win. We knew that the French would do all they could to counter our system benefits and have us marked down. It was also clear that the French had done this as they knew that no one from the UK would be in Cairo over Easter and so they would have a clear run.

After I had spoken to Adel, I rang our new marketing director, as I knew that my immediate boss was away on his Easter holiday. Gwynne had joined Marconi from Plessey some months before and I had first met Gwynne when he interviewed me for my first job with Plessey. He was ex-British Army officer and understood the need to get things done. He was struggling with the Marconi culture as much as we were.

"Gwynne, I need your approval to go to Cairo tomorrow to support Adel for final discussions with the US builders of the minehunters. The French are already there and if we are not, then the French will get us ruled out of the race."

"That's fine," said a very laid-back Gwynne. "Go ahead and book the flights on your Amex card and I will sign it all off when you get back."

So Good Friday found me on the BA flight to Cairo. Adel had booked me into the Nile Hilton in Cairo and we sat down in my room while he briefed me on the state of play. We went through the outline of the matrix and discussed all the points. We felt we had good answers to most of the points that would be discussed.

The discussions went on over the weekend and into the next week. One day, the French would be in negotiating with the builder, then we would be there the next day. It was a case of claim and counter claim. The real problem was that the shipbuilder did not understand minehunting, so every feature and benefit had to be explained and we were never sure that he fully understood the points we made. Also, it became clear that he was only interested in paying the lowest price he could and did not really care what performance the end user got from the system. All he had to do was make sure that the matrix met the Egyptian Navy requirements and would pass the US DOD rulings.

By the end of the week, however, we felt we were making progress and had a clear technical lead, but by the Friday night the French seemed to be back in the lead with an improved price offer. We spent the days in our hotel room going over the matrix, examining the price, telexing the UK for more words to emphasise some technical point, talking to the UK Naval Attaché to see what support the Royal Navy could offer and feeding that into the discussions, or seeking changes to the commercial conditions to make them more acceptable and increase their matrix rating or lower the overall price.

Finally, mid-way through the second week, the shipyard called both competitors in and declared the winner. It was the French. Sensing that they were losing technically, they had suddenly submitted a really low price to seal the deal. Adel and I were 'gutted'. We had got so near. Why did we not win? So many questions came into our minds, but in the end, after a day's deliberations on it all, we had to accept the fact that we lost and get on with life. Unless there was a clear case of malpractice, then any further action was merely time and money wasted. The Egyptian Navy were not directly involved now and we knew we could not get near the French price. In the aftermath, we learnt that the French had crashed their price to a level that they knew, correctly, we could not meet and this gave them an unassailable points lead. The only consolation was it must have been a loss-making price for them.

I flew back to the UK and went into the office feeling pretty much wasted. I was unpacking my briefcase and having the first coffee of the day, when in walked one of the senior marketing executives. His title and actual job role in the new structure were still very vague and none of us really knew what he did.

"Ah, Gordon, I hear you just lost out in Egypt. Now, did you make full use of the naval attaché and our contacts in the Royal Navy? Couldn't they have sorted it for you? They could have helped a lot, you know."

I just about exploded. "Did I do what? We have been pushing this project for months and the RN and DESO know all about it. While you lot have been enjoying Easter eggs, I have just spent two weeks stuck in a Cairo hotel room only to lose out to the French on a crashed price and you come in asking about our contacts in the RN. Unless the RN were going to subsidise our bid with hard cash, then there was nothing they, or anyone else, could do to stop a French price crash or to change the mind of the American shipyard. And, by the way, what job do you do here?"

The gentleman retreated to his office quietly before I could amplify my emotions. I apologised in the pub at lunchtime for the outburst and he also said he saw his error and apologised for his insensitivity; so all was well, and John and I became firm friends.

Time Changes

Sometime later, Bill Hawley and I were on our way to visit the Egyptian Navy in Alexandria. This time it was to talk to the navy about submarine sonars. On our way to Egypt, we needed to attend a meeting in Athens, so flew there first and spent a night there. The following evening, we caught an Olympic Airways flight from Athens to Cairo. The announcements on the Olympic flight were all in Greek, so they meant nothing to us.

Bill said to me, "Is there any time change between Athens and Cairo?"

"I am not sure, Bill, but I would not have thought so, would you? They are on a similar longitude."

"Yes, I guess so," said Bill.

When we landed at Cairo, it was quite late and we got a taxi to the Sheraton Hotel at Heliopolis, not far from the airport, so we could catch the first flight in the morning up to Alexandria. It was quite late so we agreed to meet in the lobby the next morning at 0430 to check out and get a taxi back to the airport for the 0700 flight to Alexandria.

I got up using my travel alarm clock and went down to the lobby. There was Bill already checking out. We got the taxi from the queue of sleeping taxis outside and set off for the airport. We went into the domestic terminal and found it was totally deserted. No one was manning any of the desks and there were no passengers about. "Maybe we are just a bit early," said Bill and we settled down to wait on the hard plastic chairs. We read the English adverts stuck onto the wall, we studied the flaking paint and varnish on the counters and we watched the dust and sand blowing and gathering in the corners under the chairs.

After an hour, there was still no sign of anyone. This seemed a bit odd as it was now just an hour before the flight and we were meant to check in at least an hour before the flight.

I looked around and said to Bill, "You can tell we are in Egypt, Bill, even the clocks in the airport are wrong. That one is an hour slow."

We both looked at the clock, then slowly looked round at each other as the truth dawned. We were the slow ones, not the clocks. It was only 0500 and not 0600. We had checked out of the hotel at 0330 for a 0700 flight. We promised ourselves that the next time we would ask the hotel what the right time was and not rely on each other's vague ideas of what the time zone we might be in. Unfortunately after all that, the submarine sonar contract never happened, as although we did get our system specified, in the end the Egyptian Navy did not buy the submarines.

Let the train take the strain

While there are perfectly good flights between Cairo and Alexandria, sometimes, if time allowed, it was nicer to take the train. Egyptian trains are good. They run on time, are comfortable and dependable.

Going by train allows you to enjoy a relaxed couple of hours, watch Egypt and the Nile Delta pass by the window and catch up on a snooze or two and relax. The carriages all have seats that swivel round 180 degrees. The staff turn them round at each end of the trip so that everyone sits facing the direction of travel. A stewardess comes through the train with a trolley of coffee, sandwiches, beer and other refreshments for sale so you can just sit and enjoy the ride. The train runs through the main Delta area so it is green and fertile all the way. The road from Cairo to Alexandria goes through the desert so the bus tends to be a more boring and dusty way to travel. As the train rumbles through the villages and towns, outside your window 5000 years of history passes by. The fields are still tilled by oxen; water is raised from the Nile Delta streams by Archimedean screws powered by an ox, led by a boy; and the agriculture flourishes. The towns are depressing as they seem so rundown and surrounded by rubbish tips that spill onto the railway, but as an experience of seeing the Nile Delta, it is the best.

On one trip, Bill and I had gone back to Cairo by train from Alexandria. As we got off in Cairo, a porter grabbed our cases and loaded them, with half a dozen others, onto his handcart. He then spent a good five minutes lashing and tying the cases onto the cart so they did not slip or fall as he pulled the cart along the platform to the taxi ranks. We got to the taxis and our porter carefully untied his load and handed our cases to the driver, who then heaved them up onto the roof rack. We were told to get in and we shot off at a pace, bouncing, rattling and shaking over the cobbles and off through the nighttime streets of Cairo heading out to Heliopolis.

"Bill," I commented, "that porter spent five minutes tying our cases to his trolley for a 200-yard walk along a perfectly flat platform. This character has just lobbed them onto the roof rack without any string at all and they are sliding around all over the place."

"I know," said Bill with a resigned sigh. "Egypt!"

Alexandria seafront

Alexandria Station with Bill Hawley

The Great Pyramid

The Nile

CHAPTER 10

Oman and the UAE

Oman is one of the most beautiful of the Gulf countries. It lies just outside the far eastern end of the Gulf, beyond the UAE, and faces out into the Arabian Sea. A chain of dramatic beautiful mountains runs from the Northern tip up in the Musandam by the Straits of Hormuz, down through the Jebel Akdhar, before fading and slipping down into the sea near Muscat. They seem to be always changing colour as the light changes through the day. From grey in the morning to burning white at noon, and then to deep purple and red as the sun goes down. Beyond the mountains on the eastern side are the sands of the great Wahabi Desert. To the southwest lies the vast and inhospitable Empty Quarter that stretches across the whole of the Arabian penninsula. It lies mostly in Saudi but is partly shared with Oman. In contrast, in the far south, beyond the mountains, lies the Dhofar region – the fertile and monsoon-blessed area round Salalah.

Until 1970, Oman was ruled by the old sultan from its capital Muscat. This was still a virtually closed town, well off the normal beaten track. Oman was a poor country then as oil had only been found in commercial quantities in 1962 and the benefits of oil revenues had not yet filtered down to the infrastructure or the ordinary people. Then in 1970, the current sultan, Sultan Qaboos, came to power after a bloodless coup against his father to ensure that Oman could use the oil revenue and develop into a modern society. Oman's oil reserves today are similar to those of the UK, so it is not in the same league as Saudi Arabia or the UAE. Today Oman, with a population of just three million, is a modern, clean and thriving country with wide highways good public services and gentle and friendly people.

I always loved going to Oman. Scenically, it is a lovely desert country. The main attraction to Oman, however, is the calm, peaceful atmosphere there. The people seem calm and unhurried, laid back in a way. The climate, of course, dictates the pace of life and the Omanis have got it right. The infrastructure is excellent and I believe the people are well looked after by the sultan in terms of schools and hospitals. Certainly the main roads are good. A walk through the local souks, in Muscat or Nizwa, shows a pace of life and a style of living unchanged in hundreds of years. How different from Hong Kong. Here is peace and calm, no rush, no shouting. It has adjusted to modern technology but is not ruled by it. The open-backed truck abounds and is used for everything from family outings to taking the camel to market. But once there, the farmers and merchants all squat and gossip under the trees or drink tea in the souk cafes as they have always done.

In the 70s, other places in the Gulf were just starting to see the benefits of their oil revenues. Abu Dhabi was a fishing village in 1971 but starting to develop its new port. Big concrete tetrahedron pieces were being laid along what was no more than a strip of sandy coast near the fort. Dubai, up the coast, was at a similar stage of development. There were no really big buildings or port facilities in Dubai then, let alone modern airports; just the Sheik's Fort, the British Bank of the Middle East, a few souks and various offices along the Creek. Bahrain was the modern city in the Gulf then, with international hotels, an airport and relatively large port area. But by the late 80s, that was all changing fast and the Gulf States were competing with each other.

No Objection Certificates (NOCs)

Bill and I had been in Alexandria and had spent a couple of dusty days discussing things with the navy and the agent. We flew from Cairo to

Muscat via Bahrain. We landed and entered the clean, quiet and pleasant airport where the walls were adorned with many framed colour photographs of the lovely scenery of the Oman. We passed through Immigration and Customs without any delays and stood waiting for our bags to come onto the carousel.

As we stood there, Bill told me of a trip he had had to Oman with a colleague of ours called Dick. Dick was one of life's great travellers and had been everywhere. On this particular trip, Dick and Bill were visiting Muscat. Bill, as was his practice as the senior man, always went through immigration ahead of his travelling companions. To visit Oman, you needed to have a document called a 'No Objection Certificate' or 'NOC' to be set up for you by your local sponsor a couple of weeks before you arrived and this was your visa to get in.

Bill explained, "Dick was in the immigration line behind me, as is only right. I was cleared and wandered across to the baggage carousel. I had been there a few minutes and wondered where Dick had got to. I turned round but could not see Dick anywhere in the baggage area. Then I realised that there was someone waving at me from the immigration queue. It was Dick. I thought 'What has the idiot done now?' and wandered back to immigration to see what was going on. 'Bill! Bill, I need your help!' said Dick in a slightly panicky voice. 'Why?' I asked. 'Well I have got the wrong passport with me' I looked at the immigration official. He looked as miserable as sin and had obviously just had a row with his wife. 'No joy there I thought.' I realised that there was nothing I could do, so I said 'Sorry Dick, you will just have to ride this one. I cannot help you.' And I returned to the carousel and got my bag."

"What happened to Dick?" I asked.

"Dick? Oh, they got his bag off the carousel, then he and his bag had to spend the night sitting in the transit hall and he got flown out to Dubai the next day to try and sort himself out. In fact, I told him just to go back to the UK as to try and sort it all out from Dubai would have taken too long."

Dick, like many of us in those days, had two passports, so we could still travel even if your 'other' passport was away having a visa entered into it at some foreign embassy in London. Dick had applied for his NOC on one passport but turned up in Muscat with the other passport. Quite rightly, the Omani official said, "No". Dick tried to negotiate his way in but the official was adamant. No meant NO.

Anyway, Bill and I arrived with the correct passports and NOC papers. We got our bags and went to the taxi queue. We sank back into the comfortable leather seats of the new taxi as it pulled smoothly away from the terminal. The air conditioning whirred quietly, gentle Arabic music played on the car's multi-speaker stereo system and the polite English-speaking young driver obviously knew where our hotel was. We purred smoothly along a four-lane dual carriageway with street lights that all worked.

Bill sighed, "Do you know, I am suffering from culture shock. Look at this place, this car. This afternoon we were in Cairo and compare that to this."

We had left Egypt less than four hours earlier, where if the taxi window actually wound up on the handle, you knew you had got into a good cab. If you kept your calm with the constant jolting and braking, tooting and hooting of Cairo's traffic jams and you resisted the urge to jump out and walk, then you really were a cool, chilled out sort! If, as well as all that, the driver knew where you wanted to go and that included the airport, you had really hit the jackpot.

At the time of our visits, in the late 1980s, Oman was going through a process called "Omanisation". This was where they were trying hard to get local Omanis to take over some of the responsible positions that were then held by expats. Oman and Britain have a long and strong friendship and the armed forces have helped Oman to develop its own very capable Forces. This included the navy which was run by a Royal Navy Admiral called Hugh Balfour. He was assisted by a team of RN officers with an increasing number of Omani naval officers taking on some of the senior roles.

Boat trip

Some months later, Plessey were due to give a presentation to the navy and the MOD on naval combat systems for new vessels that the navy were planning. I was going there with one of our senior marketing men, an ex-RN Captain, David Nolan, who knew Hugh Balfour well. Due to his friendship with David, Admiral Balfour kindly invited us to spend the Friday on a boat trip and picnic with him and his wife and some of the others on his team. We duly met up at the small marina near Muscat and set sail in a large motor cruiser. They told us that we were heading for a small enclosed bay that provided good shelter and swimming and was an ideal place for a day's relaxation.

After about an hour's sailing, the admiral and two four-stripe captains, both in bright Hawaiian shirts, disappeared into the wheelhouse and were busy pouring over the charts for some time as the boat chugged happily along on its own. Admiral Balfour's wife waved at the small cove off to starboard and called out "That's the place over there! We should be going that way! Gordon, go and tell them they are going the wrong way!"

I looked at her as if she were mad. "Are you joking? Me? A former mere lieutenant going in there to tell an admiral and two four-ring Captains that they have got their navigation wrong. No chance. I think it might be better coming from you."

Amid general laughter the situation was resolved and we found the bay successfully and had a very relaxing day before the work started on Saturday.

Stitched up in Paris

Later that year, an Omani Navy delegation came on a short trip to Europe to discuss command and control systems for the new ships that they were planning. The competition was between us (Plessey), the Germans and the French. Because of time constraints and as the

Omanis had visited the UK and our facilities a couple of months earlier, they were not coming to the UK; so we were all invited to visit the Omanis in Paris where they were being hosted by the French MOD. We would be given the morning slot and the French would have the afternoon slot. The French MOD contacted our head office and said that they would arrange our hotel so it was convenient for the meeting. Head office agreed. They duly did so and advised us that it was "Just a few minutes" from their offices where they were holding the meeting.

We arrived in Paris the night before and found the hotel. That night we asked the hotel to arrange a taxi for us at 0830 the next morning, as we had to be there by 0900 for a 0930 start.

In the morning as we got ourselves together, we noticed that it was raining. The taxi did not arrive at 0830. By 0845, we were on the street looking for a free cab. Not only was it raining but we learnt that there was a public transport strike of some sort there as well, so there were no taxis to be had. 0900 went by, then 0915. We called the MOD to explain the problem. "Do not worry; when you get one, it is only a few minutes away," they said.

Finally, we got a taxi. The driver was not sure where the address was and drove around for what seemed like ages. Occasionally he would call in on his radio to seek advice as to where he was to go. But, eventually, we got there. By now, we were a full hour and a half late for our presentation. The hotel was virtually on the other side of Paris from the MOD offices!

We arrived to find the Omani team irate at our tardiness and lateness. They seemed firmly of the view that we had slept round the corner, had been out clubbing all night and could not get out of bed. Certainly they had not been told we had been booked into a hotel forty-five minutes away by the French Government on the day of a transport strike. Goodness knows what the French had told them, but whatever it was I doubt that they were told the whole story. We had been well and truly 'had'. France 1. UK 0.

Concorde

Later in the process, we arrived at Muscat Airport for further discussions. The Agent met us and as we were driving away we spotted an Air France Concorde sitting at a remote part of the airport. We asked the agent why it was there.

"It's on a Round-the-World tour, is full of rich people and has stopped at Muscat for the day."

"Where else is it stopping?"

"Oh I think it has been to New York, San Francisco, Hawaii, Sydney, and Delhi."

"So why is it in Muscat?" It did not seem to make sense. "Then why is it not parked on a stand near the terminal?" we asked.

"I don't know," said that agent.

The next day, we and a few guys from the UK Shipbuilder with whom we were working on the project, attended a cocktail party at the British Embassy. This was at the invitation of the Naval Attaché who was doing a good job of promoting the British cause to the Royal Navy of Oman. During the party, the ambassador came across to a group of us.

"Good evening, what are you gentlemen doing here in Oman?" he asked. We told him. "Oh, that is jolly interesting. I have heard about this project, well good luck." And with that, he wandered off to circulate and socialise.

We learnt later that Concorde had not originally been scheduled to go to Muscat, but the stop was added at the last minute – and while the Concorde passengers were taken off sightseeing, the French had taken the sultan for a short flight in Concorde as he is a keen aviation enthusiast. You have to hand it to the French, they do know how to put on a show when they want to. Our ambassador seemed hardly aware of the project and the French supply the sultan with a ride on Concorde. Later that year, he was received in Paris by the president on a full state visit, the first of its kind. I began to realise that we were swimming against the current here.

In the end the UK shipyard did win the contract for the ships (hull and machinery), but the electronics package, worth almost as much as the hulls, was awarded to the French. I was told we had lost at a relaxed meeting with the admiral.

"Gordon. We are most grateful for all your efforts, for hosting us so well in the UK and for bringing your system out here for the demonstrations to our staff, but I am advised by our team that unfortunately it does not meet their requirements in terms of 'User friendliness'. They find the keyboard and menus complicated to operate and not as intuitive as a touchscreen system. They also much prefer the colour touchscreen display system that has been offered by your competitor. So, I am afraid that we will not be going forward with you to final bids on this project. I am sorry. Now, would you like another cup of coffee?"

How civilised can a let-down be? I was not really surprised as the Omanis had been telling us for ages that they wanted a colour display system, but we had not completed trialling our new system so were reluctant to offer it. There were a few other issues as well, but in essence, our system, while good, was not good enough. I flew home depressed and knowing that I had to go and tell the boss.

The managing director had asked for a personal debrief and he listened to my story, then said, "Well, we have all been chasing Engineering to get the colour touchscreen system sorted, but they seem to have taken too long. It seems we have been left behind on this. I will speak to the technical guys this week. Thanks, Gordon, for your efforts."

Hardly the bollocking I half expected, just a good managing director who knew what was going on.

How not to sell Hovercraft

One of the options for minehunting that the Omanis were looking at was a hovercraft. These make ideal platforms from which to operate minehunting systems. As they sit on an air pocket above the water, no sound or pressure penetrates the sea surface and so they do not activate acoustic, magnetic or pressure mines as would a conventional ship. The Royal Navy carried a prolonged trials programme over a number of years with Plessey minehunting sonars to prove the worth of hovercraft, and this was a success. However, there were, I believe, issues about the cost of running and maintaining the aero jet-engined craft used in the trials over long periods at sea.

The UK's main hovercraft manufacturer had designed a small, simple, marine, diesel-engined hovercraft that was big enough to carry a minehunting sonar system and be manned by a small crew of about six men. A normal minehunter carries about twenty-eight men. The Omanis were very interested. This led to a full demonstration in the south of England. The Omani team arrived and Plessey were asked to attend the final meetings. The sea demonstrations in the morning went very well and at the afternoon session, the Omanis basically said: "Yes, we like it and we want it." They then said to the head man of the hovercraft company, who shall remain nameless, "If you can confirm in writing the craft's performance claims made today with a full minehunting system fitted, then I think we could be in business."

Everyone heaved huge sighs of relief. This was the 'Buy' signal. We knew that the RN were supporting the deal and would provide the required data and that the craft's performance data was not really in question. It just needed to be properly documented and validated by the manufacturer to form a full performance specification for the hovercraft with all the minehunting systems fitted. While that was a lot of work, it was something that any customer would expect to be provided.

To our horror, the senior hovercraft man replied "Well, I am not sure that we can get that data as I am sure it will be classified by the navy and the craft performance data with the minehunting system fitted will take time to verify as we will need to do some more trials and measurements ourselves to be sure. Won't you take the craft without the data?"

"I am afraid not," was the only answer the Omanis could give. Without those written assurances, of course the Omanis could not proceed. So, they did not.

At 5 o'clock, the hovercraft company had a deal for selling two hovercraft complete with our minehunting systems fitted, each worth well over £3m to us. By 5 past 5, there was no deal. The hovercraft man had totally blown the sale. His whole body language and bearing was negative and the Omanis picked up on it. He gave the appearance of someone who really did not want the business. It was unbelievable.

White Knuckles

Mr Gary takes on the fastest man in the world! During this time, there was a 'Britain Oman Week' held in Muscat. This was aimed at raising the profile of British products and companies who were trying to do business in Oman. This covered all sectors, not just defence, so many high street companies from the consumer world, including Harrods, were there in force.

Plessey had previously sponsored Richard Noble in his attempt to win the world land speed record in his jet-powered car 'Thrust 2'. The 'car' was essentially an English Electric 'Lightning' jet fighter's engine with a wheel at each corner. It had been designed and built in the UK by a team led by Richard. On 4th October 1983, at Black Rock in Nevada, Richard drove the car at 650.88 mph over two runs and broke the world land speed record. As he said himself, "A real white-knuckle ride!"

As a sponsor for the project, Plessey had invited Richard to attend our stand at the British Oman week as his successful record attempt was still very much in the news. We had large display posters of the car and videos running on TVs of the runs in Nevada.

Richard arrived in Oman for a couple of days and during that time, he sometimes travelled to and from the hotel to the exhibition or down to the Muttrah Souk with me in my hire car. It was a little unnerving, to say the least, to have someone who had driven at almost the speed of sound sitting beside me as I negotiated the roads and camels of Muscat. However, Richard was an outgoing, charming guy, full of life and fun, and was great company. He was a welcome change on the stand and spent hours patiently explaining to every child in Oman and their parents how Thrust 2 worked and what it felt like to drive at such speeds.

I think I got the better of him on his last day, though. He had to catch the flight back to London that night but we had been held up at a formal dinner and we were running a bit late for his flight home. He jumped into the front passenger seat and off we went. There he sat, this all-British hero who had driven the fastest car in the world, beside me as I raced him towards Seeb Airport. Richard seemed to be rather quiet.

"Are you all right, Richard?" I asked.

Silence. I looked across at him to see what was wrong. Then, I saw them: white knuckles clutching the dashboard and eyes staring straight ahead.

I stopped in front of the departures doors and he jumped, muttering something like: "Thanks for the lift, Gordon, but I think I'll stick to Thrust 2 in future."

He caught his flight, but I never worked out what he meant.

UAE. Abu Dhabi

The UAE Navy had also been keen to buy minehunters and had invited a number of shipbuilders down to give presentations. At that time, we at Plessey were the main subcontractor to the shipbuilder. The shipbuilder called us to say they had been invited down and would we send an MCM man down too. They told us that as they were due to present on the Saturday morning, I should fly down on the Saturday and it had been arranged that I would go in on the Sunday morning to present the minehunting systems.

As I arrived at the Sheraton hotel, the favourite hotel for most UK defence people in those days, and was checking in, the shipyard team arrived back from the navy HQ and were getting out of their taxi. They did not look happy. In their dark suits in the bright sun, they looked drained. As they entered the lobby, I went over and said hello.

"How did it go?" I asked their sales director.

"Not good," was his reply.

"Then why are you so late getting back? I thought your slot was for two hours this morning?" They shuffled their feet and looked a bit sheepish. "What went wrong?" I asked, sensing that this was not good news for me either.

"Well, we thought they wanted a two-hour talk but we ran over a bit."

"How long were you there then?" I probed.

"About 4 hours"

"Four hours! To the UAE Navy? What were you talking about?"

"Well we got onto engines and things and it just sort of went on."

I was now worried, "So what about tomorrow? What time do they want me to arrive? My presentation is exactly one-hour long."

"They don't," the sales director muttered.

"They don't!" I squeaked. "I have not even checked in yet and you are saying that I have to go back and tell my boss it was a total waste of a trip?"

"I'm afraid so!"

And so it was. I made a couple of local phone calls to check but the answer was the same. The shipyard had worn them out on Saturday and the last thing they wanted, or really had time for, was a further morning taken up with MCM sales talks. The navy had thought that we would all go in together for a single two-hour session. Where the idea of a two-day session came from, we never really found out. So, I had to fly home and tell the boss. Bill was not impressed.

However, time heals and over many months we rebuilt the relationship with the navy. Their interest and need for MCMs was still strong. We were able to arrange, through the RN, for two RN minehunters – that were then based in the Gulf – to visit Abu Dhabi and take the navy out to sea for a day, and using dummy mines, show them how the RN carried out minehunting.

Fifteen Minutes of Fame

Was it Andy Warhol who said that we all get fifteen minutes of fame in this world? Well, if it is true, I had mine some years later at a defence exhibition in Portsmouth in 1987. We were manning the company stand at the Royal Naval Equipment Exhibition and exhibiting the very latest in minehunting systems as we were in discussions about it with most of the Gulf countries and it was at the time the Royal Navy had minehunters deployed clearing mines in the Gulf, so it was a hot topic in the defence press.

The opening morning, or press day, had been hectic with all the press boys and girls coming round and being given briefs on the different systems, but it had now quietened down as most of them had been taken off to lunch in the hospitality chalets. Most of my colleagues, including the boss, had departed to 'test the catering'. I was just thinking that I might have a quiet hour or two on the stand when I heard someone say, "Excuse Me?"

I turned round and a small, but smiling, man was looking up at me. "I am from the BBC Television News. We want to do a short piece for BBC News on mine warfare, who would be the best person to talk to?"

I caught sight of a cameraman with a monster camera on his shoulder pointing directly at me and a sound man standing at his elbow. Alarm bells started ringing and my lips silently mouthed "Help. Help" as I looked around. Plessey were strict about who spoke to the press and normally only a PR director would give a live interview to a TV station, let alone the BBC News. The stand was deserted.

"Well, when would you like to do it as our directors seem to have gone for lunch," I wriggled.

"Perhaps if you came back after 2 o'clock?"

"No, that won't be possible. We need to do it now as we have other equipment we must see."

Bugger, now what do I do? The Press Officer and the PR team had fled long ago and the chalet was too far away to run and get Bill from, and anyway he would not thank me if he had started his gin and tonic. Then I relaxed and decided that I must know more about minehunting than this guy. After all, I was a minehunting officer in the Royal Navy and have been trying to sell the latest systems in the Middle East, so I bloody well ought to be able to answer his questions.

"OK," I said, relaxing a little "I can do that for you, what would you like to know?"

We sat down and chatted for fifteen minutes or so while he gave me the slant they were looking for. It was, thankfully, non contentious and mainly about the prospects for UK defence sales in the mine warfare business – something I did know about. Then, he called over his cameraman and we 'did a piece to camera' as we say in the TV business. He felt I would be OK without makeup so we just went for it. I even managed to smile and quote a few impressive sounding numbers in terms of export sales potential. Then, it was 'In the can' as we also say in the trade. I am sure too that I did not give away too many national secrets in terms of sonar performance etc. It was broadcast that night on the main 6 o'clock news and most of my peers and bosses on Plessey saw it in their hotel rooms. While it was not quite a full fifty-five minute documentary, it must have lasted well over 50 seconds.

The next morning the marketing director was kind enough to announce to one and all what a good "little piece" I had done on the TV.

'Little piece', indeed. Sir Lawrence ('Larry' to his friends) Olivier would have been proud of me.

Meetings

Planning meetings in the Middle East was never easy in those days, especially if you had a boss who decided that he knew best and would try to arrange everything for you. I had one boss who told his secretary to get me on Tuesday morning's flight. She booked me on Tuesday morning's flight alright – it was 00.30. Half past midnight.

Some bosses like to show their power by sending the customers faxes and emails announcing my arrival, then failing to follow up and check that the meetings have been arranged. When I get there, I tend to find that the boss's emails have been ignored as no one there has ever heard of him, the agent will be 'out of town' and so I have to start from square one by telephone cold-calling from the hotel room.

In the Middle East, this was never easy at the best of times. Phone calls from the hotel to a Naval HQ switchboard get cut off, don't ring out, or the call is picked up by a junior security guard who just puts the phone down if you don't speak Arabic. So sometimes it is just easier to go and stand at the front gate of Naval or Army HQ and charm the guard in the security office and ask him to ring round all the contact extension numbers until someone answers their phone. Always frustrating, particularly in 90+ degree of heat. That is when the salesman will probably find that some of the people are away on duty, on leave, or overseas themselves; all of which could have been established from the UK in slow time had the boss been patient and allowed the salesman to investigate the trip himself and plan it properly.

At the debrief on his return, the salesman can also be assured that everything that did not happen will be his fault and if anything good did happen, no matter how hard the salesman had to work to make it happen, that will all be down to the boss's excellent contacts there.

The Right Plane

Once, I was in Ankara in Turkey when the boss called me. He had had a phone call from the company's Abu Dhabi resident manager asking that if I was in the area, could I get to Abu Dhabi and join him for a meeting he had arranged with the head of the navy. "Yes, Bill. Sure, no problem!" Sounded simple! Looking at the map, it did not seem that complicated.

However, when I went into the travel agents at the hotel and looked at their ABC Flight guide and started to try and work out which flights I needed, things got a bit puzzling. It appeared that there weren't any flights from Ankara, or even Istanbul, that went down to the Gulf. Everything went westwards and I could find nothing out of Ankara that would get me down the Gulf, unless I flew all the way back into Europe to Vienna or Zurich and then took a flight to the Gulf from there.

I rang the company travel office in the UK and asked the girls to investigate. They called me back later.

"Sorry, Gordon, there are no direct flights from Ankara or Istanbul to Abu Dhabi."

"OK, where do I fly to then?"

"Well you need to get a flight from Ankara to Istanbul (due west), then get another flight from there to Amman in Jordan (Southish). You change flights in Amman, but there is a six-hour layover. Then you get a flight to Doha (East) and from there you fly to Abu Dhabi (East again)."

Oh well, if that's how we get there and the customer wants to see us this week, we had better do it. I took the details and went to the airline office and changed my flights.

On the day of travel, I was up early, checked out of the hotel and was on my way to the airport by 0530. I caught the one-hour flight to Istanbul OK and headed for the transit lounge. I went to the transfer desk and was told to go to gate such and such. I was mildly interested to notice that it was in what I had thought was the domestic terminal. After a while, the Turkish Airline flight to Amman was shown on the board. It clearly said Amman and the flight number matched my boarding pass, so I was in the right place. I went to the gate indicated and waited again.

After a while, we were boarded and the flight took off. This would be a nice two-hour flight, so I settled down with my book. After about forty-five minutes, I thought I detected a drop in the engine noise as if we were throttling back to descend. We were! We had started to descend! Where were we going? The stewardess made a PA in Turkish in which I was sure she said the word Ankara. I stopped one of the girls as she walked by. "Excuse me, did you say this flight is going to Ankara?" I asked.

She beamed at me. "Yes, of course," she said and walked on.

Oh boy, I had finally done it; I was on the wrong flight and worse than that I was going back to the place from which I had started! I would also have missed my connections down to Amman and Dubai. I asked if the chief stewardess was available. She came back.

"Look," I said, "I think I am on the wrong plane. I have just come from Ankara and should be on the flight to Amman in Jordan." I was given the condescending smile that only airline stewardesses can give you. As they are always two feet higher than the seated passenger, even when they bend over and explain the basic simplicities of airline travel, they can make us feel as though we are a four year old strapped into a push chair. It was one of those 'Oh here's another idiot who can't get on the right plane' look.

Then she said, "Yes, we are going to Amman, but we go to Ankara first."

"Then why did I have to fly from Ankara to Istanbul to catch it?"

"I am sorry, I don't know," and with that she turned and walked off.

To make matters worse, when we landed, more passengers got on in Ankara too. I had just wasted about £200 and six hours flying all the way to Istanbul and back when I could have got up at a normal time and got the Amman flight in Ankara! I never did discover what I had done wrong.

Which T-Shirt?

Phone calls from the boss can be a mixed blessing. Many years later when I was working for Ultra Electronics, Doreen and I were on holiday in Dubai and staying at the Jumeira Beach Hotel. We returned to our room one afternoon from the beach and the message light on the phone was flashing. Thinking it must be the hotel with some query, I rang the message centre.

"Oh yes, Mr Gary, your office called, can you ring them urgently."

The 'urgently' part of the message set alarm bells ringing in my head. When overseas on business and I get a message to ring home or the office 'urgently', I automatically assume the worst. I would normally brief secretaries never to use the word unless there was a real family problem. As Doreen was standing beside me smiling, then I knew it was nothing concerning her. I rang the boss. His secretary Pat answered.

"Hi Pat!" I tried to sound relaxed. "What's up that you need me urgently?"

"Oh, I am sorry, Gordon. I know you are on leave, but as we knew where you are staying Terry said to call you."

"Why, what's going on?"

"Well, we had a fax this morning from the Abu Dhabi Navy asking us to go out and give them a presentation on command systems. Terry thought that as you were just up the road in Dubai, you could drive down and do it tomorrow."

"He what? Pat, firstly we are due to leave here for the UK tomorrow. Secondly, we will need to send the navy the personal details of our team for security clearances to be prepared and that won't be done by tomorrow. Thirdly, do they say in the fax that the presentation must be done tomorrow or at some time and date to be agreed?"

"The fax does not say" replied Pat.

"As I thought, Pat, nothing moves that fast out here. Anyway, you may also be surprised to know that as I am here on holiday, I do not have any work stuff with me – let alone my laptop or a C2 presentation. So what would Terry like me to do, buy a blackboard and chalk and start from scratch? Oh yes and, finally, would Terry like me to wear my Mickey Mouse T-Shirt and red shorts or my Calvin and Hobbes one with my blue swimming trunks, as my suit is at home?"

I could hear her laughing at the other end. "I told him that you would not have any stuff with you but he said to call you."

"I know. Don't worry, the boy just does not stop to think sometimes, does he, Pat?"

We left it at that amid general laughter from Pat and Doreen and dealt with the request properly when I got home.

Desert mountains of Oman

Dhows on Dubai Creek

Oman coast

Muscat bay near the royal palace

CHAPTER 11

India

What is India like?

"What is India like?" is usually the first question that people ask if they have not been there. The answer is that India cannot be described in a few words or sentences. India is like nowhere else on Earth. You cannot describe it properly, or convey what it is really like to those who have not been there. It is too big, too populous and too busy to describe. The size of India always surprises people. It is vast. It is the size of Western Europe. From the frozen wastes of the glaciers high in the Himalayas to the scorching deserts of Rajastan; from the glorious tropical beaches of Kerala to the high tea plantations in the Ghats and the plateau of the Deccan; it covers every type of topography and climate. The climate ranges from savage northern winters in the mountains to the pleasant year-round summer of the Deccan, to the summer heat of the desert; all governed by the unpredictable monsoons. Over one billion people live in India and to try and understand its history, which goes back for thousands of years, or its many religions, are lifetime studies on their own. India is commonly known as the biggest democracy on earth, but the day to day national and state politics are very confusing to an outsider. The different political parties and the personalities involved seem endless.

India is not a place that you just 'go to' for a holiday – as you might, say go to the Canaries or Barbados. India is full-on 'in your face' from the moment the plane touches down. It is impossible to go there without being totally immersed in it. India is all that the books about culture shock say it is and you are hit with culture shock on a daily, if not hourly, basis. It hits you every morning when you are there and every time you go back on a visit. From the fabulous Mogul palaces to beggars with deformed or mutilated babies tapping at the car window at the traffic lights; from superb five-star hotels to acres of shanty towns sprawling across hillsides and spilling across roads, docksides and international airports; India constantly hits notes in your soul right across the scales. Some of the world's poorest people live here and yet India has its own space programme and a nuclear capability. It has recently chartered a nuclear submarine from Russia. The distance from abject poverty to five-star international luxury is just a matter of feet. It is a film star, Hollywood lifestyle for the rich, but nothing for the masses. In India, life is cheap and the veneer of civilisation is very thin.

I recall reading a newspaper in Bangalore that had two front page stories printed side by side. One was stating that a Singaporean company was investing tens of millions of dollars in a new technology and software centre in the town. The other article was praising the town council for its decision to build some men's urinal toilets on the city streets to stop people going when and where they felt the urge. Culture shock is a daily occurrence that in time exhausts the traveller and requires him to retreat to the beaches or the hills to recover. It is, however, the people who make India a good place to be. The educated can do very well and the numbers of university graduates each year is staggering. Call centres recruit them by the thousand. For many graduates, a job in a call centre is often their first step in the professional world. In the small towns and countryside, in spite of the dust and dirt, motor fumes and the endless masses of people, the shopkeepers and stall holders in the towns and villages are always happy to explain what they are selling – whether it is colourful fruits; awful, fly-encrusted meats; or barrels of fabulous coloured spices and cooking herbs.

While many aspects of daily life can drive you mad, India with an easy relaxed attitude is great fun. But expect India to move at a western pace and it is the most frustrating place on Earth. My answer to the original question is always the same: "If you are interested in India, then you must go. If you are not at all interested, then do not even think of going there."

First Visit

At the time of my first visit, I was not at all interested in India and had only heard the usual chatter about the heat and bouts of Delhi Belly. I was working for Plessey on naval minehunting systems and the Indian Navy had contacted us asking for a presentation as they had started a new minehunter project.

The boss, Bill Hawley, decided that he would lead a small team of three; Bill, Phil Bennett, a specialist sonar engineer, and myself. Bill flew out a few days before us for a couple of local meetings and Phil and I flew out together. Our flight landed at Delhi and we found ourselves in an old building that resembled a corrugated iron barn, but which later became the main domestic terminal. Within minutes, we were confronted with Indian logic. As the carousel for baggage was too small for all the baggage from our jumbo jet, the handlers put the luggage onto two different carousels at the same time and piled the rest of the baggage in a big heap in the corner. People were dodging about from one to another to find their bags. Phil and I eventually found ours, cleared customs and then, as Bill had instructed, we found the 'pre-paid' taxi office.

A driver was allocated and he took our luggage trolley and we fought our way past the vast mass of humanity that surrounded the arrival area. Experience taught me that every airport in India is like this, whatever the hour. Half of the people were waving pieces of paper with names on and the other half yelling: "I take bags sir, no problem." "Here you use my taxi, mister!" Our official taxi driver headed off in a determined manner through the throng, pushing and shoving as he went. We followed as best we could. He clipped the ears of the child touts clustered round the terminal doors, who, we had been told, would make off with our bag if we left it for a moment.

As we left the shelter of the terminal the heat hit us and as we got out into the open, we were enveloped in dust clouds that billowed around the terminal and car parks. Our initial thoughts were drowned in a whirl of noise of car horns and yelling people. We got to the car, still with small children tugging at our jackets and begging for money. The car, like most of those in the car park, was an Indian version of the old Morris Oxford. Built in India by Hindustan Engineering and now called the Ambassador. They were ubiquitous then and virtually the only cars on the roads. We climbed in and set off still with children banging their hands on the car and with their grubby faces pressed up to the car windows yelling for money. The driver was telling us: "Do not give, sirs, do not give!" as we drove off and out of the airport.

The ancient, but immaculate, white Ambassador ground and growled its way slowly up the ramp of the hotel, its engine protesting at this slight incline. We stopped in the large, ornate, red sandstone portico of the Ashoka Hotel. The doorman opened the car door. He was a tall man, splendidly dressed in a red and gold ceremonial uniform. On his head he wore a huge turban topped by a golden plume. We stepped out into another world. The noise had gone, the heat had eased and the dust was replaced by the still cool air in the portico. The Ashoka is a massive hotel, owned and run by the Indian Government. The hotel was favoured by Bill as it was off the main business traveller's route, more traditionally Indian and it was handy for the British High Commission. As we entered its high ceilinged, cool lobby with long corridors leading off it, we were enveloped into its peace and calmness. Phil and I went into a recovery mode as we had both had our first, and by no means last, dose of culture shock Indian style.

"Glad you are here," said Bill, who was standing by the reception desk in a suit and tie watching us arrive. "I will brief you and we can rehearse your presentations tomorrow morning in my room at 0900. I am in room 207. Until then, relax, but whatever else you do, either in the hotel or anywhere else in India, do not even think of drinking the water at any time. See you later in the bar, about six?" And with that, he disappeared off for his meeting at the High Commission.

The following day, with our briefings and rehearsals with Bill over, he suggested that as the next day was Sunday and neither of us had been to India before, we should go to Agra to see the Taj Mahal. So we did. Bill stayed in Delhi as he had been to the Taj before and said he had other things to do, but Phil and I became tourists and booked a bus trip through the hotel front desk.

The tour left early and got back late. The bus seats had broken springs, some of the seat backs were broken and just flopped back into the person behind, and the air conditioning was less than good – but who cares? This is India and we were off to see the Taj Mahal. The Taj was everything that we had ever read about it. It was awesome, spectacular and magnificent. How anyone could have conceived such a marvel of architecture and then supervised its design and building is amazing. 20,000 men spent around twenty years from 1632 building it and today it is still a jaw-dropping true wonder of the world. The Red Fort at Agra was also impressive in its own way as it contained the marbled remains of the palace that became Shah Jahan's prison after his sons confined him there later in his life; and from where he could sit and look down the river to the shimmering beauty of the Taj and the tomb of his wife, Mumtaz.

Even though Phil and I were feeling exhausted after our flight out and the long day trip down to Agra, we were there, bright-eyed and bushy-tailed, to meet Bill on the Monday morning for the meeting with the Indian Navy. The meeting was to be held in Indian Naval headquarters. This is situated in the magnificent sandstone Secretariat Buildings, designed by Herbert Baker in 1911 as a key part of Edwin Lutyens' layout of New Delhi. The Secretariat is now referred to by all as North and South Blocks, as each set of buildings is a mirror image of the other across the Raj Path. The buildings also house many of the major ministries and offices of state, including the prime minister's office. Further to the west, at the end of the Raj Path, lies the even more impressive Edwin Lutyens-designed Rashtrapati Bhawan or Viceroy's House, now the official home of the President of India.

As we arrived, monkeys dropped from the many overhanging trees and scampered about the grounds. "Do not make eye contact with them," warned Bill as he marched off ahead of us. It sounded as though he had met them before. Our presentations seemed to go well. They were conducted in a high ceilinged office, across a coffee table with three minehunting specialist officers and in a formal, but friendly, manner. This meeting, in 1985, was to be the first of a number of visits on this subject over the coming years. I visited Delhi in 1990 to discuss the same subject and today India is still talking about building minehunters. Things do move slowly there. In fact, this long period of time is fairly common for minehunter systems projects. It is something that all navies recognise that they should have, but as they are, pound for ton, the most expensive ships you can buy, then it is always something that ends up taking second priority to new sexy frigates or submarines.

Lunch Date

A few months later, the Indian Navy invited us back for further discussions on the command systems and I was sent out; this time on my own. At that time agents for defence business were legally required, although they were declared illegal some years later after various bribery scandals. Our agent, Eric, a retired naval commodore, was asked by Bill to book me into the Ashoka again. I had enjoyed the hotel and its restaurants where I had had my first tastes of truly Indian food. About a week before I was due to fly out, I received a telex from a sales manager at the Maurya Sheraton in Delhi. It said that they had heard I was coming to Delhi and would I like to stay at their hotel. They would arrange a car to collect me at the airport and offered me a free upgrade to an executive room. The rates offered were very similar to the Ashoka. This was a new one for me, being invited to stay at a bigger, better hotel, so I said yes. I duly arrived and checked in. The Maurya was a much more modern hotel and much busier than the Ashoka, It was geared for international businessmen as well as foreign tourists. It had a beautiful swimming pool and gardens, and the rooms were also far more plush and comfortable than the more basic ones in the Ashoka.

On the first morning, Eric met me in the lobby and we went to our meeting. As we left Naval HQ, he said, "We need to get back to the hotel as I want you to meet someone for lunch." We walked into the lobby which was bustling with people. Suddenly, Eric was chatting to a tall elegant Indian lady with a dazzling smile and long flowing black hair that glistened in the light. She was wearing a long, bright peacock-green sari and looked magnificent. Eric then introduced me to her. Her name was Shashi and she was the sales manager for the hotel. This was the person who had sent me the telex. I had not realised from the telex that Shashi was a girl. She was a confident and well spoken lady, probably in her mid twenties. It transpired that she knew Eric through family connections and he had said that I was coming to Delhi and had been asked to book me into the Ashoka. Shashi had asked Eric for my telex number and sent me the invitation. And now, here she was inviting us to have lunch with her in the hotel's executive club dining room.

She took us up to a small, quiet dining room on one of the upper floors. The club was well furnished with mahogany tables and chairs, decorated in a pale pastel blues, and the sun shone warmly through the net curtains. It had a quiet and civilised atmosphere. From the balcony outside, we had views across the trees to the government buildings of New Delhi. I often stayed at the Maurya after that and kept in touch with Shashi. She did well over the years. The last time I was there I asked after her and was told that she was the senior salesperson for the Sheraton Group in India.

IF YOU CAN'T TAKE A JOKE...

Culture Shock over the hotel wall

The contrast between the civilised peace and tranquillity of the big hotels and the poverty, noise and dirt out on the streets could not be greater. The Maurya Sheraton has grown to be one of the top hotels in Delhi and is regularly used by visiting VIPs and heads of state. On one trip, I found that Hilary Clinton was staying there too with her daughter Chelsea. The extra added security meant that all cars entering the hotel were stopped and checked. The check was always exactly the same. The guard at the gate had a small mirror on a long pole with a pair of tiny wheels attached to the mirror. He stopped the car, shoved the wheeled mirror under the front of the car, then waved the car through. End of search.

On one trip, I was staying in a corner room on the second floor in one of the executive rooms. After I returned from a meeting, I looked down from my window. The boundary wall ran alongside the hotel at that point and there was a building site on the other side of the wall. I could see a piece of tattered, black tarpaulin attached to the top of the wall by some string and stretched out with a bamboo pole towards an open wood fire. On the fire was a blackened wok and beside the fire, a young-looking woman in a dark green sari was fussing over her two small children as the smoke billowed around them. I drew the curtains and turned on CNN. Every morning as I got up, ordered coffee from room service, switched on the TV and went into my en suite marble bathroom for a shower, she was out there: washing her children from a bucket or cooking their food on the fire. Every night as I got changed to go down to the cocktail bar for a gin and tonic, she was there, feeding rice or chapattis to the children or playing with them in the dust and dirt of the building site. At night as I climbed into the king-size bed with a chocolate on the pillow, she was down there, outside the window, sweeping the area round her tarpaulin with a bunch of twigs as her fire dwindled to a dim glow. I, or rather, my employer, paid more per night for me to stay in that room than that woman would ever see in her lifetime. Yet she, and most of the others like her, and there are literally tens of millions like her in India, seemed to accept the situation and got on with the basic priorities of life – feeding and bringing up her children.

In Mumbai the slums and shanty buildings are by the airport, acres of them spilling across the wall onto the airfield itself. They are by the railways and main roads; they are down by the docks. Totally naked children defecating in the middle of the road is a common sight. Anyone who has ever been to Mumbai, or Bombay as it was, will recognise the scenes in the film *Slumdog Millionaire*. India teaches us that the veneer of civilisation is extremely thin and that life is extremely cheap. We are very privileged to live as we do. There are millions upon millions of others in India trying to do no more than bring up their families and survive, but they have to do it from the other side of the hotel wall. Through most of our lives we are not aware of it, but in India we are made aware of it every day, everywhere.

Driving Conditions

The driving in India is something else. Everyone toots their horn, to absolve themselves of any blame; the one who has his bonnet further ahead has right of way; traffic on the roundabout must (or is that should?) give way to traffic arriving onto the roundabout. Phil and I learnt on the return trip to Delhi from Agra that at night it was better to try and sleep in the bus. That way, you do not actually see the near misses. The Delhi to Agra road was a single carriageway then. Now, it is dual carriageway. In those days, cars only put their lights on when they saw another car, also without lights, coming in the opposite direction. Then, as in China, when they saw the other vehicle, they flashed their lights on full beam, blinding the other driver then turning off their lights again. Ox carts, handcarts and wandering cows had no lights, so general chaos and a multitude of near misses and hits was the norm, as well as a good number of fatal crashes. Wrecked cars and overturned lorries were part of the roadside scenery. Overtaking was compulsory by everyone, everywhere, and on blind bends especially. Phil and I consoled ourselves that at least in the bus we were likely to be bigger than the other guy.

When I first visited India, the Hindustan 'Ambassador' was just about the only car on the roads. It could not go any faster than about 30mph, so there was a safety factor built in. If in the UK we judge passing distances in feet, in India it is millimetres. Today, with locally produced mini cars, to Korean or Japanese designs, the speed has gone up enormously but still they have near misses. More recently, many, many Indians have also taken to riding around on small 125/150cc type of motorbikes and motor scooters. They are now everywhere and roar around the country as if their lives depend upon it. No one wears crash helmets. The government tried to introduce a law to make people wear them but the Sikhs objected as they would not take off their turbans, so they were excused. Then the women objected as the helmets messed up their hairstyles so they were excused and everyone else then objected as the Sikhs and women did not have to wear them. These machines are now everywhere in India and they treat the road and traffic as a game of dodgems.

I was on a coach near Bangalore on a two-way country road. We came to a level crossing and the barrier was down with red lights flashing, so we had to stop for a train. The coach was about third in the queue with a couple of cars in front waiting at the barrier. Then, the motorbikes arrived. They weaved in and out of the traffic until they had lined themselves up along the barrier in front of the first car. Then, when there was no more space, they lined up across the other side of the road in the oncoming lane. Then, more bikers filled in all the gaps behind them. One or two cars overtook everything and joined in by trying to push into the stationery queue at or near the front. No one seemed the least bit put out and accepted it all without a toot.

When all the road space had been used up, they positioned themselves on the earth verges by the crossing. On the other side of the crossing, riders coming in the opposite direction were doing the same thing, so there were two regiments of massed cavalry of motor scooters waiting for the signal to charge each other. We all sat watching, waiting for the train and to see who would win the charge. A long, slow wail told us that the train was coming. Bike engines were revved in readiness. Another much louder whistle, then a big diesel locomotive rumbled slowly across the crossing followed by a seemingly endless line of goods wagons. Then, just as we thought it would never end, it had gone. Like a Formula 1 Grand Prix race, the red lights went out as the barriers started to rise. Up they went as riders revved and let in their clutches. They ducked their heads under the still-rising barrier as they set off and charged into the enemy. Surely this would end in carnage? Yet, somehow, and without too much shouting, blood-letting or major casualties, they all worked their way through the opposing ranks of bikes and cars, then roared off up the road in clouds of exhaust and dust. The cars and buses then followed sedately on behind. It is all totally chaotic to us but to the Indians it is normal. They expect it and drive accordingly.

Car Mechanics

I was in Hyderabad, a bustling and fast-growing city, with an Indian colleague, Ranjeev, who had recently retired from the Indian Army. He had an old army friend who was now a brigadier and the Commandant of the Indian Army Mechanical Engineering Training Establishment in Hyderabad. This is the place where the Indian Army train all their mechanical and motor engineers. Ranjeev had called his pal and we were both invited out to his quarters for a drink. He would send his car to the hotel for us at 1800.

Sure enough, at almost exactly 1800, a black, shiny Ambassador car swung into the hotel forecourt and stopped outside the main entrance. An Army pennant fluttered from a short chrome mast on the front of the bonnet and a tall smartly-dressed Indian Army corporal jumped out and ran round to open the back passenger door for

Ranjeev and myself. We climbed in. The door was shut and the driver got back into the driver's seat and started up the engine. Ranjeev and I sat back and smiled.

"This is the life" I said. "A smart army staff car and driver, just to go for a drink."

"Well," said Ranjeev, "he is a good friend."

The car pulled out into the bustle and noise of the Hyderabad streets. Other motorists recognised the smart car as military and gave us an extra few centimetres of space. We had been going for about a mile when both Ranjeev and I sensed that something was wrong. The driver was struggling with the wheel and when he used the brakes, the car seemed to fight him for control of the steering. A couple of hundred yards further on and the driver stopped the car in the middle of a busy main street. There were cars, motorbikes and trucks swerving around us and happily honking their horns. The driver mumbled something in Hindi to Ranjeev and got out. We watched as he went round to the front nearside wheel and squatted down.

"What did he say?" I asked.

"He said he has a problem, that was all," Ranjeev replied.

He opened his door and got out. I followed suit and we went to the front to see what the problem was. We only had to hold a hand near the wheel to realise that the front nearside brake pads were binding and the whole wheel was now radiating so much heat it was almost glowing. No wonder he seemed a bit disconcerted at trying to drive the thing.

The three of us looked at the wheel. Even in the dark, it still looked hot. There was no way we could do anything in the dark and with the wheel too hot to touch. So we stood and watched the people who were gathering around watching us. Then, suddenly and without a word, the driver bolted. He just started running down the road at a gallop.

"Where is he going Ranjeev?" I asked.

"Not a clue."

Now, rather than being passengers in an army staff car, we were in charge of a broken army staff car in the middle of Hyderabad and without so much as the keys to the thing.

"I suppose we had better wait and see what he is up to – perhaps he has gone for a mechanic. Or, perhaps he realises he might get into trouble and is heading for the hills!" suggested Ranjeev. Ranjeev was as puzzled by this course of events as I was.

We decided that we had better wait as we could not leave the car unattended. We waited and waited. Finally, after about forty-five minutes, Ranjeev said, "Right, that's it, we must go. We can do nothing here and the driver has clearly gone for good. Let's get a taxi."

We waited and waited but all the taxis were occupied or just drove straight past. We finally managed to stop a motor rickshaw and just as we were about to get in, there was a loud shout from a passing taxi. The taxi stopped and out got our driver.

"For yous, sirs, for yous," he kept saying, ushering us both towards his taxi.

In a short burst of Hindi, Ranjeev discovered what had happened. The driver had realised the car was going nowhere but also realised that somehow he had to get us to the commandant's house. He also had the wit to realise he was quite near the airport where there were long queues of taxis. So he ran about ¾ mile to the airport and hired one that he brought back to his car so we could continue on by taxi and he would have to sort out the dead car.

We got to the commandant's house safely and met him and his charming wife. We related the story and so the brigadier summoned another car and driver and we three men went up to the Officer's Mess for a drink. We spent a most pleasant hour or so there with cold beers in our hands and nibbling warm samosas, as the brigadier showed us the mess trophies, mementos and portraits. On the way back to his house afterwards, I was sitting in the front of the car – another army Ambassador – when, as we drove down an unlit lane, the headlights and all the dashboard lights suddenly went out. We were instantly enveloped in blackness. The driver, without pausing or slowing down at all, let go of the wheel and ducked his head under the dashboard. I grabbed the wheel with my right hand as he pulled out a mass of wires and frantically wiggled them about. As he did so, the lights all came back on. He sat up took the wheel and carried on as if nothing had happened. Ranjev and I thanked the brigadier for his hospitality, but declined the lift back in an army car and took a taxi back to the hotel.

Delhi Belly

Delhi Belly is not a lot of fun. Most people who visit India for the first time experience it at some time or another. Delhi Belly normally lasts for about twenty-four hours and people spend some hours close to the bathroom, but normally by lunchtime the next day you can recognise that you might be on the mend. There are many theories about how you catch it. The water is always the first suspect and if you only drink water from properly sealed bottles, you minimise the risk enormously. Fruit and salads are also common suspects. Regularly hand-washing is a good precaution as heaven knows who or what has just been touching anything we pick up.

I was in a hotel in Kochi sitting at the bar one evening and asked the small bar boy if I could have some more peanuts. "Certainly, sir," he chimed happily and dived down below the bar. He reappeared with a big plastic screw top jar of peanuts and undid the top, then without batting an eyelid proceeded to thrust his somewhat grubby hand deep into the peanuts and scoop them out and dropped them into the bowl in front of me. He pushed the bowl towards me with a huge smile, "Peanuts, sir." As I had not seen him wash his hands recently, I stayed hungry a little longer. I then began to wonder how many had I eaten from the first bowl! One of my rules in India is 'Always keep a packet of Imodium in my pocket' as you never know when or where Delhi Belly might strike.

I used to get Delhi Belly when I first went to India but when I was visiting India regularly, ie every month or so, I was rarely troubled. I believe it also has to do with the antibodies in your gut. Perhaps my system developed its own defences against the bad Delhi Belly bugs. However, I could be caught out. Years ago, I was told "Never eat fish in Delhi." This stemmed from the days before proper deep frozen foods were available and fish in Delhi had travelled for a few days by rail or lorry from the coast. I always stuck by this and never touched fish, especially shellfish of any kind. Whenever we attended a major exhibition in India, all the visiting staff from the UK were firmly told: "Only eat in the five-star hotels and never, never, ever eat from stalls outside or dubious cafes and restaurants and do not touch shellfish." This was genuine advice, not just a killjoy local director spoiling everyone's fun. Eating out on the streets quickly leads to an exhibition stand with no exhibitors; as well as some very sick people.

One year at a big show in Delhi, a group of us ate in the Italian restaurant of the five-star hotel in which we were staying. The Italian themed decor of the restaurant was superb and after a couple of glasses of wine, we all felt that we were really in Italy with the Italian menus, Italian food and the Italian waiters. It was all very pleasant. However, all four people in the group who had prawns that night were ill the next day.

Some years before, I had been working in Delhi for a different organisation with a colleague who was finalising a contract with a government department. The final day of negotiations were really about signing documents and did not involve me, so I had returned home. My friend stayed on to finalise things and was due to fly home over the weekend.

On the Monday, I rang his office but was told, "Graham is still in Delhi."

"Still in Delhi? Why? Is there a problem?"

"We don't know," they said. "We just had a message to say he would not be back for a day or so" This seemed strange, so I rang his hotel.

It turned out that the final negotiations had gone well and the contract had been signed. Graham, in the mood for a celebration, went to the à la carte restaurant in his five-star hotel and ordered his favourite meal. Unfortunately for Graham, his celebration was marred by having to spend the next three days and nights in his bathroom with a really serious bout of food poisoning. He had had to cancel his flight home and could only wait until he recovered before rebooking it. When I asked him what his favourite meal was, he confessed that it was "fresh oysters followed by a grilled lobster."

"What! Graham! In Delhi?" I could not believe it.

"Yes, I know, Gordon," he said, "you warned me about seafood but it was such a nice restaurant, it all sounded so good and I did want to celebrate."

Another case of serious food poisoning, not just Delhi Belly, happened a few years later. Again it was during a defence exhibition in Delhi and we had a large number of staff out to support it. Many were from corporate HQ and a few had never been to India before. On the first night, the local resident director briefed everyone, as usual, and in particular stressed the importance of only eating in the five-star hotels and avoiding the outside food stalls or restaurants. At the end of the show on the second day, one of the corporate staff guys, Phil, and a girl from the India desk in HQ, Jill, decided they wanted to go and do some sightseeing. I gave them a list of nearby sights and I told them to take a taxi from the exhibition taxi rank and said we would see them back at the hotel in a couple of hours. We went back to the hotel and got changed, met in the bar, then wandered off for a meal in the coffee shop, but there was still no sign of Phil and Jill.

The next morning, Phil appeared but not Jill.

"Where is she?" we asked.

"Oh, she rang me to say she is not too well and can't make it today," said Phil.

Alarm bells rang in my head "Where did you go last night Phil?" I asked.

"Well," he said, "we took a motor rickshaw to Old Delhi and the driver took us around the sights."

"I told you to take a proper taxi," I told him. "But then what? Why did you not come back to the hotel?"

"Well, we were in Old Delhi and decided to have a proper Indian meal out, so we asked the rickshaw driver to recommend a good local Indian restaurant."

"You what? You idiot! In the middle of Old Delhi? Do you realise that you could have killed that girl if she has got really serious food poisoning. The driver of a rickshaw knows less about decent restaurants than I do about brain surgery. Where did you go anyway?"

"Well, I'm not sure, he took us down these alleys to this place somewhere in Old Delhi that he said was run by his cousin. It seemed OK actually, but Jill did say on the way back she did not feel too good."

"Did you not listen to the briefing? The rickshaw wallah would have taken you to somewhere that was owned by some of his family or a friend regardless of how good or bad it was and he would get a cut. You really are a total a***, Phil." I was furious. It took three days for Jill to recover enough to come out of her room and four days before she could get to the show again, just in time for the last day. And this guy somehow held down an international marketing job in corporate HQ!

Hotel Customer Surveys

One of the aversions I have to modern travel is the awful habit companies now have of thrusting a customer survey form at you before you have even sat down. No matter how good a flight or stay you are having, it is instantly spoiled by these forms. They seem endless and are written in a way that ensures you cannot give a poor rating without appearing to be a thoroughly nasty piece of work who would find fault with everything.

I was staying at the Sheraton in Kolkata, where a lovely Indian lady had a role making sure that anyone in the lobby area was being looked after. She was a very attractive, tall, young lady and always seemed to remember my name and made sure everything was 'tickety boo' for me. As I was checking out and trying to sort out my bill, wondering where I had put my passport, did I have enough cash to tip the driver, where my e-ticket was and other mind-numbing things, the young female check-out receptionist handed me one of these awful forms.

"Oh, sir, please do fill in the form; we need it for our ratings."

Not only was I getting a form, it was accompanied by emotional bribery. I decided to make a stand and said, "I am sorry, but I do not do those forms," and handed it back to her.

But she persisted, "Sir, it will not take long and will help make this a better hotel."

"I am sorry, I am very happy with the hotel. If I had a problem, then I would tell you. Now I must go as I have a plane to catch."

I realised that I was sounding more and more like a peeved child. My lovely friend, who as usual was missing nothing, floated gracefully across the lobby as if on wheels.

"Oh, Mr Gary, is there a problem?"

"No," I said. "No problem but I just do not fill in these awful forms."

"But, sir, we need them for our personal assessments and to make sure you were happy with your stay."

Her big, dark eyes bore into my head and pleaded with me to fill in the bloody form. But I had taken a stand and felt I could not retreat. "Look, I am sorry, I like the hotel. Please tell your manager I am happy but I do not fill out those forms."

Her face fell and her eyes looked like a lost puppy's as she said goodbye. I took the taxi to the airport feeling like an absolute heel. I flew down to Bangalore and during the flight decided that I would take action.

When I arrived, I wrote a letter to the manager of the Sheraton Kolkata saying how I had enjoyed the stay and complimented him on the professional and helpful ladies he had in his lobby and reception areas. I hoped that that might filter down to the girls and if it did, I felt it would do them more good than filling in long forms with questions like: "How did you rate your check-in experience? Bad – please state why in more than 200 words; Excellent, superb or, out of this world?"

Frustrations

Working in India can be great fun but it can also be extremely frustrating, and the frustration is not always aimed at India. Just getting to the bidding process takes time and effort as the salesman is rarely selling to just one person. Most overseas military forces have sophisticated procurement procedures involving strict rules, many different specialists, and a number of committees who will eventually agree the shortlist of bidders. Then, there is a final bidding process that in most countries is transparent to prevent any form of corruption. So, a lot of work is needed just to be invited to make a bid.

The UK defence industry has always tried to ensure that whatever it makes for the UK Armed Forces is suitable for the export market too. However, UK MOD requirements come first and usually differ from those of overseas customers, so changes are inevitable. I have never heard an overseas customer say: "I want to buy six of the same system that the UK have got, exactly the same without any changes, and I am happy to pay the same price as the UK MOD." If that did happen, then the first cry that goes up in the office is: "The UK MOD will never let you sell that there!"

The UK MOD can refuse to allow a company to sell a system or product if any of the hardware or software is classified. Often, though, depending on the country and the system, they do allow it and give us good support too. If they don't approve it then, if possible, we must try and sell the system without the particular classified function or technology. When we have got full MOD approval to sell a particular system that is used by the UK, without any changes, and we have been selected by the Indian MOD as a credible bidder for the project, it is even more frustrating when the sale is scuppered through a lack of professionalism and disinterest within the company.

A technical colleague, Jim, from our Edinburgh simulation division was in India with me. Jim was a large, genial, easy-going rugby-playing fellow, born and bred in Edinburgh, and did not suffer fools at all. We were down in Bangalore as we had set up a teaming relationship with a successful Bangalore training software company and were putting in a joint bid for a defence contract.

Bangalore is one of India's most pleasant cities. It is situated on the Deccan plateau at about 3000 feet. Its climate is delightful with an annual temperature range of about 15 to 30 celsius. It has a long history and has been a military fort and garrison town since the 1500s and was captured by the British in 1791. Today it is one of India's major cities and the centre for IT and software, known as India's silicon valley, as well as being home to many major government-owned and private aerospace and defence companies.

After working on the bid in the UK, Jim and I flew to Bangalore to help the local company complete their part of the proposal documents and finalise the quotation. After five days work, we rang Anne, the general manager in Jim's UK Office, who had been handling the prices as the promised 'sign off sheet' for the project had not arrived and we could not submit the bid without the sheet being signed. The receptionist told us that Anne was now away on leave, but we were put through to Graham – one of the project managers who, we were told, was acting as her deputy. "Oh no, not him," sighed Jim at the mention of his name. I spoke to him. He did not seem to be too aware of what I was talking about.

"Look," I said. "All those costs have been taken from the existing MOD contract, Anne approved them last week for this bid and even briefed the board on the project last Monday.

Jim asked for the phone. "Graham, it's Jim, I have got all the original prices from the MOD contract here on my laptop and I also have the general manager's figures with the new India factors included, which is what we need signing. We can go through them together now," said Jim.

"I haven't got time," responded Graham.

"But all we need is a bit of paper to say it's OK to use what we have here," pleaded Jim. "So, can you please sign off the cost sheets for this bid and send them out to us asap."

There was a pause and I took the phone back from Jim. "I cannot do that," he said quietly. "I did not work on the MOD project so I have not seen the figures before nor studied them and I need to go through them in detail before I can sign them off."

I tried to reason with him. "Well, I can understand that, but Jim and I must have them tomorrow at the latest as we are putting the proposal together now and must have your approval sheet for the costs to go with our Indian partner's quote."

"That will take time," he said slowly.

I was now getting a bit exasperated. I was speaking on my mobile phone in our Indian partner's office so got up and walked out onto their flat roof space so they would not hear my anger. Then, I continued, "Look Graham, we are on the end stops here. This is a £3m project and if we do not get the approved prices out here in the next twelve hours, this whole project is down the pan. Our Indian partner will think, quite rightly, that we are a load of timewasters, the Indian MOD will bar us from this whole project, and Jim and I will be seen as idiots. The figures we are using are taken directly from a very recent UK MOD contract and have been reassessed by the general manager, your boss, for this bid. Can I ask you to check it now and get back to me, please. In fact, please talk to the finance and marketing directors, who both know about this bid and its importance."

This was far too much like hard work for Graham. He would not give me a straight answer but said he would ring me back. I was blazing. We had to submit the proposal and quote to the MOD in Delhi in two days' time.

When he eventually did call back the next day, he said, "I cannot sign off these costs as I have not had time to study them."

Again, I took my mobile phone and walked out of the building. "Jim and I have been stuck in Bangalore for five days to finish this proposal which we have to take to Delhi tonight and we are waiting on you for authority to submit the already approved prices we already have on Jim's laptop. Without them, we will miss the submission deadline, which is 11.00am tomorrow. Our Indian partner will think we are idiots and the MOD would be very annoyed that we failed to follow up with a promised bid for work. It has taken me months out here to ensure that we were even invited to bid in the first place. It will seriously set us back in India if we do not make this bid. You are in the UK; I am in India, five and a half hours ahead of you. Would you please speak to John, my boss, and the finance and marketing directors asap to assure yourself that this is a genuine bid and that the costs are OK to use." He said he would try. I then rang round the marketing and financial directors myself to say this was going on and ask for their help. Neither seemed too excited to put it mildly but agreed to talk to Graham when he called.

Six hours later, with no news, we went ahead and completed the proposal based on what we knew the approved prices should be. As I had to be at the airport two hours ahead of the flight, I left the guys finishing binding up the proposal and they would drive it to the airport later. I had already cleared security and the flight had been called when they arrived and the documents were passed across to me by the airport security staff.

I got back to Delhi after the two and a half hour flight from Bangalore and arrived at the hotel at about 11pm. As I walked into the room, I saw that the message light was flashing, which is always a bad sign. It was from John, my boss in the UK, telling me to call him urgently. When I called him, he said, "We are 'No Bidding' this prospect. You must not submit the bid." I was not happy to say the least. John was a good guy but I was so angry that I vented my feelings as I now had to tell both the Indian Company and the Indian MOD the good news.

At the end of it all, the reason was simply that Graham, the acting general manager of the simulation division, refused to sign off costs that he had not actually compiled himself. This was in spite of the fact that the general manager had approved them and briefed the board on the bid the week before. When the general manager returned she was as furious as I was and called a meeting to find out why it had happened. The blame was placed squarely with the acting general manager but also with the directors who failed to lift a finger to help. A bid that everyone in the company had approved was scuppered when one link in the chain went on leave. It proved one thing: It is impossible to succeed overseas without a very strong support team back at base who are all committed to the bid.

Indian Security

Having mentioned Jim, he and I had an amusing time on a later trip. We had managed to set up a meeting at one of the Indian Army's technical development centres near Hyderabad. Hyderabad is situated in the south, and like Bangalore it is on the Deccan plateau. It has a similar history to Bangalore but is noted as a centre for culture. It has its own film industry and is also a famed centre for freshwater pearls. It is a centre for some of the largest private healthcare companies in India and is increasingly becoming an IT centre as well. It is also noted as the culinary home of the biryani. A biryani is a baked dish consisting of marinated meat or fish and spiced basmati rice.

While the army base had agreed to our written request to give them a capability presentation and discuss their future requirements, they made it clear that they were required to get security clearance for our visit to the base from the army security HQ in Delhi. We duly sent off all the required personal data to India through the designated channels. Before we left the UK, I rang the base to confirm the meeting date and time. I spoke to the brigadier's staff officer, a Major Sharma.

He was most cordial and said, "Everything is fine, please do not worry; the clearance will be here in the next day or so. But, please do not be leaving Delhi for Hyderabad until we have received the clearance from army HQ."

"That's fine, I will call you from Delhi."

We arrived in Delhi and rang Major Sharma the day before we

were due to fly down to Hyderabad. "The clearance is expected any minute on the fax," he said. "But please do not be leaving Delhi until it has arrived."

I rang him later that day. "Ah, the clearance for your good selves is due here at any moment, we are speaking to Delhi now – so please carry on to Hyderabad tomorrow, but ring this number before you come out to the base to check that the clearance definitely has arrived, otherwise we cannot let you in."

We flew down to Hyderabad on an early flight and went for a coffee while we rang the base and waited for the army clearance.

"Yes. Ah, Mr Gary, you are here in Hyderabad, that is good. Your clearance will be here any moment now, I am speaking with my colleague in Delhi and all will be fine but please wait in the hotel until it is here. Please call me later."

This was all becoming more amusing by the minute. I called an hour later.

"Ah, all will be fine. We think you can come to our base so that you will be nearby when it comes through." By now, it was after 11 o'clock. We got a taxi out to the base which was a collection of small buildings tucked away down a quiet country lane. The security guard on the gate was expecting us and let us straight through without delay. He directed us to a building set back just past the main gate. It looked more like a small country hotel than an army base. It was a charming single-storied building smartly painted in whitewash with red tiled roof and with flowering geraniums in pots all along the red sandy path that led to the front door. The scent of geraniums in the sunshine wafted us along to the open front door. A warm relaxed atmosphere seemed to pervade the place.

Inside, we were met by a different officer, a helpful Major Shankar, "Major Sharma was called away on urgent business," he said. He took us into a waiting room and got us some tea. By 12 o'clock, nothing had happened.

I sought out the major. "Ah well, we think that the Delhi man has just gone for his lunch-break then it will come, be assured."

As Jim and I were getting tired of this and it was clear that no lunch was being offered for us here, I suggested to the major that we should go back to town and have some lunch ourselves, then come back at 2 o' clock.

"That is a most excellent idea. Yes. Yes, you please do that."

We arrived back at the base at 2 o'clock. The major met us at the door. "We are sorry we cannot take you into the presentation area until we have the clearance, but it will be here any minute now. I am speaking to the fellow in Delhi momentarily. No need to worry, it is coming. Please wait in the reception area." Then, he vanished. Jim and I relaxed and drank more tea and studied the walls.

After an hour, I went to find Major Shankar. "What is happening, Major? We have been waiting all day now. Has the clearance come? Is there a problem that we can help with?"

"No, no problem, we must just wait a minute or two for the fax to come."

"Can you not get a verbal clearance?" I asked.

"No, we must have the correct form for the file, you see. Delhi are very strict on these things."

I went and sat down again. Then, after a further twenty minutes, the major came in. He was smiling.

"Ah! The clearance has arrived?" I asked with as big a smile as I could manage.

"No, not yet, but it is coming, so you should set up your presentation now. Please come along quickly."

He hurried us to the presentation room as if it was us who had arrived late! We set up the laptops and projector and waited. We went through the slides ourselves to fill in the time. Then, we did it again. Something seemed very odd about all this. Then, I realised what was bothering me.

"You know Jim, this is all a bit silly isn't it? They are saying we cannot give them a presentation on our company capability because they do not yet have a faxed clearance to let us into this presentation room. Yet, here we are in the room all set up and ready to give it."

Jim just smiled and shrugged and muttered something in a heavy Edinburgh brogue that was probably not translatable, then carried on staring out of the window studying the different types of potted geraniums outside.

Finally at 15.30, the brigadier walked in with a small entourage following him. "Please carry on, gentlemen," he said and sat down in the front row.

"Did the clearances arrive?" I whispered to the major as he passed me.

"No. The brigadier just got bored with waiting for clearance."

India! Aaaarghhh!

Chris

In dealing with the Indian Army, we were really grabbing a tiger by its tail. There are over one million men in the army, which is divided into hundreds of regiments, units, departments and assorted research and development establishments all over India. BAE had developed a Battlefield Management System (BMS) for the British Army and we had exhibited at one of the defence exhibitions in India. This had caused a lot of interest from the Indian Army. The potential for this system was huge and ran into many tens of millions of pounds, even if we ended up just selling software packages. It was clear that Indian industry could and would make the hardware and any deal would be with Indian industry who would actually sell the finished system to the army. I began a round of contact building, formal presentations and meetings with the initial contacts and with the Indian defence industry. This was met with genuine interest and I immediately realised that I needed help. I was not a soldier and this was all Greek to me; I needed someone who understood, as a user, how it worked and how it was used – so I started to ask around. Then, one day, I had a call from someone called Chris Wood in BAE down at Christchurch where the army systems are developed. He said he had heard that we were trying to promote the BMS into India and perhaps he could help. I met Chris a couple of days later to explain what we had done so far and what problems I was now having as I had no user knowledge of the system. Chris was a young forty-something, tall, blond, very cheery and positive. He had recently joined BAE having retired as a major from the British Army. He was an artillery officer and had used these systems and understood them well. Chris was keen to get involved and come out to India and he supported me on a number of trips over the next few years.

The moment the Indian Army realised Chris was 'one of them' – ie an Army officer – they relaxed and opened up the discussions. We got introductions to different departments and branches that all had to be involved and approve of our system before any official requirement for it could be raised. Gradually, we worked our way up through the army until we were regularly having meetings with the relevant generals – be they of artillery, generals in charge of command and control, generals in charge of signals etc – until we knew we had spoken to everyone we needed to. Chris and I worked in India together visiting army departments and the defence industry in Delhi, Bangalore, Kolkata, Chennai and Mumbai. We felt that we were trusted and could see the huge potential for the system in an army of one million men.

On an early trip, Chris and I arrived in Mumbai from Delhi on the day the monsoon rains arrived too. What a scene. Roads that have been dry and dusty for months were now either lakes or skid pans. Trucks and cars with totally bald tyres carried on driving just as they would have in the dry, with no thought about tyre grip in the wet. Water ran and was splashed everywhere. Accidents abounded, motor rickshaws broke down in the middle of lakes leaving the passengers stranded on small metal islands. We watched from our taxi as markets became floating markets and shoppers were drenched. Umbrellas sprouted everywhere and we just hoped that the taxi did not break down. I asked our local companion how long before it stops raining and he replied, "Oh, about three months."

The following year we had a meeting arranged at a defence factory in Chennai, the new name for Madras, and it did not stop raining once during the whole three days we were there. We had to find our way out of town to the factory complex and the only access road was a pothole-riddled track, covered in brown water that was about 2 feet deep in places. The taxi driver was not too keen to carry on, but eventually, with some financial inducement, he did and we made it. The meetings were accompanied by the constant hiss and rattle of the rain as it hit the iron roof and an overall feeling of being permanently damp. After three days of solid, depressing rain, we were very glad to get the flight out of town and escape the monsoon.

We were also helped no end by a retired Indian Army colonel called Gobi who worked for a British Government defence trade organisation in Delhi and who himself had excellent contacts in the army. He also assisted in organising visits to the UK for some of the key generals and their staff to visit our facilities and have demonstrations and presentations in the UK. Until, that is, my wonderful line managers, Jeff and Guy, decided to terminate the agreement "because it might be seen as illegal by the Indian Government!" even though it was a fully legal relationship approved and supported by both corporate, the UK MOD and the Indian MOD. Bosses!

The Indian Defence industry were trying to develop their own BMS system for the army and even had an early prototype on trial. It was clear that potential for a joint development existed. Gradually, we made progress. We spoke to the Indian MOD Requirement Board, who were persuaded by the army that a requirement for the system should be issued. Draft agreements with Indian industry for a joint development project were drawn up. Our marketing director met the CEOs of the largest defence suppliers and we hosted a visit to the UK by the most senior man in the Indian Army, The Chief of the Army Staff, for a demonstration of the UK system. This was followed by a formal visit to the BAE stand by the Chief of the Army Staff at a major defence show in Bangalore where we introduced him to the BAE Corporate Marketing Director and senior UK MOD VIPs.

However, one day, my line manager – "the lovely Mr Jeff" – told me that his boss, the export sales manager, wanted to see me. He said simply, "We don't think we want to carry on with BMS to India. I want you to stop work on it." I was speechless. He did not specify who 'we' were but said 'it was a question of resources'. I knew that the managing director was not keen on India as a target market following a couple of debacles there in another division and I suspected he was behind this shutdown. To have got so far with essentially just two of us working the whole of the Indian Army and now, when there was an official requirement for the system in Indian MOD, the company decides to turn it off, was, for me, unbelievable. Interestingly, Mr Guy left us a month or so later to join a competitor company, so it was clear how committed he had been while busy finding a new job.

The People

Either I have been very fortunate over the last twenty odd years or most Indians are really very nice people. I can honestly say that in that time, I have never met or worked with an Indian person who I did not genuinely like. Over the years, I became good friends with many of them and would look forward to visiting them. This applied to both the guys I worked with on the company side and the naval and army officers I worked with on the customer side. Senior officers in the Indian Armed Forces are all very well educated and thoroughly well trained men, career officers, who all know their subjects. They all spoke better English than I did and were usually all very charming.

They also have a fine sense of humour. A group of naval officers were visiting one of our UK factories accompanied by the London-based Indian Naval Advisor, Commodore Nair, a lovely guy who I knew quite well and who everyone in the Indian Navy called 'Pinky'. as his initials were PK. As he got out of the car, I started to introduce him to our managing director who was standing beside me. Before I could say anything, Pinky said to the world at large. "Gordon! How brave you are to wear your baby pink shirt today," in a tone that suggested I had done it as a bet. He also had a wicked grin on his face as everyone else stopped and turned to look at my shirt. The Indians take their staff work very seriously and are no fools, so any discussions with them will always go to the heart of the issue.

In India, the armed forces are highly respected by the people they recruit and it is only the best officers who reach senior and staff positions. The Indian Navy had genuine requirements for our systems and held the Royal Navy and the British Defence Industry in high regard. Once we had established a dialogue with them and achieved that vital first meeting, I was never refused a request for a meeting or discussion. In fact, it once almost backfired on me.

Courtesy Call

We had had a visit to the UK by the senior technical officer in the Indian Navy, a vice admiral, and his team of officers. He was a charming gentleman who had done some of his naval training in the UK and enjoyed his trip taking time out to revisit one or two old haunts. He was happy with what we had shown him and was comfortable with the RN ways of doing things. The visit had included some of our factories as well as visits to a shipyard and RN ships where our systems were in service. At the end of the trip, as I saw him off at Heathrow airport, he said, "Gordon, whenever you are in Delhi, please do let me know." I thanked him and thought no more about it.

A few weeks later when I was next in Delhi I told a local colleague of the invitation, which I had taken to be no more than a courtesy gesture. "No, you should try and see him; certainly ring his office and let him know you are here." I remembered Ernie's teachings from many years before in London, so I did. I spoke to his secretary and said, "Please can you just let the admiral know I am in Delhi and if there is anything he wants to discuss, then I will be available." The next day, our Delhi office took a call from the admiral's office. "The admiral will see Mr Gray tomorrow at 1030. Please fax personal details for security clearance." I hastily rearranged the next morning's meetings and prepared to call on the admiral.

As I arrived in his outer office, one of his staff commanders was sitting there. "Hello Commander, what are you doing here?" I asked. "Well, I am here for our meeting," he replied with a puzzled tone. Then, two more commanders who I knew came in. After ten minutes, there were at least six or seven technical staff officers – three of whom had been on the trip to the UK with the admiral – and me, all standing crammed in the tiny outer office. By now, I was more than a little concerned and alarm bells were ringing in my head. What had the admiral told these guys about this meeting? What did they think I was here for? I thought that it would be just the admiral and I chatting about the outcome of the UK visit and the progress of various naval projects in India. But why would he need his full technical staff for that? Also, I was very aware that I had no presentational material or technical data with me either.

Five minutes later, the admiral's secretary came out of the admiral's office carrying an armful of files. He looked directly at me. "The admiral will see you now, Mr Gray." The other officers stood back and pushed me forward towards the door. "After you." "No, after you." "No, no, I insist after you!" I soon found myself pushed to the head of the group.

As I entered his large office, the admiral got up from his desk and came round to greet me. We shook hands and he said loudly, so all of those filing in behind me could hear, "So what are you going to present to us today, Gordon?" The others had all followed me in and were interested to hear the answer.

"Well, actually admiral, I had not planned to present anything new to you today as I really just wanted to make sure that you were happy with your recent trip to the UK and wondered if you had any questions or needed any more information. Of course, I am happy to discuss anything with you and your colleagues."

The admiral frowned slightly, "Oh, I see. Well, never mind, we can do that, but where is your technical team?"

"I am afraid that it's just me today, sir. I don't have any of the team with me on this trip as I am just passing through Delhi on my way to Bangalore to discuss a joint venture with a software company there."

The admiral smiled, "All alone, eh? Well, I am sure that my boys here have plenty of questions, please sit down."

"I will do my best, sir." I smiled hard as I could see the funny side of my predicament and I hoped that the admiral could too. Inside, I was screaming! *Oh Lord, what have I got myself into here.* Here I was unsupported by any engineers and about to be quizzed by the senior technical officer in the Indian Navy and his 'A' team technical staff about the deeper electronic workings of radars and command systems.

We all sat down at a big conference table in his office and the conversation moved along in a polite and friendly way until we were actually having a fairly strong discussion on the functions and capabilities of modern radars and C4I systems and the Indian Navy's requirements. I tried to keep the discussion away from software codes, volts and amps, and keep it to user aspects, functions and benefits. Luckily, most of the officers had already attended earlier technical presentations by our engineers or had been on the UK trip so they knew I was just a marketing guy and not an electronics engineer, and were gentle with me. The admiral was charming and allowed his staff to probe and question but protected me by always drawing them back from any deep technical issues with comments like. "Mr Gray is not a software designer. That is not his field, but I am sure he will take note of the question."

My twenty-minute courtesy call and a coffee with the admiral turned into a one and a half hour discussion with the whole team. I left Naval HQ totally drained but also feeling somewhat elated as I did not think I had made a total fool of myself. I don't think I lost too many points for a non technical marketer, but it was a bit stressful for a while in such educated and capable company. In hindsight, though, I am sure it helped as I now knew them all a little better and they had a lot of their user questions answered.

Earlier in my time in India, I had been asked to give a presentation to this particular admiral and his staff. The presentation was given in a large boardroom in naval HQ. It was midsummer and the room was hot in spite of a series of old and very noisy wall-mounted air-conditioning units. I therefore had to project my voice to the other end of the boardroom to where the admiral was sitting, over the top of the noise of these air-con units. By the end of the forty-minute presentation, I could feel my throat screaming at me to shut up, but I still had a bit to go. Then, as I began to sum up, I realised that nothing was coming out of my mouth. I had totally lost my voice. One of the Indians, seeing that I was drying up fast, passed me a bottle of water from a sideboard. The golden rule with water is: 'If the top is still sealed, then it is probably OK. If it is not, then do not touch it.' I started to unscrew the top from the bottle but it just lifted straight off taking the sealing ring as well. Aaargh! No way could I touch it. After a few embarrassed moments, I managed to get a squeak to come out, enough to gesture to my technical colleague that it was time for him to take over.

Lifts

I arrived for a meeting with a company whose offices were on the fifth floor of a tall office block in Delhi. I went to join the crowds waiting for the lift to take me up to the fifth floor. The lift lobby was open to the outside and the area was dark, hot and sticky. The lift was a long time in arriving and the local office workers were getting restless. As it was hot and humid, they were reluctant to walk up the stairs. Then one of them walked over to the wall where a small metal junction box was labelled 'Fireman's Switch'. The cover was swinging loosely, held only by one screw. It had a small flicker switch on one side. He casually opened the box and a mass of tangled wires fell out. He then happily started to waggle them about and pushed them back into the box. He then flicked the switch itself on and off a few times while watching the lift indicator arrows. Everyone else stood and just watched, including me, as this guy handled the cables with a 'live' lift with people in it on the other end without any idea of what he was doing. The lift eventually arrived and the doors slowly opened. We all got in. The doors closed again and it moved upwards, but very slowly, and ground its way up to the second floor. It stopped, but about 2 feet short of the floor. The Indians in the lift had had enough and they prised the doors open against the forces trying to keep them shut. Those wanting the second floor scrambled up and out through the gap on hands and knees. I looked at those of us that were left and decided that getting out was a good idea and followed the others. Once out, the Indians left the lift to its own end and carried on into their offices as if this was a normal event. Whether anyone reported the lift fault or indeed if anything was ever done about it is a whole different matter. I walked up the remaining flights and although hotter and sweatier than I wanted to be, at least I was there.

Company takeovers and joint ventures

While I was spending a lot of time in India, I was working for BAE Systems, but we were not helped in the export market by changes going on within the company. Before BAE had bought Marconi, Marconi had set up a joint venture with an Italian company called Alenia and the joint venture was called Alenia Marconi Systems or 'AMS'. The old Alenia Company had been very active in India. After BAE bought Marconi, the naval radar and command systems divisions of BAE were joined up with this AMS joint venture, which also made similar systems. We were then relocated to the AMS UK offices in Surrey and found that our new bosses were now all Marconi people and our managing director and directors were all Italians based in Rome. Our business cards said we were AMS but our work contracts were still with BAE. We then had to explain all this to the bemused Indian customers. "Yes, we are still part of BAE, but we work within a part of the old

Marconi and Alenia joint venture called AMS." "So you are now an Italian company with an Italian boss, yes?" "No, well, yes, sort of, but we do now work closely with the Italians." It was all very messy. This tie up meant that on many occasions we had to give joint presentations with the Italians to try and explain the logic and benefits of the tie up, even though they were selling similar and 'competing' systems to ours. Parochial and national loyalties and interests meant that each half was trying to sell its own product irrespective of which system was the 'best system to meet the customer's requirement'. All the while we heard our corporate master's cries telling us all to "Ensure that we only offered the appropriate system to meet the customer's requirement – but be sure it is ours!" It caused a lot of market confusion and internal friction and frustrations. Then, after a couple of years, BAE Systems thankfully decided to split from the Italians as the joint venture was clearly not working and they reabsorbed some of the old BAE parts of AMS back into BAE Systems. We were glad to become part BAE Systems again and the Italian half of AMS went off on its own. Now, of course, a company which had been telling the market it was a close sister to the Italians had to tell them that they were a direct competitor. It was all a bit confusing. If we were confused, then one can imagine how the customers felt. "Would you buy a naval radar system from this lot? I don't think so." Things that perhaps make perfect financial sense in the boardroom can be an absolute nonsense in the market place.

New Bosses

Once we were back in the BAE Systems fold, we had a new set of senior managers and directors drafted in. My first BAE boss, Andrew Humphries, had had a lot of overseas sales experience. At the time, I was struggling to get our divisional directors enthused about India. He began our first conversation by saying "I have spoken to the corporate marketing guys covering India and they think India is worth pursuing. They are obviously well aware of what you have been doing there and they seem happy with that so you have my full support to carry on." That made life a lot better. Andrew was a great boss. He wanted to know what we were going to do, offered guidance and help with strategies, then let us go and get on with it with little interference. He came out to India with me and met all the players and showed interest and corporate commitment to the region. When we wanted senior management support to get a point across at a board meeting, he was always there and supported us.

However, unfortunately for us, after only a few months, Andrew was promoted to an overseas director's job and we had more new bosses brought in. This included not only a new marketing director, but an export sales executive and a deputy to the export sales executive – though it was never totally clear what his role was. None of them, from what we could see, had very much, if any, overseas sales experience and they came with a "risk averse" approach to everything from expenses and overseas travel to signing MOUs and agreements with overseas industry and other companies. This made marketing in India even more difficult as it already had its own local challenges and difficulties. I believed in getting on with the job, setting up the right arrangements to move forward and doing all the right things while staying firmly within both Indian and BAE Systems laws and rules, but I think I was probably still seen as a little bit too 'cavalier' for their liking.

The approach we had taken so far in India, with the blessing of HO corporate marketing, had got our division well known in the Indian defence markets and created a lot of interest in our capabilities. We were now being approached directly by government-owned and private defence companies, as well as departments of the MOD and we were included on many new tender lists as a compliant and capable overseas supplier. We were recognised and respected. We had good relations with many of the senior staff in the Indian MOD, the armed forces and the senior directors of the major Indian defence manufacturers, both public and privately owned. In spite of the new management and its approach, we had, over the years, managed to put agreements in place to take a number of projects forward with Indian industry and it was only a question of commitment, time and effort before we enjoyed success. All we needed was an order. However, in spite of a strong 'Pro India Lobby' in corporate marketing at head office, the directors of our division of BAE were not committed to India. They had not been there and did not understand it, or if they had been there, did not like it and could not be bothered to put any effort into making it work. Fiascos like the earlier cost-sheet sign-offs for a final quotation were not isolated incidents and certainly did not help us. They did not want to wait for projects and relationships to come to fruition and did not want to make the investments needed. They wanted fast rewards without the long-lead times and the effort on the ground that is so vital in the export market.

Security Search

"Is this your bag, sir?" I groaned inwardly. My bag had been pulled to one side for a random search by security at Gatwick Airport and it very nearly caught me out. I had just got back from India and Doreen and I were off to Scotland for a long weekend's break to celebrate our wedding anniversary. "Can you open it for me, please?" The security guy asked his standard questions and then started to take out various items in a slow and deliberate way. They have a wonderful way of holding things they remove by their fingertips as if they are about to catch something very nasty off my paperback book. This was obviously going to be very thorough. Doreen was standing beside me, watching with amusement as item by item my weekend bag was emptied.

A couple of years earlier, Doreen's engagement ring and other jewellery had been stolen when the house was burgled and I had just had a replica ring made for her in India, which I had collected from the jeweller before I left Delhi. She knew nothing about it and I was going to give it to her as a surprise over our anniversary dinner in Scotland. It was to be my attempt at a romantic surprise on our short break. I suddenly remembered that the ring, in its velvet box, was tucked in a jumper in the bottom of my bag. Now, unless I did something, this guy would find the box, take it out and open it right in front of Doreen. Not what I wanted at all.

I waited until the security guard was well inside my toilet bag and examining the colour of the toothpaste, then I slid my hand slowly inside my bag while trying to look as though I was helping him by repositioning the bag a little further away from the toilet bag. I felt quickly around inside, luckily found the jumper with the ring box inside, palmed it into my hand and slid my hand back out and into my jacket pocket. I waited for him, or Doreen, to spot me but they didn't. At last he pushed the bag across to me and with a "Thank you for your cooperation, sir, have a nice trip," we were on our way. Phew! Made it. I furtively dropped the ring box back into the bag as we headed for the bar and that gin and tonic.

Jeff, there is always one

Unfortunately you can always depend on some bosses to let you and the company down. One of the new ones brought in shall remain nameless, but for the sake of the story we shall just call him Jeff. He was my new line manager. Jeff was in his mid forties, a large man, brash, loud and over confident. While being bright enough, he was lacking a certain amount of diplomatic flair and had a bullying approach to life. Jeff liked to give the impression that he would be the next marketing director, so do not cross him. He had a spiky 'worn out wire brush' hairstyle and because the sales director tended not to wear a tie, neither did Jeff. My first sales boss Ernie would definitely not have approved. Previously Jeff had run a service support division in Essex, but he had higher ambitions. I had actually met him once before but he chose not to recall that. We had been seated next to each other at an AMS company dinner two years earlier. Sitting opposite Jeff was the managing director of our division. Jeff spent the entire meal trying to keep a conversation going with the managing director, enlivened by dodgy, smutty jokes and personal 'How I saved the World' stories. He did this to the total exclusion of everyone else at the table. Other than a curt hello when he sat down, I do not recall one verbal exchange with him during the whole meal. It was obvious to all at the table that he was trying desperately to 'impress' the managing director. However, in spite of, or because of, all his obvious and odious crawling, he was still given a senior position in export sales and marketing by the managing director and when Andrew left, he appeared as my line manager.

During his first months with us, I had had few direct dealings with Jeff as I had been travelling and he had shown no interest in discussing India. However, one day while I was in Delhi, he phoned me to say that he had decided that he would come out to India the following week for five days and see what I was up to. I am not sure what that meant to him, but to me it meant that I needed to make sure he met all the key people with whom we were dealing. That meant that, as was usual when any senior manager or director came into the territory, I needed to set up a series of meeting with Indian Navy, Army and Indian MOD customers, Indian defence industry, BAE Systems staff in Delhi as well as with the key people in the British High Commission. That way, they would get a full and fair picture of what we were doing. At a few days notice, there was no way that I could set up the necessary meetings and I also knew that some customers would not be in town. Jeff was far from happy when I asked him to delay his trip so I could set things up properly. After some comments about what was I trying to hide, he reluctantly delayed his trip for three weeks but left me in no doubt that he thought I was keeping him out of India and was vocal in telling others in the office that I did not want him in India as I was up to something! He reacted as though I should be able to get admirals, generals and CEOs to change all their plans instantly, including foreign travel and leave, just for him to meet them.

Jeff arrived in Delhi and we met up in the hotel bar of the Maurya

Sheraton late on a Sunday night. The bar was smart and dimly lit with soft music playing. Various items of golfing memorabilia decorated the main walls of the bar and a couple of silent sports channel TVs were suspended from ceiling. The plush, dark leather seating, arranged in small booths, provided an intimate and relaxing atmosphere. However, in spite of this relaxed and pleasant atmosphere, his very first words to me as he walked into the bar – even before I could say hello or offer him a beer – were "Look, we all know that you work less than 30% of the time when you are out here, so you need not try to tell me otherwise." He made it sound as though all the directors of BAE Systems had had a special meeting and agreed that I was out here just having a good time. I am afraid that my reaction to such a crass comment was less than diplomatic. "Well, Jeff, either you are having a joke or you really have no idea what this job entails." Jeff could not seem to decide which of these two options applied.

The fact is that people actually work more hours when they are overseas and away from the office than they do when they are in the UK working from nine to five. Keeping up to date on the many different navy and army projects and keeping them moving forward, with all the customer departments involved, government-owned defence suppliers and local private industrial partners scattered all over India, from Delhi to Bangalore and Kolkata to Mumbai, made the ten or fifteen working days of a normal trip pretty hectic.

However, I did not feel that this was the time to explain the basic facts of life to our Jeff. I hardly knew him at all as we had never had a proper conversation, either business or personal, even though he was my line manager, so I was even more surprised with his next question. "Why did you and your wife not have any kids?" As this is something that we have never discussed with anyone, I can only assume it was his attempt to put me at ease and establish a more warm and intimate friendship building on the relaxed atmosphere of the bar. This comment, following on from the "you only work 30% of the time" statement had my hackles bristling. My immediate reaction was

"Mind your own bloody business." I joked that we never had time with me being away in India so much.

The next night, he asked me something about my background and from his surprised reactions it was very clear to me that he actually had no idea about my naval background, what I had done, which companies I had worked for, or what my professional experience actually was. He seemed to think I had been born last week, never sold a brochure before and had started the India job yesterday, but that he, Jeff, was going to teach me everything.

"You have read my CV, haven't you, Jeff?" I asked. "No?" he said in a bewildered way without even blushing, as if my CV was totally irrelevant. I sighed and wondered how any manager of a team of salesmen can send them halfway round the world without knowing at least what they have done in the past?

The following morning, we had a meeting arranged with a vice admiral in the Indian Naval HQ. It had taken me three weeks to get the meeting set up, security papers submitted and meeting confirmed as he was one of those who had been out of the country. The admiral was in a key position for us and it was vital that he formed a good impression of our Jeff. I knew the admiral well from his time in London at the High Commission of India where he had been the naval advisor. He was a highly intelligent, articulate and extremely dedicated officer and known to be a high flyer. He was also an extremely courteous gentleman. I had briefed Jeff on the topics to be discussed and the key questions to ask, so was totally taken aback when after just ten minutes in the admiral's office, just as we were starting to discuss business matters, Jeff decided he would tell the admiral a dirty joke. I shuddered as he began, as I knew what was coming. It was not funny, even at a schoolboy level, and it put the admiral in an embarrassing position. Not surprisingly, after just a few more minutes, the admiral drew the meeting to a close. We had not covered the topics or gained any information that would help us in our projects. Jeff said afterwards, "I think that all went rather well, don't you?"

Lunch that day was with a senior defence officer from the British High Commission in one of the Delhi hotels. And Jeff's first question on being introduced? In a loud voice for all to hear, he said, "Ah, so are you a real spy then?" As I said, Jeff lacked certain diplomatic skills!

He had said he would stay for the week, so I had arranged meetings for the Thursday and Friday. By Tuesday, he had met half a dozen people, but was bored and decided on Wednesday morning that he had seen enough of India and wanted to go back to the UK. He changed his flights and left me to cancel the meetings arranged for the Thursday and Friday. He flew back to the UK on the Thursday but not without first needlessly upsetting the young girls at the hotel reception as he checked out by being rude to them over a petty issue about how his magnetic door key card hadn't worked two nights before. This is also the man who openly boasted that he had secretly taped his job interview with the marketing director so if it did not go the way he wanted it to, he 'had evidence'. Such was the calibre of our 'management'. I left BAE about a year later and a few months after that I heard that Jeff had been sacked by the new managing director, so perhaps there is justice somewhere.

The patience and commitment needed to win major programmes is best illustrated by BAE Hawks in India. It took BAE, as it was then, led by the resident BAE man in Delhi; a super guy called Peter Ginger – over sixteen years to secure the Hawk jet trainer contract in India. People in the UK used to say, "Well if it takes that long in India, perhaps it is not the right market for us." In fact, this was not just one bidding process. Because of competitor wrecking tactics, changes in the requirements and other local issues, all of which had to be properly investigated by the Indian MOD. It took a number of re tenders and re bids, and numerous visits by senior company directors and technical teams, before the deal was finally agreed and closed. It was the focus, patience and commitment shown by BAE and Peter Ginger that won the order. However, if we looked at the UK MOD procurement, they would see similar time scales. The main combat system contract for the new Type 45 'Daring Class' destroyer was awarded in 1999.

However, work actually started on the design for the new combat system in the 1980s when a NATO project called NFR-90 or 'The Nato Frigate Requirement for the 90s' was set up. That project then changed and became Common New Generation Frigate (CNGF), before changing again to Project Horizon and finally becoming the UK Type 45 Project. A lot of this was due to changing views and requirements of our European partners, as well as the RN and the UK MOD. Even so, UK suppliers were spending money on design work, visits, meetings, prototypes, demonstrations, trials etc for over sixteen years before they saw the final supply contract. So maybe India is not that slow after all. Both projects are, however, large and are probably the exception to the rule, but they illustrate that companies must be prepared for the long haul if they want to become successful.

On the bright side, once a major contract has been secured, then the company should be able to look forward to many years of support contracts, upgrades, supply of spares, training courses, replacement systems, refurbishment and the next generation back fit contracts – provided, of course, that they can satisfy the customer with the initial systems. In addition, success in country A helps to breed success in country B.

Monsoon

In the height of summer Delhi does get very hot, but with air-conditioning in all hotels, cars and offices, it is not really a big problem. You know it is a hot summer in Delhi when it is too hot outside for the visiting air stewardesses to lie out by the hotel swimming pool. However, it is probably the monsoon rains that cause the most inconvenience.

The monsoon caught up with me again in Delhi as I came out of Naval HQ. I handed back one of two passes and my escort waved me out of the building. Before I had walked 10 paces towards the gates, the heavens suddenly opened. I now had no choice but to carry on and get wet. I just hoped that the taxi and driver were nearby and watching out for me. To get to the main gate, I had to walk about 75 yards and hand in my other pass; then once outside, try and find the car. Parking outside Naval HQ was very limited and the MOD police moved cars on all the time. I had told the driver that I would be outside at about 1200, so to look out for me coming out. It was just after 12 now. I was very wet by the time I got to the gate and the security guard looked at me as if I was mad, but there was nowhere to shelter. I set off through the vertical rain to search for the driver. I skidded and slipped, stepping into huge puddles as I squelched along. I looked along the road immediately outside the HQ. He was not there. I set off along the adjoining street and finally after walking the full length of the road, found the car in a small side road and fell in. The driver was, like most Indian drivers waiting for their passengers, fast asleep. By now, I was totally sodden right through to my skin. My suit looked and felt like a wet chamois leather. The driver looked at me incredulously.

"Sir, you are wet!" was his illuminating utterance when he was awake enough to look at me.

"A little," I growled. "Now, back to the hotel. Anyway, why were you not driving round the roundabout at 12 o'clock so I could see you?"

"Sir, I did not think anyone silly-billy enough to walk outside in such terrible rain, so I wait here safely until it stops!" He said this with a smile of totally happy innocence.

"Thanks" I said as I sullenly sunk into my sodden suit and shoes.

When I got back to the hotel room the only thing to do was to remove everything and call the laundry.

Goodbye Lunch

Before I left the company, the three senior officers of the defence staff at the Indian High Commission very kindly invited me out for lunch in the Quilon Indian restaurant in London. This is one of the best in London and a rare treat. It was a very kind thing to do and very much enjoyed and appreciated. Thank you, guys.

BAE Systems' Marketing Director Mike Routh and Mr G welcome General J.J. Singh to the BAE Systems stand

Demonstrating the latest Command system to an Indian Admiral

Elephant at The Maurya

Old Delhi

Roadside repairs

CHAPTER 12

USA

New York

It was nighttime and dark outside; there was not much to see except the dark edges and banking along the urban freeway as the taxi sped away from JFK Airport. It was 1980 and I had been sent out to the USA to give presentations and demonstrations of the new ARPA computer radar to the New York shipowners. It was my first time to New York. Suddenly, we came over the top of a rise on the freeway and there in front of me a panorama of light erupted. Through the windscreen I watched in awe as the golden, white lights of the Manhattan skyscrapers rose magically out of the freeway. Great cliffs of bright sparkling lights filled my view. As we got nearer, I could make out the few famous buildings that I recognised: the Empire State, the Chrysler Building and the twin towers of the World Trade Centre. We entered Manhattan over one of the East River bridges and the taxi worked its way across and down through the one-way grid system until it stopped outside my hotel.

I was booked into the Summit Hotel on Lexington Ave. After twenty-four hours, I was into the New York speak and was staying at "The Summit on Lex at 51st". The hotel was not the greatest and the room was simple, small and overlooked a side street off Lexington; but I did not care, I was in New York. Across the street from my window was a NYPD (New York Police Department) precinct office.

IF YOU CAN'T TAKE A JOKE...

Now, I was living the TV shows. I explored my room. It had a multi-channel American TV and an empty fridge and a big bed.

The images I had of New York as a small boy were still clear in my mind and undimmed by the real thing. There were no jumbo jets or cheap air tickets back then. The only way to get to New York was by sea, preferably First Class on Cunard. For me as a ten year old, New York may as well have been on the dark side of the moon, it was so inaccessible. I remember hearing the voices of Frank Sinatra and Peggy Lee on the radio with the magic Big Band sounds of the day. I used to try and imagine the skyscrapers, the big cars and the 'fancy apartments'. I remember seeing newspaper photos of glamorous film stars setting out for New York on one of the Cunard Queens. All this built a fantasy city in my child's mind and I was delighted to find that when I finally got there: It was exactly as I imagined it would be.

Once I had unpacked and showered, I went down to find a beer. Downstairs at the front of the hotel was a lobby bar with dimmed lighting and a fairly comfortable sitting area. I decided to sit at the bar for a while and take in the scenes of New York passing by on 'Lex'. The barmaid was a tall brunette. She was an attractive, well proportioned lady of about thirty, wearing a smart and bright, colourful cocktail dress and obviously not a shrinking violet. I ordered a 'Bud', being into the American lingo already. Too late, as I was spotted as being a Brit even before she had poured the beer! I confessed. I learnt she was called Brenda and was a native New Yorker. She was straight out of a TV show. She had a thick nasal NY accent and took no prisoners. More than one late-night drinker felt the rough side of her tongue and her highly developed sense of sarcasm. I was sitting having a last beer one night and the bar was quiet. Brenda was looking forward to closing up and going home to her flat down on the East Side (wherever that is). A guy came in off the street, wandered slowly in and sat up at the bar. He was fat and a bit dishevelled and had obviously been out drinking and was looking for a night cap. He leaned on his elbows and called for a beer without waiting for Brenda to come over and serve him. This got him a look. His accent told me instantly that he was from the UK. She served him a beer without a word, but she looked at me and inclined her head at the drunk as if to say "Is this one of yours?" I just shrugged. Then a couple of minutes later, he called out at her, "Say, is Washington North or South from here?" She looked at him hard, then said, "South". He grunted. A minute or so later, he called down the bar again, "Is Boston North or South from here?" She stopped what she was doing, turned and looked him in the eye. "If you go South round the bottom of the world up the other side, over the top and back, then it is South, but to us clever folk that live here, it's North."

The guy looked at her as he tried to work out what he had been told. Was she taking the mickey? "OK," he said, (obviously a glutton for punishment, this guy) "if I wanted to go to Chicago from here, which way would I go?" Without drawing breath, she turned on him, "Look, arse'ole, you come in here a huffin' an' a puffin' an' a chugging, an' asking dumb arse questions. You go whichever way you like, but just go!" She then turned and carried on polishing the glasses. The drunk downed his beer, sighed heavily, paid and left. I knew I was definitely in New York.

I spent the next day, a Saturday, exploring the 'Big Apple'. New York was exactly as I had imagined it would be with the traffic, the sirens and the skyscrapers. What I was not prepared for was the physical size of Manhattan, nor the size of the skyscrapers. It was all on a vast scale, whereas in my head I thought that it would all be much smaller. It was all the TV 'American Cop' shows rolled into one. New York is unique, a one-off place. The contrasts here are more of the rich and famous alongside the historical crime rates in the city. The all out aggressive 'Go! Go! Go!' of the New Yorkers and the mad noise of police sirens. They have no time to slow down, they just go. The big yellow taxis are big, until you get in and find that the security screen round the driver cuts the available space in the back down by half.

On the Sunday night, one or two Racal Decca sales guys from out of town arrived at the hotel for the presentations. We met up and sat in the lobby for a beer. Brenda was on form as usual and took their orders. Then, she just turned to me with a smile, "Your usual, Gordon, I guess?" The newcomers looked at me! "How long have you been here?" "Just since Friday night, honestly!"

The radar and demonstration equipment had been flown across to the Racal Decca Office in Battery Place in lower Manhattan. I was due to set up the equipment on the Monday and start four days of demonstrations to the New York shipowners on the Tuesday.

On the Monday morning, we waited for the radar equipment to arrive from the customs warehouse. It finally arrived at about 4pm and we manhandled the 5 foot by 3 foot by 3 foot crate into the cargo lift and up to the offices. I set to work to unpack it and set it all up. As soon as I opened the case, I could see something was wrong. The console was tipped to one side and jammed against the side of the crate and the wooden pallet under it was broken. We finished unpacking it and I gingerly opened the front panel. Gloom fell on me like a cold shower. It seemed to me that the whole packing case had been dropped and this had shattered the wooden pallet and some of the electronics in the radar. I could immediately see that pieces of the electronics were broken and some of the printed circuit boards badly twisted. Heaven knows how many of the solder joints had been broken or cracked. Some items at the base of the cathode ray tube had clearly been snapped off. Oh hell! There was no point or sense in trying to switch it on. It needed a careful dismantle to see the full extent of the damage and then a rebuild with new boards where necessary. The NY guys were eager to help and to let their engineers "Have a go at fixing this limey thing". Fortunately, I was resolute in forbidding anyone to touch it as I knew no one there had even seen the electronics of this radar and the last thing I needed was for them to make things worse out of goodwill and ignorance.

Until I had spoken to the engineers back in the UK, there was nothing we could do so I went back to the hotel feeling decidedly dejected. I tried to think of a way we could save the week's presentations that the local guys had set up. By now, it was early evening in New York and even later in the UK. There was nothing that anyone there could do tonight so I would be better to wait until the morning and call them then. NY was five hours behind the UK so 7 o' clock in morning in the UK would be 2 o'clock in the morning in NY. I went to bed and set my alarm. At 2 o'clock I called Louis, my boss, at home.

"Louis, I am sorry to disturb you at home at breakfast but," I began and then explained what I had found.

Louis interrupted me, "Gordon, what time is it there?"

"What, oh it's 2.15 in the morning, but we need to act fast if we are to save this week. The New York guys have over 80 shipowners and superintendents all due to come this week."

"What do you suggest?" asked Louis,

"Well, we need Mike Pope over here. Mike was one of the chief design engineers and knew the radar inside out. If we can get Mike onto this morning's Concorde flight from London with some spare boards, that arrives in NY at about 1100 NY time this morning. We can then work on the radar all day today and into tonight if necessary and we may be OK for Wednesday's demos. But if we let him come on the normal flight, he won't get here until late tonight and then we can't start work until Wednesday. The system MUST leave here on Saturday for the next demos back in London and while we can hopefully delay Tuesday's guests until later in the week, we cannot cancel Tuesday *and* Wednesday and get everyone in by Friday. Also, everyone will realise that we have had a problem with it. We are looking at a lot of potential orders here Louis. If we cannot get it up and running, then we will blow our start on the US market."

Louis was silent. *Oh Lord* I thought. *He thinks I have totally lost it!* "Yes, I agree," he finally said. "Leave it with me, but first tell me exactly what you have found inside the radar."

Finally, about four hours later, after Louis had had chats with Mike's boss, Tony, the R & D director who had come to China, and a long chat with Mike trying to describe to him what I had found, I got a call back from Louis.

"Mike is on his way to Heathrow to catch Concorde now, but the managing director is not at all happy and the finance guys are going ballistic."

"Why?"

"Well, under Racal rules only managing directors can fly on Concorde and it is unprecedented for an engineer to go on Concorde."

"You are joking Louis?"

"No I'm not, that's how they looked at it. It was more important to retain the perk for directors only than save the week of ARPA demos! However, they finally saw our logic. It actually took longer to get the finance director to sign off the travel chitty than the flight itself will take. Mike will be with you at 1100. Good luck!"

"Thanks Louis, I will be at the airport to collect him."

Mike walked out of Concorde Arrivals at JFK with a big stupid grin on his face, his head full of Concorde stewardesses and champagne and a large, bulging grip bag. This was, thankfully, in the days before the endless security screening and searches of today's airports and Mike was able to hand carry all the spares he thought he might need in the bag. On the way to the office, I sobered him up by telling him again what we had found in the console. It worked, as his expression had turned from happy to puzzled to worried. He had filled his hand baggage with as many spare printed boards and tools as he could and we hoped that somehow we could sort it all out. The main concern was that if the cathode ray tube itself was damaged or cracked, we were sunk, as it was a special one that we knew we could not get in the USA and we did not have a spare. Mike set to.

He decided fairly quickly that the whole packing case must have been dropped, possibly off a forklift truck. However, in spite of the Concorde champagne, he worked hard for the rest of the day, testing and changing boards, dismantling, examining, measuring voltages and things and then reassembling various modules. I could do nothing but get him lots of coffee or pass him a screwdriver now and again. Fortunately, most of the damage was in one area near the base of the CRT and he had the boards to fix that. It was, however, a key area that controlled the rest of the radar display. The display console design had ensured that most of the shock was absorbed by the console framework. By 7 o'clock that night, Mike had done it and we had the radar working again.

Meanwhile, the New York team were busy on the phones and all Tuesday's guests were rescheduled to come for later in the week. So at 10.00 on Wednesday, the first of six half-day presentations and demonstrations was under way. None of the customers realised there had ever been a problem. Mike stayed until Friday morning 'just in case' then flew home on a normal economy class flight, much to his disappointment.

Mike's Concorde trip saved the week. We did not let anyone down, all the invited guests arrived and in the weeks following the demonstrations, the American office took a number of large fleet orders for the radar. The Concorde flight for one engineer suddenly seemed very cheap.

Now, years later, I know that arriving by sea is still the best way to arrive in New York. We have been lucky enough to have done it a couple of times. There is nothing like arriving in New York in the early morning after passing under the Verrazano Bridge, passing into New York Harbour and seeing Manhattan emerge from its slumbers as the sunrise strikes the pink sides of the skyscrapers. A peaceful, distant grey silhouette that slowly grows as the ship approaches the city and the sun climbs higher until it becomes a solid tangible thing. The skyscrapers finally tower above the ship and cast their shadows over her as she slides up the Hudson River and into her berth, assisted by the ever busy Moran tugs. Only when finally alongside the wharf do the sounds of the city intrude onboard the ship and alert the traveller to the real New York waiting over the bow.

Washington. R&R Weekend

A few years later, I was back in the States. I was with Plessey by then and we were bidding to supply the US Navy with naval command and control systems for the new Avenger Class minehunters that they were having built. These ships were over 1000 tons each and all built of wood, including the funnel casing. We were invited to give presentations to the shipbuilder and visited the Peterson Shipyard up in Illinois. It was a family-run yard with heaps of character and we were welcomed personally by the owner and managing director and after the formal presentations, we were shown round the yard. It seemed to consist of lots of pale blue wooden buildings and did not immediately appear to be at the cutting-edge of technology. However, they certainly knew how to build wooden ships, and big ones too. The yard had a long and illustrious history of shipbuilding. The wooden hull frames for the minehunters were enormous and made up of laminated wood strips about 18 inches wide and all bent into shape in huge 'steam boxes'. These were vast metal chests about 3 or 4 feet high, housed in one of the wooden buildings. The dark interior stretched away and steam hissed ominously at us as we peered into the gloom. The proof of the pudding lay tied up at the fitting out berth where the first hull was waiting to have her main equipments installed.

I was then sent across to Syracuse in Upper New York State where GE, our American partner on the project who made the minehunting sonar, had their facility. After a week working with them, writing the final proposals for the command and control system, I had to get down to Washington to meet my boss who was on his way out from the UK. It had been agreed that I was to be flown down to Washington on the Friday afternoon by one of Plessey's US guys, called Ed, who had his own small single engine plane that he flew around the States whenever he could. He had flown it up to Syracuse during the week and was now going to fly back to Washington and take me too. We went out to the airfield and Ed pointed out his plane, his pride and joy. I was not happy. It seemed to be very small and although he told me what sort it was, I instantly forgot. Normally I am very happy to fly on comfortable big airliners with nice stewardesses, but with one guy and a single engine, I felt a little exposed. We took off.

The thing was so noisy so I could not hear a word he said and it was also cold and draughty. I had a fear that the little flappy door thing that I was wedged against would give way and I would plummet down into someone's backyard. I kept my seat belt tightly fastened on the trip. To complete my enjoyment, the guy had a bad touch of B.O. as well. There we were crammed into this little thing that seemed to be made of perspex and tin, while he kept fiddling with switches and things and tapping gauges. The engine noise kept changing and the whole thing seemed to swing and shake about in the sky. I could not see out of the front at all as the instrument panel rose above my eye level. I asked him how he could see where he was going. "I can't," he shouted. "I look out of the side and work it out from that," pointing sideways out of his window. Maybe that explained the feeling of flying sideways! Not exactly confidence building! We eventually landed on one of the main runways at Washington Dulles airport and taxied off to a private aircraft parking area. Boy was I glad to get out. Commercial flights for me from now on I vowed.

I was meant to meet my boss in Washington over the weekend and brief him on the trip etc before he flew on to Los Angeles, but when I got to the hotel and checked in, there was a message from him to say he had been held up in the UK over the weekend and would I wait in Washington until the Tuesday when he would now arrive. I should now plan to fly home on Wednesday night.

Great! I now had a whole weekend on my own in Washington. I had been booked into a super hotel, the JW Marriot, which was the boss's favourite, so settled down to enjoy Washington as a tourist. Life sometimes throws you a double six. And enjoy Washington, I did. I went on a Grey Line tour, watched the American football on TV and walked all over the city. I ate well on burgers and steaks, drank American beer and popcorn and slept well in the king-sized bed and felt very relaxed. After that flight down from Syracuse, I felt I deserved it. However, the pleasure we all got some months later after winning the contract made me almost forget the flight.

I always found America refreshing, fast-moving, go-getting and the people all very friendly and helpful. They always seemed to know which admiral or senator we had to get on our side and it would be done that day. I loved the soft music, easy listening and country music radio stations. I loved the automatic gears on their cars and I loved the supermarkets where you could buy anything. I loved the huge lean steaks in the butchers section and I loved American football, weak beer and popcorn. The Americans were a breath of fresh air with their 'can do, will do' approach.

CHAPTER 13

Some Final Thoughts

Head Hunters

"Mr Gray? My name is James, we have not met, but are you able to talk at the moment?" The voice on the end of the phone was cultured, calm and confident. I recognised the use of the words. That was always the code signal for 'This is a headhunter calling', or executive recruitment consultants as they were more properly known. They would continue something along the lines of "Our client company is a UK-based, blue-chip company, trading internationally in the electronics industry; they need to expand their markets and are looking to recruit an experienced international salesman." After a few guarded questions and answers, with no company names ever mentioned, they would then say, "If you feel it would be of interest could you come in and see us to discuss it further?" The answer usually was "YES."

Such calls, while rare, were always good to get. Even if I was happy in the job and had no intention of leaving, a head hunter's call always made me feel good. Somebody loved me, or at least was prepared to see if they loved me! Maybe it was worth following up anyway, just out of interest. It was always good to go and meet these headhunters as firstly that was the only way to find out about the company who were looking for a salesperson, and secondly it revealed a lot about my value in the market place and what other companies were prepared to offer. If this job did not suit, then perhaps they had others on their books that did. So I would find myself visiting the headhunter. Their offices tended to be smart, comfortable and in the better parts of London's West End, often looking out over the trees of quiet London squares and always with beautifully spoken, smartly dressed and attractive receptionists. It was a very different world from offices I had worked in, like those out in the suburbs by New Malden Station or the old concrete buildings off Feltham High Street.

It also worked the other way as well. When I was looking for a new job, I always contacted the headhunters as it was a good idea to make sure that they had your CV on file for any future requirements. Those that specialised in defence manufacturing industry placements had a unique view of the industry. If a company wanted to find a certain type of person to fill a particular role, then they went to a headhunter to get them to trawl the market for the best candidates. In the process, the company revealed to the headhunter a lot about their structure, perceived market position, plans and aspirations as well as their salary scales etc. Equally, an executive working for that company who was fed up would go to the headhunters to seek alternative employment. So, the headhunters often heard the other side of the story. What was wrong with the company, what sort of management culture they operated and why people wanted to leave. Over time, theses headhunters knew an awful lot about most of the major companies.

The typical headhunter was usually a charming, articulate person, who might be wearing casual light-coloured suits and burgundy loafers with tassels. He would always start by taking my CV and questioning me line by line on its contents with open questions. "What did you like about school?" "Why did you leave the Royal Navy?" "What made you decide to move out of the Harbour Radar department?" "You say here that you did such and such. Tell me about that." "What salary were you on then?" "How did your wife feel about you changing jobs?" "Tell me about your achievements while you were with Thorn?" "What career benefits did you think you would get by moving to a defence consultant?"

So it continued as they dissected me and my career, line by line,

Some Final Thoughts

to be sure I was the same person that had compiled the CV. This could take about two hours, but I knew at the end that they could not say I was trying to be somebody I was not and hopefully they felt I was the ideal person for whatever job it was. Only then, once they felt that they were comfortable with me as a candidate, did they ever tell me anything about the position that they had been asked to fill. Often though, it ended in disappointment as it was not a job I would want or a company for whom I would not want to work. If it was not what I wanted, then nothing lost and the headhunter had my CV on his database for any future requirements.

Sometimes it would be a direct approach from the company themselves. I was sitting in the departure lounge of Abu Dhabi Airport waiting for a flight to India. In walked a man I knew fairly well. Adam was the owner and managing director of a small defence consultancy company and we had worked with him a few years earlier in Plessey. He was a jovial, friendly, outgoing guy who always seemed to be in good spirits.

"Gordon, how good to see you. I am so glad to have bumped into you as there is something we need to discuss," he gushed. He was treating me like a long-lost son! He put his arm on my shoulder and led me across the lounge to a quiet corner with no other passengers nearby. "Let's sit over here and have a quiet chat." He went on, "We have been watching you and believe that you are one of the best guys around in the industry. We have big expansion plans as we are looking at new markets and we feel you would make an excellent addition to our small team. Other people who know you well are working with us and agree you are the man to have onboard. Would you be interested in joining us?" Before I could think or reply, he continued, "And don't worry about the salary, it will be much better than what you are on at the moment."

"How do you know what I am on at the moment?" I asked.

"We know what your company pays as we have done work with them."

"What about Kelvin, your deputy, does he agree to this offer?"

"Of course! He is with me 100% on this. Look, I must go now, but I will call you when you get back to the UK." We shook hands and he left to board the London flight. I boarded my flight to India with a feeling that life was going to get better and trying to see myself as an 'International Defence Consultant" rather than a "sales rep". I believed him and his sales pitch. I took the job, the higher salary and the big new car; but it was a mistake. What he had failed to mention was that his sycophantic deputy had never wanted me onboard at all and he spent the next twelve months undermining me and backstabbing me to Adam whenever he could. I was not really aware of this until it was too late. I was made redundant and had to start again back in mainstream defence sales. Working in a consultancy, however, gave me a fresh and interesting perspective on the defence market as I got to know a number of different companies and saw how they operated, as well as getting a clearer view of the market from the customer's viewpoint. But I also found it a frustrating position to be in. A consultant is neither the maker of the product nor the buying customer; he is neither the poacher nor the gamekeeper. He sits somewhere between the two, trying to bring the two sides together and to a deal.

Once I was called by the managing director of a small marine electronics company who I knew pretty well. He wanted me to join his export sales team but he wanted me to meet his sales director first as I would be reporting to him. A one to one meeting was set up. The sales director, who was called Eddie, strutted into the office. He was a short guy with a prominent stomach. He had bright red braces, green striped tie and was not wearing a jacket. He was brash and loud and immediately told me that he used to be a photocopier salesman. He continued by telling me what a great copier salesman he had been, how many awards he had won and how only the very best salespeople succeed in the copier business. "It is the toughest sales job anywhere." I was clearly meant to be impressed. He had not asked me one question about myself at that point or told me anything about the company or the job. He really was all mouth and lots of big talk of what *he* had sold, the high targets *he* had always met and the bonuses *he* always won. This was not the sort of man to whom my old mentor Ernie would have taken! He finished with the motivating challenge of "I drive the team hard and set good targets that you will meet 'cos I'll sack you if you don't. You'll find me a tough guy, but fair". He even said at one point, "I am a good boss as I will never bollocks you in public, only in private." Charming! At the end of the interview, he offered me the job by saying, "Now, do you want the job or not?" I said I needed to think it over and discuss it at home. This clearly annoyed him.

I rang the managing director the next morning and said basically "Thanks, but no thanks." He asked why and I told him there was no way I could ever work for that man. The managing director did not sound surprised. I learnt later that the sales director and the company parted company a few months later.

On one approach I received, the headhunters said the client company wanted a sales manager to sell their new range of small boat marine electronics in the UK. It was not clear which company it was, but at the meeting with the headhunter it became clear. I was not very excited. I rang a friend who worked for a South Coast marine company and asked his views of the company and its products. "Look Gordon, they have had a whole load of these things made on the cheap in the Far East and think they can dump them on us to sell them. The product is not very good, they have a poor performance and are not selling. I cannot tell you anything about reliability as we have hardly sold any. Actually, we have heard on the grapevine that if they cannot make some sales soon, then they may get out of the market as they do not really understand it."

Out of interest I went along for an interview, but was not overly impressed. As I walked into the offices, I got a negative feeling from the drab decor, all greys and browns and the characterless look of the reception area. The HR person I met seemed preoccupied, distant and disinterested and I detected a lack of any enthusiasm. To her, I was

IF YOU CAN'T TAKE A JOKE...

just a nuisance on a busy day. I then sat down with the general manager, a middle-aged man of short and dumpy build, called Mr Clarke, in his small, untidy office. He wore a crumpled brown suit and his shoes had not seen any polish in a while. He did not seem very happy.

Without any preamble, he began. "Tell me about yourself." His tone was bored.

"Well, I am 33, married and have worked in the marine industry since leaving the Royal Navy."

"No," he interrupted. "Tell me about your current job. What do you do? How many people work for you? What sales have you made?"

"Oh, I see. My current job entails running a series of sales demonstrations," I continued, but I found his brusque approach together with the lack of any common courtesies irritating.

He cut me off after a couple of minutes. "We need a good salesman to sell our products to the marine leisure market, local dealers, yacht marinas, that sort of thing. Can you do that?" he demanded.

After some short questions and answers regarding the product itself and bland statements from Mr Clarke about "On target earnings over a strong base salary", it became clear that Mr Clarke saw it as a simple direct selling operation and he had no feel for the end users, relationships with dealers, or customer and product support. I did not see any real interest in, or knowledge of, the marine industry in anything he said. The meeting was quickly terminated as Mr Clarke told me he had lots of other candidates to see. I left knowing that I did not want the job nor did I want to work there. I was a little surprised to receive a job offer a few days later. I turned down the offer even though the money was a lot more than I was on at the time.

Then a few days later, the phone rang at home one evening. It was Mr Clarke, "Look, we think you should reconsider your decision not to accept our offer," he began. "Oh really! Why?" "Well, we have reviewed the salary and are now prepared to offer you £5,000 more." I refused. I wondered what had happened to all the other candidates. Three nights later, the phone rang again. This time he offered an even higher salary, about 50% more than the one I was on. I still refused. I came off the phone and told my wife I had just turned down a 50% pay rise! The more they rang me, the more convinced I was that I was right to refuse. Time proved me right as the company soon vanished off the marine electronics map.

Many meetings with headhunters led nowhere, but even so they always seemed to give my self-confidence a boost. Some, however, did lead somewhere and that always made it all worthwhile. In terms of 'hit rates' then in job hunting, I found that roughly for every 100 application letters I wrote then I might get about ten invitations for interviews. Of those ten, maybe one might result in an acceptable job offer. It makes it sound as though the odds were low. They were. The job market is a busy place and in sales there were always lots of applicants for any job. Sometimes I would hear others looking for work saying, "Well I have written to the two electronic companies in my hometown and they have both said no so I cannot do any more." Looking for a new job is a full-time job and can take months. When I was redundant, I wrote letters to every defence, naval or marine company in the country, and more than a few overseas, to whom I felt I could offer something, wherever they were. I applied for anything in the papers that I thought I could do, regardless of whether I was qualified to do it as defined in the advert.

Many adverts were quite ridiculous in their demands. Some seemed to read "Leading naval company requires a junior sales manager to join sales team. Must be educated to degree level, have full Masters Mariner's ticket and not less than five years command experience at sea. Must be under thirty and have previous international sales experience with blue-chip company". Clearly such people do not exist, but part of the fun of applying to such adverts was to go and see where the company was out of tune with reality.

Then, when all the companies had said no, at least I knew I had tried and I could start again with another set of companies.

Company Cultures

Surely, in an industry like defence manufacturing, most of the companies would be pretty similar to each other. In fact, they were all different and had different approaches to how they treated their staff, how they valued their customers, viewed their products and how they saw themselves. From the big boys of the day like Racal, Marconi, Plessey, Thorn EMI, BAE, etc to the many smaller "niche" companies, each company had its own 'culture' or 'atmosphere'. In some companies, this was a good positive atmosphere; in some, it was not. Some looked after their staff well, respected and trusted them. Others treated their staff poorly, did not trust them, did not encourage initiative and generally demotivated everyone. Interestingly, it seemed to be those companies that looked after their staff that also tended to ensure that the customer and his needs were the priority. It was the companies that treated staff poorly that tended to see the customer as an irritation. You could often tell which culture a company had after a short visit and quiet observation of the staff and their mood. Would I want to work in this atmosphere?

Decca Radar was a good place to work. It had a family atmosphere where loyalty and trust worked both ways and lifelong friendships were formed. In fact, over thirty of us, from directors to sales reps and engineers, still meet up every couple of years for a reunion nearly thirty years after the company was taken over and we all went our different ways. Plessey had a great culture, especially in the naval systems group. At one stage in the early 1980s when I was looking for work, I was repeatedly asked by different headhunters "You have applied to Plessey, haven't you?" When I told them which other companies I had also applied to, they would answer, "Well, we can leave Marconi as a backstop." The message was clear and I was very grateful to be offered a job with Plessey. Ultra Electronics always had a good professional culture and was a great 'niche technology' house, run and managed professionally as a series of separate, small niche technology companies within the parent group. These companies had bosses who had a passion for their technology, treated their people well – not necessarily just in terms of salary, but in terms of giving them the chance to improve themselves through training and making them feel that they belonged and were valued members of the company.

If given a choice, then I feel that it is often better to accept a lesser job and lower salary with the company that feels right, rather than the grand title and more money in the wrong company. The wrong job will not last long, while the better company will offer the right chances to grow and progress successfully and happily.

Final Thoughts

Much is made in some sections of the media about the 'defence industry', or as they like to refer to it, 'The Arms Trade'. It is seen as something verging on the illegal and certainly immoral and they have a tendency not to differentiate between those employed on genuine government-backed defence export sales to friendly nations and those smuggling guns and explosives to terrorist organisations. A government's first duty is the defence of its people, so for any country a defence industry is a vital asset. To ensure that the costs of development and manufacture of sophisticated systems are minimised for the home customer, it is important to be able to sell these defence systems to friendly countries with similar requirements. However, this must be offset against the needs to maintain a technical and military lead over our adversaries, so the UK Government has strict rules and a very strong say in what can be sold to whom. The UK

Defence Industry is one of the last remaining major industries left in the UK with strong R&D, manufacturing and technology capabilities. I worked as an international salesman in the marine and naval defence industry with many companies between 1977 and 2007 and I found it a professional, honourable and satisfying industry in which to work.

During the 1980s and 1990s, the UK defence industry went through some major contractions as government defence spending was cut in response to the end of the Cold War, the changing of perceived threats and other world events. These contractions caused many companies to be bought out, sold or merged with the associated redundancies along the way. Between 1980 and 2000, the UK defence industry shrunk from employing over 750,000 people to about 300,000. In the face of these corporate changes, then to maintain some sort of career in the industry I often needed to move on, or I was forced to move on. I changed defence companies six times; I was headhunted for three of those changes, while three were forced on me by redundancy. However, the shrinkage of the UK defence market did force companies to look to the export market for their future and that gave an opportunity for those of us in export sales.

Every country is different. They all have different ways of doing defence business and different rules for potential suppliers to follow. All have different defence system requirements and during the course of a project, the cultural, ethical and legal differences became apparent and had to be incorporated into the sales strategy and tactics.

International selling is not a science. It is not a case of "If I do X, Y and then Z, an order will pop out on Tuesday. It is more of an art. Do as many of the 'right things' and as few of the 'wrong things' as you can and it *may* result in success, or it may not. There are no certainties. In export sales, the cry should be: "If we keep doing the right things long enough, then we MIGHT win; if not, we certainly will NOT win". It is a marathon race, not a sprint. It often takes years to get to an order with many of the key factors and personalities affecting the project changing over that period – some of which will help and some of which will hinder. Some of the factors will be under the company's control but many will not be, so it is important to recognise the factors that can be controlled and those that cannot.

When I look back over the years at the good and the bad times, they fall into two clear groups. The good times always happened when I had a good boss. Life was so much better with a boss who had actually experienced what the salesman was going through. He would understand and could often offer valuable advice and guidance. The salesman could then concentrate on the job and did not need to worry about what was going on back in the office. The bad, or frustrating, times seemed to happen when the boss did not understand what was entailed in the job I was trying to do.

Thankfully, there have been far more good times than bad. I have been involved in many successes around the world and I have been honoured to work with a lot of good people as bosses and colleagues, customers and agents, both in the UK and overseas, and I still keep in touch with a lot of them. I have had great job satisfaction from so many aspects of the job, not just when the team won an order. Satisfaction came from just knowing we were doing all the right things, even if it seems that little progress was being made as we worked our way 'one step at a time' through a project. Each small positive step along the way boosted our confidence and commitment, as well as job satisfaction. As new doors opened, so we met new people, new opportunities emerged and new ways of winning presented themselves. It all added up and kept us going.

However, all good things must come to an end. I realised that my end was coming when a new sales director, fresh from a desk in corporate HQ, appeared in the division. On our first meeting, I was struck by his casual 'no tie and open collar' look and his youthful face. He was chatty and friendly and was, I discovered, just thirty-four. I was fifty-seven. As he studied my tie, I had what Bill Hawley used to call a 'BGO' moment (a 'Blinding Glimpse of the Obvious'). My boss was young enough to be my son and I am sure he must have been looking at me and thinking "Why have I got this silly old codger working for me?" *Time to move on*, I told myself, *Your work here is done and your time here is over.*

And so it was. I took a voluntary redundancy package a few months later. At fifty-seven and with the industry contracting, I was not going to find another export sales job in the industry so I retired from the game. However, I had enjoyed myself and had always tried to take the frustrations, or jokes, that life threw at me along the way. As long as the salesman remains honest to himself, does his absolute best, then he can sleep well at night. Anyway, "If you can't take a joke, you shouldn't have joined!"

Brief CV of Gordon Gray

Between 1977 and 2007, I was employed by the following companies:

1977 – 1983: Decca Radar/Racal Decca. (Sales Manager and Far East Sales Manager).

1984 – 1985: Sperry Marine, European HQ. (Sales and Marketing Manager).

1985 – 1990: Plessey Displays, then Plessey Naval Systems. (Naval Export Salesman, Middle East Area Salesman).

1990 – 1991: Marconi/ Alenia Marconi Systems (AMS). (Middle East Area Salesman).

1991 – 1994: Thorn EMI Electronics. (Export Sales Director, later Regional Sales Director. Far East).

1994 – 1997: Ultra Electronics. (Export Sales Manager, Command and Control Systems).

1997 – 1999: Capitex Ltd. (Marketing Director).

1999 – 2007: BAE Systems. (International Sales Executive).